Praise for Tim Traver's

Sippewissett: Or, Life on a Salt Marsh

Tim Traver has created a wonderfully unique piece of genre blending in his elegant rumination on Sippewissett, the Cape Cod salt marsh he has known since childhood. By including both a rich history of the nearby Woods Hole Oceanographic Institute (along with fascinating profiles of the many scientists associated with it over the years) and stories about his family's long relationship with the marsh, he provides the reader with a work that is equal parts natural history and memoir. As he ponders the accomplishments and impact of naturalist luminaries Louis Agassiz, Spencer Baird, and Rachel Carson, he places their historic research in the context of the marsh's present condition . . . *Sippewissett* is a rare book, as it both informs and entrances. A delight from beginning to end.

   —*Booklist,* *Starred Review*

Biologists . . . have long been drawn to the patch of Cape Cod marsh where Traver spent his boyhood summers and to which he still returns. His reflections on the fauna, flora, habitats, and human culture eloquently weave together ecology, history, and memory. He offers enticing discussions of tidal flows, spawning runs, eelgrass beds, clam hunts, and even the microbial communities in the muds. And his treatment of sometimes contentious conservation issues demonstrates his recognition of the challenges facing those who wish to sustain their sense of home.

   —*Science* Magazine

In this wonderful blend of natural history and memoir, Traver details both the ecology and the history of Sippewissett, describing the people and creatures that he encounters, and chronicles the daily turning of the tides. Educational, touching, and highly relevant in today's changing ecological world, this marvelous book is highly recommended for public and academic libraries.

   —*Library Journal,* *Starred Review*

Tim Traver has written not just about a salt marsh, but also about the experience of living near one. He reflects upon what others—scientists, poets, philosophers, relatives, local residents and even occasional visitors—tell him about Sippewissett marsh. And, while the book is focused on his marsh, it is really about a man's relation to nature on a large scale.

   —John Teal, co-author of *Life and Death of the Salt Marsh*

This lovely book made me miss a bus. The sounds of the motor and the opening doors were lost in the ebb and flow of saltwater, migratory fish, and family, and in Traver's combination of humor and natural history with a deep meditation on the ecology of home.

—John Elder, author of *Reading the Mountains of Home*

Rarely can so much be so happily learned. Tim Traver takes us deep into the microcosm of Sippewissett, but more so, explores with us the idea of home. Traver leaps into his salt creek home and where it takes him is never dull.

—Janisse Ray, author of *Ecology of a Cracker Childhood*

Tim Traver's *Sippewissett* is a brilliant accomplishment replete with insight, wisdom, understanding, and passion. The author marvelously combines natural history, science, culture, conservation, and enduring qualities of the human spirit. The reader is continually moved by Traver's eloquent blending of personal narrative and rational reflection; we find ourselves traveling with the author through his coming of age cum personal and professional odyssey. This is a book that is likely to endure, enrich, and inform for many years to come.

—Stephen Kellert, Tweedy Ordway Professor of Social Ecology,
Yale University School of Forestry and Environmental Studies

Sippewissett is a salt marsh with history, and Tim Traver is an ideal guide who steers his readers through layers of birth natural and human, personal and expansive. The science of home is a noble pursuit, and Cape Cod has spawned some of our finest literary naturalists. With *Sippewissett*, Traver joins the legacy of gifted seaside storytellers John Hay, Henry Beston, Henry David Thoreau, and Robert Finch.

—Ted Levin, author of *Liquid Land: A Journey Through the Florida Everglades*, winner of the 2004 Burroughs Medal

Tim Traver's *Sippewissett* speaks to us about matters of extreme urgency and does so in a voice we want to hear. It's a powerfully smart and likable book.

—David Huddle, author of *The Story of a Million Years*

The road home leads through dirt, mud, saltwater and sand in this wonderful, storytelling book about a man and a salt marsh. It is lovely to read a book in which deep reflection on self, science, and community are woven with direct, lived experience.

—William Bryant Logan, author of *Oak: The Frame of Civilization and Dirt: The Ecstatic Skin of the Earth*

Lost in the Driftless

Trout Fishing on the Cultural Divide

Tim Traver

Crooked River Press
Taftsville, Vermont

Book interior and cover created by suewheelerdesign.com

Printed in the United States
First printing, January 2017

ISBN: 978-0-692-75616-4

www.timtraver.net
PO Box 45
Taftsville, Vermont 05073
totraver@comcast.net

To my wife Delia Clark
with love and gratitude

ACKNOWLEDGEMENTS

To the extent that you can't "stir a flower without troubling a star," a story about declining trout fishing in America has its broader contexts. This is what I have sought to uncover. To that end, I want to thank Roger Kerr. Without his obsessive passion for all things trout, I could never have finished this work or even undertaken it. And thanks to Mary Kerr for the good meals, including trout fried with Fryin' Magic, Green Bay Packers games, and stories from her childhood on the farm.

I also want to thank the organizers, compilers, and presenters of the Wild Trout Symposia over the years, beginning in 1974. In particular, researchers Robert Carline (Pennsylvania) and Dan Schill (Idaho), as well as Wisconsin trout manager and researcher Jordan Weeks; senior Wisconsin trout researcher Matt Mitro; fish manager Gene Van Dyck; and Wisconsin Department of Natural Resources social scientist Jordan Petchenik. Thanks also to Richard Seibert, who provided research assistance on Native American use of brook trout in Wisconsin; Ray Richardson and Ray Danders, worm trout-anglers extraordinaire on Michigan's Pere Marquette River; and Mark Tonello, biologist with the Michigan Department of Natural Resources.

My thanks to Trout Unlimited volunteer, fishing guide, mentor, and friend Marty Banak in Vermont. Also, to supreme fly-fishing guru Jay and his faithful sidekick, sheep farmer, rodeo photographer, and wife June Doolittle of Pray, Montana; Driftless fly angler Mike Juran; Trapper, who has introduced trout fishing to allcomers in the Driftless, whether worm or fly, old or young; farmer and teacher and trout-regulations protestor John Slaney; historian and author Jen Brown; Vermont fisheries biologists Ken Cox and Jud Kratzer; and Vermont natural-resource social scientist, Richard Kirn. Also, New Hampshire fisheries biologists John Magee and Diane Timmons; White Mountains stocking manager John Viar; Vermont Trout Unlimited stream restorer and researcher Joe Norton; Elise Tillinghast, director of the Center for Northern Woodlands Education; Christine Woodside, editor of *Appalachia*; and Margo Baldwin, Michael Metevier, and their colleagues at Chelsea Green Publishing. Special thanks to the employees of the American Museum of Fly Fishing in Manchester, Vermont, for allowing me unlimited access to their library. Many thanks as well to the Federation of Fly Fishers for generous access to their library and museum in Livingston, Montana.

I could not have gotten far without the support and patience of my wife Delia Clark and my daughter Mollie Traver, editor in chief of all my trout misadventures. Also, my other two children, Toben Traver and Kal Traver, for their vital advice, encouragement, psychological support, love, and inspiration. I owe my sister Ann Swardlick and brother-in-law David Swardlick a debt of gratitude for invaluable copyediting and marketing guidance.

[Rural] people mattered then, and provincial citizens had waxed confident in the knowledge that they represented—in movement and thought—the soul of the nation.

—DAVID RHODES, Driftless

Contents

Lost in the Driftless

INTRODUCTION

Everglades City, Florida

When people ask me what I have been writing over the past three years, I tell them it's a book about trout fishing culture and a battle over regulations in a remote rural region of Wisconsin. The trout fishing there has greatly improved, thanks to the fundamentals of improved water quality, wild trout genes, creek habitat restoration, and management. But despite improved fishing, a local trout fishing tradition is rapidly disappearing too. Beyond that, if they are still interested, I have a lot of explaining to do. When their eyes glaze over, I comment on New England's fickle weather.

Why write about trout regulations squabbles? Should we care? Isn't that a tempest in a teapot? Old news. Sport fishing is infamous for fights over rules. Isn't the real story, at least from the social perspective, the declining numbers of Americans who hunt or fish, who even have a memory of stalking game and rural life? Or, say, the decline in the biodiversity treasure trove in America and the world? State natural-resources departments face a continuing onslaught on air, water, and habitat; a declining public interest in hunting and fishing hits them in the pocketbook where it hurts the most. Eighty percent of us now live in cities, many with no notion of why some water is warm and some is cold, or what a native brook trout is. And this is a barrier to understanding not only the basic tenets of nature, but the values of disappearing rural life.

And why write about an argument over fish regulations in a postage stamp of a place, when it's climate change that is the hot and pressing issue everywhere? A warming planet is potentially devastating to cold-water fisheries from the Rocky Mountains to the Appalachian chain. Because down there in that *nowhere* rural place is the smallest theater of human existence—just above the solitary mind and the extended family. Inside a small community of people who live together, go outdoors together, and work together, we can learn something about the nature of cultural change and the values of fishing; every person who gets outside, including the urbanite on a racing bike, is hunting for something after all. Massachusetts politician Tip O'Neill said that all politics is local. So is trout fishing. Unless you examine the small, you'll never really get the large. That's what I set out to do here.

Whether we scan the Internet or read the newspaper, it's clear that cultural differences can give variety, a break to sameness in social life, and have tremendous economic value. In difference and variety is resilience, whether rural or urban, biological or social, familiar or foreign. Or, cultural boundaries can be inflamed, damaging, violently disruptive—cultural divides can set us back or stall us out. Ruin us. They can get in the way of what we need to do. Worst case, they can send us spiraling into warfare.

When it comes to political divisions, equally divided red-and-blue Wisconsin—where I was headed—knows them well, long a national leader in natural-resource protection and restoration (including the coldwater fishes), with founding conservation visionaries like Sigurd Olson, John Muir, Aldo Leopold, Senator Gaylord Nelson, and Governor Warren Knowles. But a country divided is a country that fails, and a once-great progressive innovator in resource-stewardship fields now struggles to fully fund the warden service.

The social conflicts around trout fishing in America may be part morality tale for why, when it comes to managing nature, we need to pay closer attention to culture, but trout fishing today also contains a powerful restoration story that is a model for how in the coming decades we might restore much of the damaged world. For trout stream restoration to work, nature and culture must dovetail neatly together. At the heart of ecological restoration everywhere is a collaborative society and a new kind of people.

My doorway to trout fishing in Wisconsin's Driftless Area was a retired county fish manager named Roger Kerr—an unlikely hero to some and an obnoxious gadfly to others who work and live in the world of wild-trout management in the Midwest. The proof of the pudding is in the eating with Roger. He's been officially blacklisted by the Wisconsin Department of Natural Resources (DNR)—number three on a confidential do-not-respond list, a group of sixteen people singled out because of repetitive or abusive communications. To me, he is someone I have gotten to know and respect as a friend through letters and travels over the past four years, a remarkably informed and, yes, at times gallingly persistent voice of protest in the arena of trout fishing and rules.

To explain how I landed in Kerr's net—coulee country is in the backwaters of southwestern Wisconsin—I have to backtrack to Everglades City, Florida at a bridge over the Barron River. That's where I first met Roger. The Barron River bridge connects Everglades City to Chokoloskee Island, a shell heap island made by the ancient Calusa Indians. Everglades City isn't a real city. Rather, it's one of those places that wanted to be. Today it's described as either a small fishing town with a drinking problem or a drinking town with a fishing problem. The nineteenth-century founders had other grand designs, if the town hall is any indication. Drinking town or no, Everglades City is an angler's paradise, an appropriate destination if your style of sport fishing is to disappear, as is mine. Peter Matthiessen's *Killing Mr. Watson*, the first of a trio of books about the shadowlands of the Ten Thousand Islands region of the Everglades, begins and ends at the Smallwood Store and post office in Chokoloskee, a museum that looks the way it did in the 1930s, when DDT was sold in five-gallon drums there and when Mr. Watson was riddled with bullet holes behind it. In Everglades City you can still hire a fishing guide named Smallwood. The killers, a group of men who'd been harmed one way or another by Watson, were never charged.

I ran into Roger and his wife Mary as I was laboring my way in a kayak against the tide to get under the low Barron River bridge and out to mangrove islands across the bay. They were sitting in lawn chairs by a bridge abutment scattered with oyster shells and old bait. They had a white, plastic scraps bucket half-filled with blue crabs. Florida fishing regulations allow anyone with a valid fishing license to catch up to a five-gallon bucket of blue crabs any day in season, if they are able—that's a lot of blue crabs. Few are lucky enough to fill even a half bucket, but these two retirees were having a good day, with a net and raw chicken parts for bait. They reeled in their lines for me, but I pulled up onto the abutment before I got to them, eased my way out of the kayak, brushed aside a seven-weight fly rod, and stopped to chat.

"Having any luck?" Roger asked. I held up a pair of speckled sea trout I'd just caught on a fly tied to look like a shrimp. Roger shook his growing pail full of crabs in response, and that's how things got started. Roger, a tall, rangy guy with a jowly smile, was seventy plus some years. Mary—quiet, compact, and tan—a good bit younger. The retired Kerrs, I learned then, are old-school Badger State anglers. They have been traveling together for years to fish some of America's fishiest places—from South Texas reservoirs for smallmouth bass, to North Dakota's Devil's Lake for northern pike and walleye, to Alaska for halibut and salmon. At home, they catch and freeze trout, bluegills, and walleye head-down in plastic soda bottles filled with water. Trout fishing is fun and it's also food to them. Catching, cleaning, freezing, cooking, and eating fish keeps them vital in retirement. They also process a half dozen deer each fall for friends. And they make excellent elderberry wine.

Some people have a fishing gene. It makes a protein that transports serotonin when triggered by the shape of a fish. Fish obsession makes you a bit touched in the head maybe, but also childlike happy. And there's something especially satisfying about connecting sport to putting food by. I quickly pegged Roger and Mary as people of this type. And they must have instantaneously recognized the same in me. Later, I learned that they are both natural connection makers. They have friends scattered across the Midwest and beyond—people they've met on the fishing road by the sides of rivers and lakes.

I would venture to say that Roger and Mary are modern heirs, as unlikely as it may seem, to the indigenous Miccosukee of the Everglades, being part of the marginal rural culture that has carried into the modern era an artisan-food fishing and hunting tradition, in spite of the roadblocks. The Kerrs' love of fishing includes a big interest not only in the fish in their freezers, but also in their community—the tribe of friends and family who fish rural creeks and often eat together, who scope out the good fishing spots and share the information with the clan. When meeting a stranger, first they want to know his name and to whom he is related before they might ask about his work. They fish the same creeks time and again, often across generations, and their methods—more often than not, drifting worms—are tried and true. These are not my people per se, though I do have a once-removed family connection to rural Wisconsin, which is secondhand to say the least. My maternal grandmother's second husband Harold, the man who adopted my mother and her brother, was born in Kenosha and worked his entire short adult life for Nash Motors, founded in Kenosha in 1916. It is not an exaggeration to say that Harold lived for trout fishing (I still have his bamboo rods). As for my grandmother, a Virginia-born farm girl, she grew up wild-crafting fish, oysters, and crabs, and hunting squirrels, as did my mother. My grandmother's the one who taught me how to bait a hook and wait patiently for a strike. My mother's the one who cooked everything I brought home, from eel to flounder. While an ancestor's rural pedigree doesn't qualify one as rural, a rural life in Vermont for the past thirty years doesn't either. I have lived, if not in, then beside rural life for all these years, and my work and side interests have at times roped me into the values and practices of a rural life and farmer people—often the people my work as a professional conservationist served.

But the fact is, Roger Kerr knows trout and he can catch as many as he wants without even thinking about it. He spent twenty years managing trout for the Wisconsin DNR, then worked as a land agent for the department, securing over two hundred miles of fishing easements and river corridor lands. He was cofounder of Wisconsin's wild-trout stocking program and has received awards from the Izaak Walton League, Trout Unlimited (TU), and the state's Bureau of Natural Heritage Conservation. He has published papers on wild trout and has kept a watchman's eye on everything in the popular press on trout during his years of retirement. He knows the land of trout as well as anyone.

The Kerrs aren't the only Badgers with an interest in fishing. Wisconsin is a fishy place; it's one of the most visited by out-of-state anglers (third to Florida and Minnesota) and home to the second-most-traveled anglers in the country (after Texas). Surprisingly, those anglers visiting Wisconsin are generally not fishing for trout. It's lake fishing for walleye, musky, and pike that's the biggest draw. Bluegill and ice fishing for perch are highly sought after. So are Great Lakes salmon. Trout, then, are somewhat mysteriously overlooked, which is surprising because Wisconsin has some of the best trout fishing in America.

"If you like trout fishing," Roger told me at one point in our conversation, "you should visit our corner of Wisconsin. We have hundreds of spring creeks there, filled with brown trout. The Driftless Area is a fly angler's heaven. I'll draw you a map." We made a plan to meet late in the day at the Everglades Seafood Depot, so he could draw me a map and I could deliver my catch to the Depot's kitchen. For about seven dollars each, my wife and I could eat our fresh-caught fish and all the shrimp we wanted from the salad bar, a cheap meal—until you consider fishing license fees, hotel rooms, flights to Florida, tackle, and the kayak rental.

Over drinks that night, retired fish manager Kerr, in a most expansive and happy mood, drew me an elaborate map of southwestern Wisconsin on the back of a paper placemat. It showed their town, Boscobel, on the Wisconsin River; the Mississippi River; Madison (state capital); and La Crosse, a small city on the banks of the Mississippi, almost at Wisconsin's southeastern border with Minnesota. It also showed two dozen or so squiggly lines: spring creeks flowing into each other, into the Wisconsin River, or into the Mississippi. The creeks had names like Kickapoo, Timber Coulee, Black Earth, Little Green, Blue, Big Green, Crooked, Avalanche, and Castle. Clearly, it was a country he knew well. Describing the sheer number of wild, catchable brown trout per mile—from two thousand to five thousand in many creeks (hundreds of pounds per acre of water)—and over thirteen thousand miles of trout creek statewide, he got my attention. I'd never been to Wisconsin.

His corner of the state, he explained, had never been covered by glaciers. Hence the name "Driftless." Drift is the layer of unsorted rocks, gravels, and till that glaciers leave. The Driftless is limestone karst terrain. That means coldwater springs. Small, sharp limestone bluffs, never ground down by ice, and narrow valleys called coulees hide a system of spring creeks. Thanks to soil conservation efforts beginning back in the 1930s and the conversion of farmland back to forest, the creeks, once choked with eroded soil, again run steady and cool. Stemming erosion set the region up for a major renewal of not only agriculture, but also wild-trout populations. Kerr had been involved personally in managing a trout boom that included moving wild strains of brown trout from creek to creek, so that now, with little artificial stocking, wild brown trout reproduce and grow rapidly throughout the region in hundreds of miles of Class 1 creeks. These fish have all but replaced native brook trout in the Driftless Area, but no one seems to be quibbling over Latin names and DNA (there are efforts underway to protect remaining native brook trout with upper watershed refuges). There are dozens of creeks, he added, where you'll never see another angler. The towns are mostly small in the Driftless, some nearly forgotten now that the number of dairy farms is way down.

His description of the Driftless had me thinking of the ancient disappeared Calusa and their labyrinth of mangrove islands that I'd spent the day lost in, scratching only the surface of a watery fishing paradise stretching clear down to the tip of Florida. The Driftless seemed to have some of the same qualities: vastness, convolutions, rich in fish, and light in people.

But then, as if laying out a view of a trout fishing Mecca was only a kind of teaser—only half of the real story—Kerr switched modes. Went dark, describing a world of regulatory woe. Fish Paradise Lost. Wisconsin's trout fishing regulations, he declared in a matter-of-fact tone, with over a thousand special regulations, had driven as many as a hundred thousand local anglers away, favoring wealthier urban fishermen, most with fly rods. It was no wonder the Driftless Area was depopulated of local anglers, many of the worm-plunking variety.

"They were zoned out," he said.

He looked sideways at me—a fly angler—somewhat accusingly. Having positively assessed the fish knowledge, map-drawing skills, and outgoing friendliness of my new friend, now I wasn't so sure. Clearly, there was a mania working in his mind. He was angry—maybe obsessively so. But could what he said be true? Could regulations alone have scared off nearly a hundred thousand anglers from Wisconsin trout creeks? Could locals have been gentrified out of their own creeks because new rules favored anglers from far away? The "new rules" Kerr was talking about, I soon learned, were more than twenty years old! What he was describing was a kind of colonization, an occupation of the countryside by a foreign, urban army. I got his point, and I got curious.

Absolutely, regulations can discriminate, and discrimination can discourage certain people from fishing, Kerr promised. He had the data to prove it, and said he'd send it if I was interested. I was, if only because the story of the depopulation of the middle of America had been on my radar for a long time. Everything from a Buffalo Commons to vast wind farms and biofuel perennial grass collectives has been proposed for a Midwest that is losing farms, losing communities, and losing biodiversity; it was a part of the country I knew almost nothing about.

But why so angry? Roger's one-man protests have translated into thousands of hours and hundreds of letters to newspapers, fisheries biologists, state administrators, and sympathetic fishermen across the years, as well as full-page ads and deliberate lawbreaking. His narrative includes an enemy cabal of anti-local interests: urban TU chapters, entrenched old-boy networks, tourist business/agency collusion, DNR biologists in the pockets of fly-fishing groups, and a trout lobby and Wisconsin Conservation Congress aligned against the once-common rural angler. Does this sound like conspiratorial thinking? To a certain extent, it is.

But it's a cheap ploy to pass off Roger Kerr as a conspiracy theorist. That is not the Roger Kerr I have come to know and appreciate, though he is not without the whiff of disgruntled employee about him, and he has his bitter personal vendettas. Kerr's been on the ground for a long time, and he's seen a lot of change, a lot of anglers come and go. He's marshaled an impressive file of evidence showing the relationship between trout-fishing regulations and the loss of rural anglers. His problem, he said, is that no one listens to him; no one cares. The root of the problem, I thought at the time of our first encounter, could be the force of shifting culture. Or Roger's problem could be Roger, as the bureaucracy would have us believe.

I do confess to an interest in stories that have *some* conspiracy attached, as long as they are tethered to certifiable reality. I came of age as a fly angler in the first years of the 1970s, when most good fishing literature was politically subversive and more about sex, drugs, or spiritual enlightenment than fishing. Fly angler writers then were more often than not loners drifting across the West or South, bums really, dreamer-outlaws, philosophically tainted and overtly influenced by Jack Kerouac or Hemingway, not to mention politically marginalized. Or they were from a powerful privileged class, easy to make fun of. Trout fishing, from Theodore Gordon to Thomas McGuane, has had an antihero tinge mixed with an aesthetic that millions of words from writers writing about trout fishing can't seem to quite capture. They keep trying. In the mid- to late 1960s and early 1970s, if you weren't anti-something, you weren't nobody. Trout fishing was subversive like reading Henry David Thoreau's *Walden* or Richard Brautigan's *Trout Fishing in America* was subversive. Writers took their trout rods into the wilds, from Patagonia to Siberia, in search of beauty, meaning, and ego trips. It was a sign of resistance.

Kerr's subversive nature is different. It's rural backlash, populist, anti-urban, and in his case, a well-researched curmudgeonry. He's not angling for nirvana or heaven. He's simply angling for dinner, fairness, and the rights of rural worm-fishing anglers to fish their own creeks using the methods they know.

Early in his career, Kerr was paying attention to the social side of trout fishing when most were not. The ears of a rural county fish manager, as well as the shrewd warden, have to be pretty close to the ground. Both need to know the minds of the people they serve, so they can provide the type of fishing experience that law-abiding people want while catching the poacher too. When regulations on keeping trout and using worms clamped down on some of his creeks—early experiments in catch-and-release "fish for fun" streams—Roger began hearing from the locals. He took note, and he has followed that thread of story for years, never letting go. No one, in my research, has linked angler dropout to special regulations as convincingly as Roger Kerr. Is he obsessively caught up in his beliefs? You betcha. But the bigger story is what's happening to the quality of life in a rural place when people stop fishing.

Making Kerr's story relevant beyond Wisconsin politics are the facts of dramatic trout-angler decline across the nation. There is a general decline in all fresh-water fishing in America. But trout fishing is dropping faster. Trout anglers today are an aging demographic, white, middle class, and male. We don't look much like the emerging face of America. And children are not taking up the rod. This does not bode well for a natural resource that depends on users for its protection and restoration. In trout fishing, as in much else, we rely on the experts to tell us what we can and can't do, and the experts are listening more and more to fewer and fewer of us—to the members of affinity groups that care the most and have the most money and clout. In an age of dwindling resources for natural-resource conservation, they have to.

If you consider agricultural and economic trends, loss of trout fishing in many parts of middle America is another nail in the coffin of fading rural culture. Trout fishing was once considered an all-American way to connect families to each other and to the beauty and wealth of the natural world. If you wanted your children to connect early on to the language of the seasons, you gave them a fishing pole on opening day.

Can trout fishing become that again? When it comes to the decline of trout fishers in America, is this question about regulations even the right one? Or is something else going on?

In social science circles, angler decline is usually assumed to be caused by shifts in cultural attitudes and behaviors. Anyone can look around and see that we've become an urban people cut off from rural ways. Fewer of us are interested in stalking, killing, and eating wild animals. Kids are too busy killing zombies popping out of trash barrels on computer screens to think about stalking and catching a trout. They're texting or selfie-taking, not casting. Technology is shaping values as well as computer chips. Today, if a thing doesn't exist online (virtually), it doesn't exist at all. What is real has become a kind of fading myth.

We have more factual information at our fingertips than ever before, but less reality. Gaming zombies is more real than catching brook trout partly because of proximity. Values are simply what we love—what's close to us. We can't love a trout, because a trout is no longer real, no longer close.

At the Seafood Depot, into a second round of margaritas, we continued to talk about fishing regulations and shifting cultures. Even the ancient Calusa—whose culture, destroyed by Spanish steel and disease, was built on the backs of fish—had fishing rules, seasons, and protocols designed to sustain them through lean times.

Regulations are important, and they are needed more than ever. To the extent that the political processes allow, rules are based on scientific knowledge. That we often don't get them right in the ocean is evidenced by massive overfishing and depleted stocks, with populations of the largest pelagic fish reduced by 90%, and 85% of the six hundred commercially targeted fish "fully exploited." If not depleted stocks, we have in South Florida's inland waters a dramatic reduction in sizes and weights of caught fish, and a "shifting baseline" of angler expectations when it comes to size and fish population densities. Aquatic ecosystems are complex, and oceans are being impacted by legal commercial overfishing, illegal pirate fishing, acidification, chemical pollution, and habitat destruction. This makes rule-making difficult, to say the least, but vital.

To confuse things further, in South Florida there are overlapping jurisdictions, with different constituencies vying for power and access. Florida's regulatory framework is dual; waters more than nine miles out into the Gulf are under federal jurisdiction, while waters within that perimeter are controlled by the state of Florida.

Fish don't abide by political boundaries. When the National Oceanic and Atmospheric Administration (NOAA) makes rules that apply to federal waters, based on their population data—a closure on red snapper, for instance—commercial boats with permits to fish both federal and state waters have to abide by the federal rule in both jurisdictions. Federal rules trump state rules. As they should. State regulations, more easily influenced by partisan politics, tend to be more liberal. On the hopeful side, countries are waking up to the ocean crisis. Thanks to federally mandated ocean sanctuaries, fishing stocks in many parts are making a comeback.

In Wisconsin, when it comes to setting fishing and hunting regulations, they have something called the Conservation Congress. It's supposed to make rule-making a democratic process, Roger tried to explain, by giving citizens an advisory role. "But everyone knows good sense breaks down in a democracy—especially ours." The loudest interest group or the one with the most money wins, Roger claimed. "We have a rule-making system," he went on, "that gives a small group of the most active participants—the old-boy network and a politically expert minority—undue influence. Why is that?" I couldn't answer his question, and I couldn't argue with his assessment.

After dinner we drove uptown to a row of pastel-colored boxy condominiums on the river by Jungle Erv's Airboat Tours. We parked and made our way in the dark to the mosquito-infested edge of the Barron River—the branch that Barron Gift Collier built with his dredges—and peered into the water. Underwater light attracts small fish, and small fish attract larger fish. There they were, the shadows of large snook cruising in both directions in and out of the light. There is something mesmerizing about watching shadow-fish at night cruising through lit water; it's as if we'd come across a stage and the fish were actors in a timeless play, though not a particularly dynamic one. We watched until it became impolite to stay, given that our wives were less interested and the mosquitoes thick.

It was out there at night on the edge of the black Barron River, watching snook shadow-play, that I decided I'd travel to Wisconsin to visit the Kerrs the following summer. I wanted to see Kerr's spring creeks. Look at his thousand special rules. I wanted to see what swam in the shadows of his half-lit landscape, where conspiracy ran rampant, the brown trout were thick, and the world hung upside down.

When we arrived back home to Vermont a few days later, my first handwritten letter from Roger Kerr was waiting. Hundreds were to follow. His first letter simply pointed out to me that the sea trout I'd caught on a shrimp fly in the Barron River were two weeks out of season. To prove his claim, he'd included a snip from the Everglades

City weekly, *The Mullet Rapper*, on the new season for sea trout.

Congratulations. I was a lawbreaker. Just like him, though he can claim civil disobedience, the higher ground.

What I learned in Wisconsin, I now know I already knew: When it comes to conserving and restoring wildlife, soil is the fundamental building block. Aldo Leopold said as much in the 1920s. But there's something even closer to prime when it comes to stewardship and restoration: human attitudes, values, cultural perceptions, and behaviors. Our success depends on what we believe and how we express our values. Restoring the health of the world may be the work of soil and water chemistry, but human values are the fuel. Leopold put the challenge this way, in a letter to his former student Douglas Wade: To conserve land and restore nature, "we need a new kind of people."

CHAPTER 1

Wild Brook Trout
and the Social Rule

Trout management, more than any other fisheries program, has been clouded by the desires, demands, emotions, and ritualisms of trout fishermen.

— J.R. FATORA, 1975

This summer I guided several parties to the Pond [Ethan Pond]. The first time I went there, we caught in a short time about 70 salmon trout; they differed a little from our common river trout, as they had a redder appearance and taste and flavor was delicious. On the bank of the pond we struck up a fire and after dressing a sufficient number of them, we cooked them in a real hunter style. I cut a stick with three prongs to it, and put the trout on these prongs in the form of a gridiron and I broiled them over the fire; then I would cut pieces of raw pork and broil them in the same way and lay them over the trout and that would give them the same relish. I always enjoyed these and similar feasts in the woods, as in such ways I suppose our forefathers lived when they first came and settled this country.

— ETHAN ALLEN CRAWFORD, 1830

Catching trout is a sport. Eating them is not.

— LEE WULFF, *Trout on a Fly*, 1986

Trout fishing, since I began casting flies for trout in the spring of 1973, has gone through a remarkable transformation, both in terms of the new scientific knowledge driving native-trout conservation efforts and the strange and often failed attempts to manage what researcher J.R. Fatora termed the varied social "ritualisms" of trout fishermen. Let's face it, trout anglers can get weird and the social rules weirder, even less rational than the customs of the dedicated scientific angler. The backstory of rule making in trout fishing, I had begun to realize during the intervening months between meeting the Wisconsin political worm angler Roger Kerr and leaving for a fishing trip to the Driftless Area in his backyard in Wisconsin, was shaping up to be a major theme of my fishing venture to the Driftless region.

I'd been receiving letters from my new Badger friend, sometimes two a week. Almost always attached to his handwritten missives were scientific studies, creel censuses, and trout electroshocking studies going back forty years. I was learning a lot about Wisconsin's trout and Roger Kerr's strong feelings about them. Kerr sent me copies of his letters to government officials. He sometimes got an official response. That was rare. He regularly sent copies of his letters to papers like the *Wisconsin State Journal*, Madison's main daily, which were ignored and remained unpublished, and to local weeklies from little towns across the Driftless counties, where his letters were often welcomed and published. There were also clips from *Wisconsin Outdoor News*, editor in chief Dean Bortz's territory, where Roger Kerr, unless he wrote under an alias (which I was soon to learn he often does), was persona non grata.

His communications included articles about chasing monster brown trout by fishing writer Len Harris, and fishing writer Jay Thurston's forays into what sounded like a limitless and underutilized brown-trout fishing paradise. The picture emerging was of an incredibly stubborn retired fish manager and equally stubborn TU members and Wisconsin DNR staff. It was not clear who was smarter, brown trout or anglers. Brown trout remain hard to catch for most of us. The trout rules hard to fathom and hard to change.

Often attached to his letters were articles about politics in Wisconsin, too. Politics in Wisconsin are as divided as its trout anglers; on the one hand, Tea Party governor Scott Walker was proving tough on pregnant low-income women, the unemployed, blue-collar workers who belonged to labor unions, and the state university's tenured professors, while singing protesters occupied the Wisconsin statehouse nearly daily. On the other hand, Wisconsin elected ultra-progressive Russ Feingold to Congress many times and has recently elected Tammy Baldwin, the first openly gay member of the US Congress. Madison loathes Walker, while the countryside quietly reelects him, even when it is against their self-interest to do so.

Social divides are common when it comes to trout fishing, and the scientific literature is well populated by social analysis of human trout-fishing group conflict, most famously but not limited to the Au Sable River in Michigan, the Wood River in Idaho, and many others, from Minnesota and Pennsylvania to Arkansas, Montana, and Colorado. In each of these places, groups fought to expand catch-and-release fishing, outlaw live bait, and promote fly-fishing destination fisheries, with their promise of improved and restored ecosystems, bigger fish, "quality"experiences, jobs, and tourist dollars. Bait-preference groups eventually organized and fought back, sometimes erasing a fatuous rule, other times curtailing rules placing limits that were biologically justified and needed. Such was the history and current circumstances that my stance in Wisconsin might turn out to be less angler reporter and more war correspondent.

Trout anglers, as testy and pugnacious as they appear to be, are still poorly known from a social science perspective. This has been noted by many top biologists and social scientists over the years. We simply don't know who we are. We believe what we believe regardless of the facts. Our beliefs shape the facts. Roger Kerr once said that if fish managers devoted as much time to segmenting different user groups as they do to writing complicated regulations for segments of creeks, we'd have a lot more anglers than we do today. Too little effort, he believes, is spent on the social side of resource management. Game is easier to manage than people, and natural resource managers are caught in the middle; they really need to know their audiences, but that takes money they don't have, partly because their traditional funding sources, license sales and taxes on sporting equipment—in other words, hunters and fishers—are in decline. Rule making designed to protect natural resources can quickly devolve into political struggles with losers and winners. There's a corollary when it comes to combating climate change. Environmentalists today wonder why they are reviled, their global warming message spurned by half the US population. Too little effort is made to cross political, psychological, and cultural divides, to understand the mindsets and culture, or for that matter, the common ground of the opposition.

Roger's letters whetted my appetite for a plunge into the state of social science in trout fishing, but also for a taste of Wisconsin's spring creeks. Some of the electrofishing numbers in the fish reports were, frankly, shocking, notwithstanding the politics of Wisconsin, whose noteworthy personalities include Joe McCarthy of communist witch-hunt fame and John Muir, who saved Yosemite Valley from the dam builders.

Before heading to Wisconsin, I gave in to my own trout fishing obsession with a trip back in time. Ethan Pond, a small pond high in the White Mountains of New Hampshire, is not only where a trout fishing addiction began for me, but it's also where some of the earliest observations of recreational trout fishing were made in northern New England. At this one high outpost of wilderness, you can gaze backwards and forwards and get most of the entire span of trout fishing history in America.

Ethan sits at an elevation of 2,900 feet under the dome-like summit of Mount Willey, by the cliffs and ledges of a west-running ridge. A wild place in the upper Pemigewasset watershed, Ethan gets its water from intermittent streams plunging off the steep sides of massive Mount Willey and from springs seeping up through the broken stone of its floor. Life for the small brook trout that live there is a risky proposition. Should the shallow pond heat up or dry up or freeze solid, there isn't much room to move. Close to the top of the divide, Ethan's inlet soon disappears into cliff and scree slope and its outlet heads west, cascading over nearby Thoreau Falls and into the East Branch of the Pemigewasset River, a tributary to Henry David Thoreau's Merrimack River, and then onward to the Atlantic. Hemmed in by a waterfall and a mountain, Ethan's brook trout somehow endure. I'm glad they do.

My own relationship to these denizens of cold highland brooks began when I was seventeen and on my way to climb Mount Carrigain deeper in the Pemi. Halfway there, I ran into a group of whiskered, sooty fellows fishing below Thoreau Falls. They had bottles of Jack Daniel's, a fire, and a bacon-greasy cast iron frying pan, in which they were cooking small fish with the enthusiasm of twelve-year-olds playing with firecrackers. They bragged that they had caught a hundred brook trout over the course of a few days. Would I like some fish and whiskey for breakfast? I stayed, ate, and drank. It was a pungent affair involving unwashed holiday fishermen, the perfume and sizzle of frying fish, and warm, be-spitted whiskey going down and almost back up. Later, we walked down the river, the men showing me how they dropped their baited hooks into clear pools where brook trout lived. It was my first encounter with living eastern brook trout, *Salvelinus fontinalis*. Eastern brook trout are the only native trout in eastern Appalachian waters. They are true coldwater specialists—char, closely related to Arctic char—able to eek out a living in the shadow of glaciers, upland streams, and high mountain ponds. Seeing those bejeweled fish with their patriotic anal fin, their bluish and red spots, fining in their crystal-clear pools, was a game changer that I have not forgotten. The boozy trout feast made for a crooked walk down that I do not much recall. I never climbed the mountain, but I did throw up in a friend's car.

And I never saw those drunken old-man-anglers again. Public lands management was changing rapidly by 1971. (The wilderness designations first came to areas within the White Mountain National Forest in 1973. The so-called Pemi, comprising the upper watershed of the

East Branch, was made wilderness in 1984.) New rules created camping bans near waterways and trails. Volunteers cleaned up blighted campsites, and fishing encampments all but disappeared. New trout regulations were changing the face of trout fishing all over the country beginning around then.

But those old guys and their fishing camp had captured my imagination, and by the next summer, thanks to a twist of fate and a new friend fresh back from fishing in Wyoming, I'd bought a fly rod. I caught my first trout on a fly at nearby Shoal Pond in 1973, and then a second at Ethan. Over the next five summers, hooked on fly fishing, I fished every stream, river, puddle, and backcountry pond I could float, drive, or walk to in the White Mountains. Later, I lived and worked at the Atlantic salmon hatchery in Milan, New Hampshire, and got a whole new view of the native-fish restoration world. After college, I worked for a storied saltwater striped bass fishing guide named Bob Francis on Nantucket, and much later I guided trout anglers in Vermont with the best guide in our area, Marty Banak. There almost always has been a fish in my head. But other than a failed attempt at the age of six to land my little sister's big rainbow under the watchful eye of my grandmother, the Pemi is where the first trout entered.

I arrived at Ethan Pond late in the afternoon, the sun still blazing, the air cool, and walked around to the boggy outlet. I wanted simply to catch a few fish, check them out, release them, and then head down, hopefully getting to the car before the dark set in—but as for that, walking through the evening and into the dark on a June night can be a very fine thing, and with a full moon, no headlamp would be necessary.

I made my way further down the shoreline, through bog mud smelling of sulfur and past little islands of pitcher plants and yellow cinquefoil, onto a stony edge, where the pond narrows and a spindly stand of stunted black spruce grows. I found good purchase there and began to cast to rising fish. The ones I caught and held were each as dark backed as the black waters of Ethan. I could hardly make out the vermiculation, but the red was bright and the bellies, pale pink.

Going back to a time long before I first made my way up to Ethan Pond as a greenhorn angler with a few spangled country-store-bought flies and an L.L.Bean spin/fly outfit, Ethan Allen Crawford and his cousin and wife Lucy, whose book *The History of the*

White Mountains captured that early era, were homesteading in Crawford Notch. It was the early 1800s and life at Hart's Location was no piece of cake. The Crawfords' only neighbors, the Willey clan, were killed by rock avalanche just before the Crawfords arrived.

"Wild" during Crawford's time still meant forbidding and dangerous. This was hard country to navigate. Guidebook writer Moses F. Sweetser, referring to the Pemi circa 1876, writes of "a vast primeval forest . . . [whose] inner solitudes should be entered only under the guidance of experienced foresters; and traveling will be found very slow and arduous." It was a country where "trout increase and multiply almost undisturbed in the brooks and ponds."

Underneath a four-hundred-year-old red spruce forest, deep organic soils had formed from thousands of years of deadfall and decomposition, and the shade and humidity created by the canopy of giant red spruce had a profoundly moderating effect on forest microclimate and water flows. Under old-growth spruce, long before stormwaters hit streams, they percolated through feet of what writer Jack Noon, author of *Fishing in New Hampshire: A History*, describes as "sponge mats" of sphagnum moss, rotting wood, and duff. The pre-settlement forest floor filtered, buffered, and cooled water, and provided a continuous water supply to rivers throughout New England. This was very good for native brook trout.

But already by the 1830s, what was wild was rapidly disappearing in the White Mountains, and so were the old-growth fish. Crawford wrote in his journals about the drop in size and number of trout in the main river stems by 1844. Pioneers had long since fished out lowland lakes and rivers. Jack Noon cites numerous early records of abundant brook-trout stocks throughout New England, including John Josselyn's assessment from 1674: In New England, there were trout in "good store in every brook, ordinarily 2 and 20 inches." Noon also finds records of ten- to twelve-pound brook trout in the Rangeley Lakes and great numbers of large, spawning brook trout in brooks connected to large lakes. Native lake trout—and in a few lakes, arctic char, dubbed golden trout by early writers—had disappeared by the early 1900s. Those fish, in the absence of fish science and regulation, were speared, netted, pickled, and smoked into extinction by eighteenth- and nineteenth-century food anglers. Nineteenth-century dams on

New Hampshire's Merrimack River blocked the passage of Atlantic salmon and other anadromous fish, including massive runs of sea lamprey spawning in the highest reaches of the Pemigewasset watershed.

To me, the most surprising observation in Ethan's journal is that even by the early 1830s, with hardly a footpath through Crawford Notch, where horses had to be elevated by a pulley system to get them through, Ethan was guiding urban travelers up a foot trail his family had created (the Crawford Path is still widely in use and is part of the Appalachian Trail through the White Mountains) to the top of Mount Washington, the highest point on the East Coast. By the 1830s, some new urbanites were already eager for trips back to the still-untamed Acadian wilds of northern New England. The most famous among them is Henry David Thoreau, who made his trip up the Merrimack River with his brother in 1839.

These early urban adventurers, guided by Ethan, would catch their dinner of trout on the way back down the mountain to the Crawfords' inn and tavern. The yearning for escape to the American wilds by a new urban class may not have hit its zenith until the first half of the twentieth century, but the roots of trout-fishing tourism were back in Ethan's time.

To put Ethan's era into the frame of early American trout-fishing history, the first state fish commissions—with their hatcheries and fishing regulations—were thirty years away. The first federal fish commission was nearly fifty years distant. Famed fly-fishing genius Theodore Gordon, who shaped the direction of modern American fly fishing, wasn't born until 1854. Gordon received his first English dry flies from the British entomologist Frederic Halford in 1890. Ethan Allen Crawford was a tweener; the earliest American pioneers had come and gone, and trout as modern urban recreation was just over the horizon. Brown trout introductions from Germany and Scotland were nearly sixty years out.

There is another vivid piece of trout-fishing history worth noting from Crawford Notch, its impact arguably far greater than the overharvest of native trout by pioneers. Beginning about a hundred years ago, Ave Henry built mills and logging railroads deep into the Pemi, following the East and West Branches of the river, into Zealand

Valley and up and over Carrigain Notch. They stripped the old-growth spruce forest that had developed on the heels of the last ice age, ruining more than fishing. Pulp and sawdust piles polluted rivers, log drivers straightened them, dams drained streams, and railroads and roads cut them off. Fires and erosion burned off those deep soils that had been ten thousand years in the making, washing away the future. What occurred was a type of cataclysmic land use being repeated throughout the forested regions of eastern North America. The losses to wildlife were enormous. On the plus side, forest destruction in the Whites led to the formation of the White Mountain National Forest. But old-growth forest recovery, if at all, is a five-hundred-year prospect. In Michigan, grayling went extinct. In Vermont, we lost the last of our arctic char by the late nineteenth century. It's not just overharvest that kills native trout; it's soil, sun, and water that grow fish after all, and everything else from lynx to purple fringed orchids. Soil erosion, water and air pollution, *and* overharvest kill off trout populations.

A lot began changing in the 1970s. We're seeing some of the benefits of that change nearly fifty years later. Thanks to a reduction in acid precipitation caused by smoke stacks to the west, red spruce is growing and regenerating at a faster rate now in the White Mountains. Scars from the rail lines that shipped old trees away are more obscure than ever. Many mountain ponds once stocked with domestic hatchery fish are getting a dose of wilder genes. It was a put-and-take domestic fishery in these ponds forty years ago. The trout I caught was a ten-inch hatchery fish dropped by fixed-wing aircraft. The first fish-stocking pilots here had flown Liberator bombers in the Second World War; now, it's by helicopter.

The ultimate measure of the new world of trout may be the quality of native trout habitat research and restoration going on today. Researchers are working collaboratively across regions now under the specter of climate change. They have new massive data sets, regional collaborative approaches, and technologies unknown just ten years ago. Using remarkably powerful new tools for landscape-scale monitoring and for tracking fish, researchers are opening new doors to the mysteries of trout lives. Regulations reflect this new knowledge, and thanks to them, we're seeing a resurgence of native fish populations and the restoration of entire ecosystems. In the White Mountains, researchers like Joe Norton are reconnecting watersheds so brook trout can move again, from tiny spawning stream to main-stem river. Fish need whole watersheds to guarantee a complete life cycle and a healthy gene pool. Other researchers are creating new habitat by dropping tree trunks into stream beds, once straightened for the log drive. The trees move with the flood and jam up downstream, creating new pools and a good food source for the insects trout eat. New regulations play a role in recovery.

At Ethan Pond now there is a Wild Trout Pond special regulation in place. It calls for a release of all trout caught. It mandates single, barbless hooks or lures (debates rage over lure-hooking mortality) and flies only. Worms and other bait are not allowed, based on research that shows higher rates of mortality when fish caught this way are released.

At least at first blush, the Wild Trout Pond designation seems to make sense, especially given the region's history. The new regulations appear to fit a new knowledge landscape, not to mention a radically different fishing culture. Old fishing practices—embodied by Crawford and the men I met, camped in with worms, Jack Daniel's, and cast iron frying pans—feel retrograde and seem no longer sustainable.

Back when I caught that first brook trout in these high haunts, legally you could keep and eat a dozen. But the whole orientation of the sport of trout fishing was shifting, beginning in the late 1960s and early 1970s. The old objective of managing for maximum sustained yield was giving way to other ideas that referenced subjective words like "quality" and "wild" and the sport angler's "total experience." Thanks to thought leaders like Lee Wulff, it was becoming rapidly out of fashion to even eat a trout. Old-time methods and the guy who caught trout for a meal using worms—dubbed the "folk angler" by some—were being left behind. Good sport fish were simply "too valuable to be caught only once." Lee Wulff's famous bromide proved an incredibly sticky message, and even if it needed to be seriously qualified to be true, catch and release remains a rallying cry for trout anglers to this day. Wulff's message spread rapidly. A trout is too valuable to kill and eat—it's a sport fish, not a food fish. Say that or read that a thousand times, and the belief begins to feel part of your DNA. Even when it's not true. The great trout taxonomist Robert Behnke more than once found himself in the position of correcting Lee Wulff's often exuberant misuse of science. Behnke, a powerful voice for catch and release, nonetheless qualified the practice, writing that the long term survival of a trout depended on a lot other than its release back into the water.

As the likes of Lee Wulff were busy taking the meat out of recreational trout fishing, emerging social values that elevated ecosystem thinking were taking hold. The concepts of whole-watershed planning, energy conservation, clean water, earth resources as limited, and land as sick and ailing were just around the corner. We were crowning some new heroes in the conservation arena, including Rachel Carson and Barry Commoner. In trout fishing, the chase, not the meal, became the prevailing aim. Kill less, catch more. Cleaning up our pollution messes was of the first order. As the culture was shifting, so were angler demographics. What had been a decidedly rural tradition was giving way to urban recreationalists with larger wallets, more leisure time, and different appetites.

Every aspect of the Wild Trout Pond designation at Ethan Pond—from the word "wild," to the bait ban, the barbless hook, and the catch-and-release rule—fits the ecological aesthetic and desires of the new group of fishing conservationists, with a strong association to fly fishing, that began emerging in the early 1970s.

But things are not always as they seem. Scratch the surface some, or stand on your head, and the world looks different. Take the idea of wilderness. Though Ethan Pond sits on the edge of a federal wilderness area, a better frame for viewing this White Mountains wilderness is of the highly disturbed landscape slowly recovering from massive disruption described above. What was truly wild in the 1830s may have existed in Ethan Allen Crawford's day, though even by then it was fading. Wild has always been a relative concept. Even the wild brookies here, genetically anyway, belie their "wild" moniker. The last fingerlings stocked at Ethan came from Kennebago Lake genetic stock, trucked over to New Hampshire hatcheries from Maine.

Wild or not, the Wild Trout Pond designation with its no-kill rule seems to stand on reason. The regulation is understood as a way to protect what is described often and widely perceived as a threatened native species from overharvest, while allowing sport anglers their pleasure. Yet, biologically speaking, the rules' benefits to this local population are not a slam dunk. Studies show high brook trout natural-mortality rates. Water temperature, water and air chemistry, water depth, available nutrients, and water supply control the destinies of brook-trout populations throughout their range, especially high up in the watershed—not whether the occasional angler catches a bite to eat. The remote location of Ethan Pond and very light fishing pressure guarantee that human predation will not be a major factor in trout natural mortality any time soon, possibly ever, the way things are going. That's not to say the trout population will survive at Ethan. Weather and food supply will decide. There are economic benefits to ending stocking here and promoting a wild trout population—it's cheaper and smarter than growing and flying in hatchery trout—but ending fishing with bait or outlawing trout sushi on the shore contain dubiously limited ecological benefits. Brook trout, thanks to evolution across thousands of generations can survive in these harsh mountain places, even when annual natural mortality rates reach as high as 90% for every year class. They're an r-selected species designed for disturbance. That means small numbers of them are capable of repopulating their places following even cataclysmic loss. They're a boom-and-bust, highly migratory fish with a knack for finding cold spring water in drought years. They have few aims in life outside of survival, growth, and spawning. They're excellent at adapting, even in the most challenging places and times. But they thrive best in well-connected watersheds where main-stem rivers are seamlessly connected to tiny tributary brooks, shaded pools, and eternal springs. And they absolutely need cold water of good quality. Mortality brought about by hooking injury and harvest by anglers would have to approach 40 to 50% of the population to change this basic formula. That's simply not going to happen three miles up a rocky trail at a remote pond with small fish. In other, more accessible locations with greater fishing pressure, brook trout may need greater protections.

There is also the biological concept of "compensatory mortality" to consider. It says that in general, the greater the human harvest of a wild trout population, the less natural mortality. And the reverse is also true. Less human-caused mortality means higher mortality by other means, including primarily a limited food base. Nature will always get her pound of flesh, whether that nature includes the human predator or not. Even with big swings in mortality, brook trout will—in high quality, connected habitat—endure. They will die in great numbers too, feeding otter, bear, microbe, and the like. If our taking less leaves more for bears, then there's a biological justification to wild pond rules that's worth exploring (this has been amply illustrated with native cutthroat populations in heavily fished areas like Yellowstone National Park; they are vital sources of food to grizzly bear populations and highly susceptible to angling pressure).

The real threats to brook trout populations in the White Mountains and up and down the Appalachian chain are cloud born and landscape scale, including acid and nitrogen precipitation and other airborne pollutants, mining tailings, a warming planet, mass land use changes, logging, road building, and losses to development by urbanization and suburban sprawl. The way to save brook trout is to deal with corporate greed and exploitation, repair fragmented habitat, dechannelize rivers, remove dams, improve cover, clean up mine tailings, plant trees, curb acid precipitation, and cool an overheating planet. It's salvage and restoration work, both. The conservation-minded angler knows as much and should cast a very cold eye on Wall Street, corporate developers, industrial loggers, energy company air polluters, and mining conglomerates. But without broad public knowledge, support, and organization, the aware angler is helpless against these. So are trout. And the public's perception of the value of wild trout is fading, not growing.

Up here, the Wild Trout Pond designation is a social rule, empty of meaning except for its natural symbolism. So, why such a rule? I asked John Viar, who's been in charge of stocking these fisheries in the White Mountains for a long time.

"Some people," he told me, "want to fish for wild trout." Who are those people? One thing about them is known: Few live in the White Mountain region year-round. They may have a second home in Bartlett, but they probably don't have a permanent address there. Distinctions in angling methods come down to differences in physical address more often than not—even when, broadly speaking, cultural values are closely shared.

The Wild Trout Pond rules at Ethan restrict one type of social user (the bait angler who doesn't resort to other methods). Such rules are designed to reduce hooking mortality. They fit a category of rules called special regulations because they exist outside the norm—they add a layer of protection. In a recent survey of the role of special regulations in wild trout management, researchers from Pennsylvania found that 61% of the biologists surveyed in the fourteen states believed special regulations in trout management are warranted based solely on social preferences (Detar and Carline 2014), as opposed to biological need. For the user groups that lobby for them, such special regulations mark a type of quality fishing experience that their members highly value and will travel far to find. Of the biologists surveyed in the Detar/Carline study, 56% believed special regulations increase fishing pressure, providing a kind of road map to good fishing. Biologists polled also indicated that they understand special regulations often reduce participation by other, less organized angler groups, and that this can lead to feelings of disenfranchisement. What results is resource partitioning, where some of the best trout fishing resources are made off limits to anglers who use live baits, even though 89% of the biologists surveyed believe that both fishing with bait and some harvests can be compatible with special regulations water.

As Detar and Carline point out, one of the biggest problems faced by fisheries biologists is explaining what special regulations can and can't do. They are no panacea, and are generally not able to make a poor fishery into a good one. Special regulations that are put in place for purely social reasons, to satisfy a particular group's sporting objectives (say, catching a trophy animal), compound a conundrum of culture. Trout anglers have strong-set beliefs, sometimes contradicted by the evidence. The least helpful belief is that their particular group is being zoned off water—in some cases, the best water—because of rules that have no biological merit. The result is resentment and conflict.

It was surprising to me to learn that a majority of New Hampshire's trout anglers use worms and other live bait when they go trout fishing, not fly rods and flies. This is also true in Vermont and in most rural states. In my old universe, everyone was a fly angler, or if not, should be. That's because it was the group I belonged to. In my teens and early twenties, I papered my bedroom walls with pictures of big trout from *Fly Fisherman* magazine. I had recurring dreams of trout streams so vivid that for years I thought they were real. It wasn't long before I began traveling west. I've sought catch-and-release waters from the

North Ram in Alberta to the South Platte in Colorado. But size doesn't matter to everyone. For the local angler living in Hart's Location or Twin Mountain—a grandfather, maybe, who fished Ethan Pond with worms once a year for forty years, and who brings his grandchildren there—the social rule at Ethan is limiting. And since native trout and the sport's survival are deeply rooted in the hearts and minds of future anglers, the influence of rules on participation is worth a hard look.

Wild trout—all native animals and plants in all the wild and domestic places, for that matter—are slung between the poles of society's love and neglect. I came of age in the early 1970s thinking that a bright fish dangling from a thin silk thread is "beauty as well as bread." John Muir penned that idea once about wilderness itself. But sadly, in today's world, wild trout mean nothing much at all to most people. Few Americans—less than 3%—go trout fishing. The social dimension is never separate from a conservation goal. Trout fishing isn't only sport for sport's sake. That may be the value of listening to pissed-off small-town worm anglers like Roger Kerr. For native coldwater fish to survive, we may have to eat them.

CHAPTER 2

Trout Fishing and the Diminishing Rural Class

The diminution of the fish is generally ascribed mainly to the improvidence of fishermen in taking them at the spawning season, or in greater numbers at other times than the natural increase can supply. It is believed moreover, and doubtless with good reason, that the erection of sawmills, factories and other industrial establishments on all our considerable streams, has tended to destroy and drive away fish. . . . It is probable that other and more obscure causes have had a very important influence in producing the same result. Much must doubtless be ascribed to the general physical changes produced by the clearing and cultivation of the soil. . . . It is certain that while the spring and autumnal freshets are more violent, the volume of water in the dry season is less in all our water courses than it formerly was, and there is no doubt that the summer temperature of the brooks has been elevated.

— GEORGE PERKINS MARSH, Report to the Governor
of Vermont on the Artificial Propagation of Fish, 1857

On the eve of leaving for Wisconsin, knowing I'd be away for a few months, and with hopes of catching a last supper with my wife, I went down to the Ottauquechee River to fish. There were fresh mushrooms in the woods, garlic just harvested from the garden, and fingerling potatoes to throw into the mix; in the river there was a large rainbow trout hanging out by a drowned tree. I didn't really have time to go fishing, but it's always good luck to say goodbye to the river you know best, and I might catch that fish. Part of my rural rootedness is that crooked river, and my rod and an old squeaky reel connect me to it. It's the memories of fish and people that help remind me that I live in a rural place, that I raised my three children in this place where a boulder in a river is as familiar to me as it is to them. City people may be fond of particular street corners and food vendors. We have rope swings and dirt roads.

For hundreds of years, writers have drawn connections between hunting, fishing, and their importance to maintaining rural culture, class, and character. In Vermont, one of the most rural states in the union by population and land mass alone, we have an early and powerful voice for that connection in George Perkins Marsh, author of *Man and Nature* in 1854. Marsh was one of the first to write about the social benefits of hunting and fishing to rural people and culture. He knew that if you want to rile a Vermonter, take away his work; to thoroughly ruin him, take away his game. He believed an urbanizing Vermont needed hunting and fishing because, even though these activities risked contributing to rural lassitude, they built character and fought back against the softening influences of urban existence.

During Marsh's time here in the mid-1800s, Lake Champlain fisheries were collapsing, thanks to the gillnetting of spawning rivers. As Marsh pointed out, it wasn't only overfishing, but changes in land use, land clearing, and pollution from mills, mill ponds, and settlements that destroyed fish and game. By the 1850s, deer, moose, catamount, and beaver, along with the land's capacity to produce abundant game, were gone from Vermont. As for Marsh's confluence of nature and culture, and the value of fish and game—not only to nutriment, but to the spirit of the nation—Marsh foresaw a parallel loss of rural people and culture along with rural nature. One hundred and fifty years after the publication of Marsh's *Man and Nature*, his predictions have been borne out. Rural culture has been long in decline.

Do we even have a rural class anymore in America, or is rural life slipping away, fading to myth, so backseat as to be all but invisible? I think if you asked most Vermonters, they would say yes, Vermont has genuine elements of rural culture, quite distinct from the mere rural lifestyle hawked by real estate agents around here and not to be confused with the real thing. Yes, Vermont is a great place to settle if you have a fortune, and people do, but there are elements of deep rural community values that drive our transactions, habits, beliefs, and control of our local schools, politics, and economies; our ways of being that can seem closed up and unfriendly at first to outsiders, but that in fact are generous and welcoming once you get to know us. While tourism may be a dominant force in the Vermont economy today, local agriculture is experiencing a surprising resurgence; so is forest-based manufacturing. We still have town meeting. It's likely that we know our state representatives on a first-name basis. If we don't know the governor on a first-name basis, it's likely we are only one or two degrees of separation away.

Indeed, we are proud of our rural roots here—even if we aren't technically from here (me: no, wife: yes). To be sure, as much as we celebrate our agricultural history, at certain points, history has been particularly unkind to rural Vermonters, especially new arrivals. And I'm not talking about the weather. Rural persons in Vermont have treated each other poorly in the past and been treated by the political elite as backwards, indifferent to ambition, unholy, and quite possibly imbecilic. For example, there was a time when the KKK was part of the Vermont social landscape, focusing hatred on French Canadian Catholics settled in small Vermont towns close to the northern border with Quebec. Vermont had its active eugenics promoters too (mostly urbanite elites from New York), with its forced sterilizations of rural people from the 1920s through 1940s. But these are exceptions, not the rule of rural life, where large extended families and neighborliness—especially during hard times—get you through. In spite of it all, rural life continues and, in some respects, thrives in Vermont.

But here's the question: Does a trout-fishing tradition contribute in any measurable way to the health of rural culture here? Does trout fishing really matter at all? If it goes the way of the two-person saw, will anyone notice? Will there be some effect on the quality and resilience of rural life?

If I drill down into my own relationship to trout and rivers in Vermont over the past thirty years, I find memories of family outings, fish, swimming holes, found objects (my oldest daughter had an incredible knack for finding buck knives that anglers had left behind), and conversations with farmers who said I could park on and walk across their land, or who had stories of better fishing gone by. You meet people. Strange, solitary anglers appear. Once, an elderly woman decked out in battered waders and vest with an ancient cane fly rod and woven creel, came ghosting by, flinging expert casts downstream.

My haunts were the miles and miles of the undammed White River, with its multiple branches growing far up into the very heart of rural central Vermont. In this part of Vermont—and this is true the farther north you get in the state—there are fewer and fewer with fortunes and more and more living in trailers, following the hatchery truck, fishing for dinner, and ready to share their bread and spin their theories of trout fishing along with their favorite lures and fish worms.

I suppose trout fishing is what also originally exposed me to rural poverty, to people living off the back *back* dirt roads with deer in the freezer. Vermont, for all its rural chic, has alarmingly high rates of poverty, addiction, and illiteracy. It's also true that rural Vermonters are ingenious at getting by through thrift, hard work, and family connections. The old culture of harvesting from land and water survives. What looks like poverty to a city person isn't always impoverished. I've seen it firsthand. In that sense, trout fishing gave me an opening. Thirty years ago I was using trout fishing both as family entertainment and as an occasional way to escape the endless work of little children, demanding jobs, and low non-profit wages, to see what could be discovered abroad in the forms of water, hatchery rainbows, wild brookies, and the rare lunker brown. Trout fishing helped construct a personal culture, a new kind of language, a bilingualism, and a multicultural view inside me. It helped me better understand where I really lived. Does trout fishing sustain rural culture? Yes, if culture is sustained by memory as much as by practice and food. Yes, if rural culture is part of the reality we construct inside.

George Perkins Marsh, an enthusiastic reader of books, including Alexander von Humboldt's *Cosmos*, and certainly a member of Vermont's small intellectual elite, was never content to look solely at the economic and ecological utilities of natural resources. Fish, like Catholic saints and the camel, were a type of opening for him to an understanding beyond himself. His curiosity drew him far outside Vermont to serve as ambassador to Turkey and then Italy. Back home, he'd already conducted a study of the state of Vermont's fisheries, and influenced his good friend Spencer Baird's classic study of fish declines in southern New England coastal waters in the 1870s. Baird was founder and first director of the US Fish Commission, precursor to the National Marine Fisheries Service. Marsh foresaw the need for a federal approach to regulation and fish culture. He passed that on to Baird, and Marsh's ideas became, in addition to Baird's work describing the fishes that lived in New England waters, Baird's charge.

Marsh had some wrong-headed ideas too, including his thoughts on human racial hierarchy, and that we should follow the Romans and French by growing and releasing exotic fish into our waters to bolster native stocks (oops!). But the foundation of the idea of fish culture has its strong upside too. Hatcheries can grow native fish and help build back threatened stocks. They can teach, in addition to providing cost-effective recreation.

So who goes trout fishing these days in Vermont?

Like much else when it comes to living in Vermont, there are at least two types of Vermonter in the world of trout fishing, and everything in between. Generally speaking, only one is locally born. That is to say, a growing majority of Vermont residents are not; they moved here and bred. People like me. Traveling anglers are welcomed here, but Vermont doesn't have much of a well-developed destination trout fishery (the Battenkill River maybe, but quality is way down there), outside of Lake Champlain's lake trout, bass, and landlocked Atlantic salmon. We have more blue-ribbon trout-fishing literature than actual trout fishing. Vermont's fishing writers include John Merwin, who edited and published collections of Lee Wulff, A.J. McLane, and Ernest Schwiebert. He lived on the banks of the Battenkill in Dorset and ran the fly-fishing museum for a while. John recently passed away. Northeast Kingdom novelist Howard Frank Mosher wrote about the Willoughby run of rainbows out of the Lake Memphremagog in stories like *Where the Rivers Flow North*. Closer to home, we have the never-identified Vermont river in a book of the same name by W.D. Wetherell. *Vermont River* is an homage to a decent country trout stream here in the Connecticut River Valley and the exceptional love one fly angler holds for it. Annie Proulx lived nearby once. Trout occasionally make a cameo appearance in her stories (read "The Wer-Trout"). Actual trout fishing can be okay too, if you work at it.

One type of local angler is part of an older fishing culture epitomized by a friend I'll call Brook Trout Bob. Bob works at our local landfill and specializes in fishing small brooks for wild brook trout, using worms. He collects useful junk, and I've brought him old fishing gear gleaned from relatives' basements. No, he told me, when I asked him if he ever fishes with a fly rod, "I ain't no elitist." (Recently, he told me a friend has given him a fly rod and he is learning to become a fly-fishing elitist.) He is kind of an elite worm fisherman, working his worm fishing into a science. He has his favorite holes—some, you might drive by every day and never suspect they hold brook trout. Or, using GPS and detailed aerial maps, he hoofs it into remote beaver ponds and quickly catches his limit of twelve wild brook trout (which he eats with satisfaction, preferring the standard hot-oil-in-a-frying-pan method). Most worm fishermen I've run across are older, well-seasoned anglers and hunters. They fish in May, when bouncing a worm down a spring-cold brook is a deadly approach for brook trout and hungry rainbows. Bob fishes all summer. He's also a proficient morel hunter. When the apples bloom and we get a slug of rain, he's out looking under old elm trees. Like fishing—and fiddle-heading and wild-leek gathering in late April—his trout fishing is a place-based affair. Mushroom hunters have their spots. Brook trout fishing, the way Brook Trout Bob approaches it, is a forager's art, as old as the Abenaki and their distant kin.

At the other end of the spectrum is Thomas Ames Jr., an elementary school teacher. He's well educated, erudite, a prolific fly angler, and a writer and photographer. His fine, large-format photo books on aquatic insects are classics of trout-fishing literature, the product of a fly-fishing passion combined with a trained photographer's eye. Tom travels across New England, hauling fly rod, bug box, and camera equipment, searching as much for aquatic insects as for the trout that eat them. I never get tired of looking at his photos in *Fishbugs: The Aquatic Insects of an Eastern Flyfisher*. I doubt Tom eats trout, but he may. He may have eaten the bugs, too. Plenty of Vermont fly anglers of Tom's ilk keep a trout for the table; not a few have sampled naked caddisflies.

Fishing culture is reflected in the state's history of private trout fishing clubs. Around the end of the nineteenth century, private lodges cropped up on lakes well stocked with trout. The two clubs closest to my hometown of Woodstock are a study in contrasts. The Lakota Club was founded in 1874 by prosperous Woodstock merchants, lawyers, and other successful businessmen, many with ties to New York, railroads, and gold-prospecting fortunes. Today, you have to be invited to join, and the annual fee is several thousand dollars, on top of which you agree to spend a certain amount on food and drink. Built in the Adirondack style—with large sitting rooms, a wraparound porch, and a view of a placid, trout-full lake below—Lakota strikes that perfect balance between primitive and luxurious. The food and drink are excellent, and the historical photos exhibited provide a direct line to the early development of fly fishing as a gentleman's sport. To top off the storied history, Teddy Roosevelt visited Lakota in the early days of the twentieth century and gave the club a pair of mounted deer heads with their antlers locked in a deadly embrace. Lakota embodies the conservation ethic and aesthetic of the first American fly-fishing elite, with its emphasis on social intercourse, aristocratic hues fascinated by Indian lore, and a return to the Acadian dream. While children might be allowed the use of a worm to catch a trout at Lakota, one member wrote, they would be gently weaned away from the "vicious practice of fishing with bait or treble hook" as soon as practical, and taught the "gentle art" of fishing with a fly. My favorite artifact there is a fly tied to look like a hummingbird.

Twenty miles away as the crow flies, near the once-brawling mill town of Bridgewater (the town that periodically dyed the Ottauquechee red), is a trout club with a bluer-collar tinge. The Meccawe Club was founded in 1900. Calvin Coolidge was once a member. Worms and lures are okay, and members, who pay an annual fee of $1,500 bring and prepare their own food. The club building is an old schoolhouse, very quaint. It sits on a rise overlooking the lake and nine hundred acres of wild land. The manager told me they throw in some very large trout, just so "young anglers get the feel of catching large trout." These have to be returned to the water. There is a quote from Richard Brautigan's *Trout Fishing in America* on the wall. All in all, the club is beautifully unassuming, the water quality and fishing similar to Lakota.

Good rule making strikes a balance. It's a mistake to believe that one type of angler is more local than another or more entitled in Vermont. Like every other state, Vermont has trout anglers with different needs and values. As is the case with all cultural divides, there is far more that joins trout fishing enthusiasts than separates them. Locality, sense of place, favorite spots, expertise, and hard-won knowledge are all shared values, whether it's worms or flies or lures that are sworn by. Vermont anglers love where they get to go, sometimes in spite of the backdrop, and they keep their secrets. One music teacher I know fishes on midsummer evenings from a canoe on the Connecticut River, somewhere behind the big-box stores of a busy retail strip. He sings snatches of opera while fishing for large rainbows, almost exclusively using size-sixteen Parachute Adams. He would never tell me exactly where the holes are. He would never even tell his wife. They are now divorced. Another friend has gotten to know a secret *Hexagenia* hatch in the corner of a certain unnamed nighttime pond. There are sets of riffles vaguely located on the Black River where very large brown trout can be found; and in the floodplains of the White River, hard-to-walk-to nightspots where giant browns engulf mouse imitation flies. These are places seldom shared, and fished by a select few. Brook Trout Bob, on the other hand, is constantly offering to show me his latest stream.

Vermont's trout fishing regulations reflect the mixed, mostly local makeup of her trout anglers. The general regulations in Vermont are considered liberal by many who would prefer more restrictive regulations, but liberality in trout regulations, like in politics, is the rule in Vermont. It's a nod to old culture, actually, that Vermont allows for the harvest of up to twelve brook trout in most rivers and streams (fewer if brown trout or rainbows). Twelve wild brook trout may sound high, but as Vermont fisheries biologist Jud Kratzer put it, allowing anglers to keep twelve fish potentially makes use of fish that are bound not to make it through the winter bottleneck or a summer drought or flood—the latter two increasing in frequency, thanks to climate change. Few anglers actually catch anything close to their limit. Kratzer described to me an interesting kind of reverse psychology when it comes to lowered limits. Since "limiting out" is a traditional goal that seems to keep many anglers returning to the stream, he said, lowering limits may actually increase angler effort—a four-fish limit may feel within reach, while a twelve-fish limit may not. But Cedric Alexander, an old University of Vermont classmate and chief moose biologist for the state, put it this way: "You can't make a meal of four tiny brook trout!" Of course he would think that—look at the quarry he's comparing trout to.

But many anglers I know vehemently disagree with the assertion that wild brook trout should be caught and killed by the dozen. Surf the web, and you'll find the majority web-housed belief that wild brook trout are so precious and rare that not even one should be kept. That opinion is still in the minority in Vermont. According to Vermont's most recent angler survey, Vermont resident anglers were twice as likely to use bait and keep some of their catch than not.

Vermont regulators, in fact, have used special trout regulations on streams sparingly. Some claim Vermont Fish and Wildlife is kowtowing to old-school fishermen who hold up tradition as a kind of sacred cow (that would be the Holstein). But the state policy document on special regulations is clear and based on good science, noting that special regulations often do not produce the desired results—more trout, larger trout, and greater catch rates—where they've been applied. Most of Vermont's trout streams do not have the nutrient productivity for trout growth or longevity or great enough fishing pressure for even a severe special regulation, say no-kill, to have a positive influence on the trout population. What *has* been shown on special regulations water is dramatically reduced angler effort. On the New Haven River, for example, angler hours went from 1,963 to 700 when a no-kill zone was imposed on three and a half miles of stream. On a section of the White River that went to an experimental rule of one trout per day, with an eighteen-inch minimum limit (this is effectively no-kill), with the objectives of increasing the catch rate and size of rainbows, angling hours didn't change, but bait anglers dropped out and fly fishermen increased. The trout population changed very little.

Sometimes, special regulations are justifiable, and Vermont uses many of them on heavily fished ponds and lakes, but in a state that is losing anglers thanks to demographic changes and shifting public attitudes, pushing more anglers out by regulation is costly.

Just how dire is trout fishing in Vermont by the numbers of anglers? Pretty dire. In Vermont, angler surveys conducted in 1990, 1999, and 2010 show a 30% decline in sales of fishing licenses—for all types of fishing—over the past twenty years. According to the US Fish and Wildlife Service, New England has 7% of the nation's trout anglers and it has experienced a 12% decline in numbers over the past twenty years. From the results of Vermont Fish and Wildlife's own angler census work, of the people still fishing in Vermont, small- and largemouth bass have overtaken trout fishing in popularity for the first time. Trout fishing, in terms of days fished, is down (out-of-state anglers put in more hours on the stream per visit than Vermont locals—this is also true in New Hampshire and reflects a national trend—but anglers fishing for other freshwater fish spend more days fishing).

On the other hand, bluegill fishing has increased from 17% to 38% in ten years. Ice is also hot. Ice fishing for perch, a family affair, is way up, along with the aforementioned black bass. Residents and non-residents alike appear to support both put-and-take, hatchery-based trout fisheries and special regulations like lower creel limits and higher size limits in trout management. Bait anglers would like to keep eating those twelve wild fish for breakfast, if they could only catch them; most, with the exception of a few prodigies like Brook Trout Bob, cannot. Those few who can, do "catch and release 'em into the frying pan," as the saying goes, with virtually no impact on the fishery. What about me? Can I catch a fish on the Ottauquechee and bring a rainbow dinner back to the clan? It's never guaranteed. But it's worth a try.

I'm one of those lucky anglers who's gotten to travel to fish, thanks to an understanding spouse. But there's no place like the home river. There's a path only I use, hard to find; virtually no one fishes where I fish, so I have come to feel a sense of ownership of a place that is technically not mine.

By the time I got to the river, the sun was low enough to put long shadows on the north side of the hills. It had been warm and dry, but I could hear a toad trilling, and the leaves of the trees still had some of their early-summer green fullness. There was a kingfisher chattering across the river, and I could hear cars up on Route 4, hidden from view by the south bank and tall trees.

Standing on the pale sandbar, I recalled my old dad. He was going strong until recently, when a combination of illnesses hooked him deep and brought him down. Fathers and sons who fish or hunt together often have a strong bond. It was fathers who traditionally initiated their sons into the blood sports. For many, trout fishing brings memories of youth and of the father, long after he is gone. Social scientists think this may be what keeps some men and women fishing, even as they begin to struggle with aching joints and poor balance. To be clear, that is not the case with me. I may be aging into decrepitude, but my father wasn't an angler; fish were too slippery for him. He was a lifelong golfer—a state champion in his younger years—and he had a different concept of the lie (for you non-golfers, this means, among other things, the location of a golf ball at rest) than we fishermen do. Dad could drive a golf ball long, straight, and true, and he tried to teach me that trick. But golf is beyond me. Actually, I'm dismayed by golf; I think of it as simply a frustrating abstraction of fishing. Casting my fly to a fish is like his drive to a flag on a green. My sweet, old, five-weight Sage fly rod; his five iron. Rod to club. Fly to ball. Cast to drive. Line to lie. Good fish on to a birdie putt. Giant whopper beached to hole in one. My dad got two hole-in-ones in his life and many club championships. That's rare. That's how good he was. When he stopped playing golf is when he started to die.

This river has seen the likes of some excellent fathers in the past. For example, George Perkins Marsh's lesser-known cousin James Marsh, a religious philosopher considered a father of American transcendentalism and much more. He lived on the river too, just downstream a few miles from us. It was James Marsh who brought to the attention of New England's elite thinkers, including Ralph Waldo Emerson and other Concord religious philosophers, the mystical writings of English romantic Samuel Taylor Coleridge. As one of UVM's early presidents, James taught and inspired John Dewey. He spoke German and made

some of the first English translations of the German romantic philosophies of Immanuel Kant and Georg Wilhelm Friedrich Hegel while at
Dartmouth College. What I love best about cousin James is his idea
that, through the powers of the mind, *Mind* itself can be transcended
to the divine realm. That's a paradox of the highest order, if you believe. That through ourselves, we have the power to overcome ourselves. We may think that managing trout is all about fish science and
aquatic biology, hydrology, and molecular biology. But both Marshes
believed real human progress in any scientific or industrial field was "a
condition," as George said (Marsh 1847), of inward being, not a mani-
festation of outward science, technology, and action. The real action is
in the human heart and head, not the dancing rod. Both would agree
that cleaning up rivers and protecting native fish starts with an inward
transformation—cleaning up the mind—to integrate ecological thinking and social goals with a moral outlook. They bemoaned the "clang
of hammer and forge," mindless industrialization in the absence of balance. Balance and integration are what George Perkins Marsh, dubbed
"father of the American conservation movement" by his biographer,
imagined could be reflected on the land as the balance of open lands,
forests, and urban development. To James Marsh, balance referred to
inner balance too, divine rational thought and passion-driven action.
Artful land stewardship started with right thinking. A balanced people
was needed. Not only a scientific elite and the legislators in its grasp, but
a widespread ordinary community that broadly understood the public
good. If you think about it, this blending of the practical science of George
Perkins Marsh with the spiritual landscape of James explains a national
pastime such as has evolved in fly fishing—a thinking man's reflective
occupation, as much meditation on the fly as on the conditions of
social life, the science of resource conservation, and landscape-based
stewardship.

The Marsh cousins' ideas taken together argue against trout
fishing as sport only. Trout fishing is more. There is significant room
for a broad basement of understanding through different angles of
view. There's room for a gastronomy of wild trout and strong rural
traditions, where fishing for a meal survives and wild animals are
hunted and consumed, even as they thrive and multiply in a landscape
well cared for. Eating a wild fish, rather than catching and releasing it,

can bring sport closer to home. We tend to take care of what's closer to home. And that's why I took the ghost of my father fishing. My father may not have been a trout angler, but he understood that we had to take care of the land. He took good care of his.

This pool with my big problem trout in it was long, straight, and deep, and it flowed into the branches of a downed tree before turning sharply left and deflecting back into the shallow center of the river. I wanted my fly deep by the time it got to that tree. The fly wasn't an earthworm, but it *was* a woolly worm—a black yarn body with green, sparkly chenille threads, grizzly hackle, and a bead head to get it down. Some purists feel the use of a woolly worm is cheating, but it's a popular fly around here. The cast would require aggressive mending, distance, and accuracy. With Dad watching from my shoulder, I put a decent cast where it needed to go.

Watch that rod tip, Dad. See the deft sideways push at the end of the cast, how it sends line upstream? That's deliberate. Watch the fly hit the water and disappear, now mend, mend, mend! Follow the line, and imagine the woolly worm sparkling deep by the branches of that submerged tree. Get ready, get ready. Face that tree, rod tip high. Right there! Strike! Fish on; birdie putt.

The big ones are scarce and special.

And they taste good too. Leaving home for a long fishing trip to Wisconsin, it's a good practice to cast some thanks into a home river before you go. You can cast prayers for children and farewells to fathers, both. The casting of the mind—the transcendence of the mind, the transformation of it by the Mind of the river—is a marvelous, dependable, and necessary thing.

As for eating a two-pound, eighteen-inch, rainbow-hued fish, don't forget the wild mushrooms. Does a trout matter to rural culture? It does when baked with fresh garden dill.

CHAPTER 3

Worms and Trout and Hooking Mortality, Oh My!

Let's have a standing ovation for the worm, the lowly little critter who is all things to all fishermen . . . and so much maligned. When a man takes his son fishing for the first time, what do they use for bait? A hundred to one, they use worms. . . . [Yet] the whispering campaign is always going on against the worm.

> — LEE WULFF, "The Lost Art of Fishing with a Worm,"
> *Collier's*, 1954

It was the bastard in the backseat without any underwear that he hated. The bastard who had ruined most of our summer fishing. The bait-fishing bastard. The bait-fishing bastard who had violated everything that our father had taught us about fishing by bringing a whore and a coffee can of worms but not a rod.

> — NORMAN MACLEAN, *A River Runs Through It and Other Stories*, 1976

Contrary to the claims of many prominent anglers and angling authors, no-kill is not a sure cure for all the ills of trout management. There are many trout waters where no-kill is not a suitable management approach. If habitat is not suitable for the maintenance of an exceptional trout population, then no protective regulation will produce more than the environment can sustain.

> — DELANO R. GRAFF, *Trout Magazine*, 1978

Until about a score of years ago, this Country's basic management goal was MSY or "maximum sustained yield," measured purely in pounds without regard to size and without taking into consideration that an angler who fishes for sport might rather catch one fine trophy fish than a greater total weight of small ones. Only recently did "quality" become a point of consideration in our research. . . . The ultimate tool for the development of quality fishing is the NO-KILL regulation.

— LEE WULFF, "The Trout Fishing of the Future,"
Wild Trout Symposium II, 1979

On the way to Wisconsin, I took a slight detour to meet with retired fisheries expert Robert Carline on his home river in State College, Pennsylvania. I wanted to ask him some questions about regulations at Spring Creek and hooking mortality studies. Spring Creek may be the best example of a resurrected urban cold-water fishery anywhere in the country. It also has an unusual special regulation. While it's strictly a catch-and-release river, there is no bait exclusion. You can fish with worms if you want to, or lures, or flies, except for a one mile stretch of flies-only water called Fisherman's Paradise. This wormy fact may seem vanishingly irrelevant in the greater scheme of trout management. But Pennsylvania's decision to allow bait at Spring Creek back in 1980 represented a break in the catch-and-release narrative of the day—a small revolt, in fact. At the time the decision was made to allow bait, the drive to ban live bait from high-quality fisheries like Spring Creek was at its peak. While a good game fish may be too valuable to catch only once, a good angler is also too valuable to lose. Pennsylvania, thanks to strong leadership in the fisheries division—Ralph Abele and later Delano Graff—seemed determined at the time to hold onto its trout anglers, and to base fishing regulations on sound biological and social science, not hearsay and politics.

Nestled in the Alleghenies, an Appalachian range of north-south-trending ridges and valleys, Spring Creek flows out into Amish country, where all manner of white-, yellow-, and black-hatted Amish families live, worship, and farm together, each with their own distinguishing style of worship. The ridges are of sandstones and shales, the eroded remains of an ancient Pangaean continental collision and uplifted seabed. It's a landscape that's rippled like the outer rings of the rise a trout makes when it lifts for a mayfly. Underlying the shales is calcareous bedrock—dolomites and limestone materials. This is karst terrain, characterized by fractures and sinkholes that provide ample opportunity for groundwater infiltration at the base of the ridges; the same fractured bedrock that stores groundwater and gives outlet to flowing springs throughout the valley floors. At least seven large springs feed Spring Creek, including the unusually large spring at Bellefonte (giving Bellefonte its name) and many smaller springs and seeps, all of which provide a steady supply of cool groundwater and dissolved nutrients for much of the creek's twenty-two-mile run to Bald Eagle Creek. From there, it's on to the Susquehanna River.

With the strong fundamentalism of calcareous bedrock, clean, cold water, low sedimentation, a high pH, and plenty of dissolved nutrients, Spring Creek's native brook-trout population thrived into the early years of the twentieth century. Then urban development caught up with Spring Creek. Sedimentation, pollution, overharvest, and competition from brown trout killed off the native brook trout. In his 1885–86 report to Congress, Spencer Baird, head of the US Fish Commission, reported on the first German brown trout, sent to Pennsylvania in the form of ten thousand fertilized eggs. Between 1887 and 1888, another thirty thousand fertilized brown-trout eggs came from Loch Leven, Scotland, to the Corry State Fish Hatchery in western Pennsylvania. The stocking of Spring Creek brown trout probably began in 1892. Browns can live in warmer water and they're much more resistant to angling pressure. American anglers didn't take to them right away, but browns adapted well, and soon enough became accepted citizens, a quarry worthy in their own right.

I met Bob Carline for breakfast on the morning I arrived over the ridge from Amish country. Carline started his career with the Wisconsin DNR in 1967, working under trout researcher and trout-stream restorer Robert Hunt. By 1984, Carline had moved to the US Fish and Wildlife Service as leader of Pennsylvania's Cooperative Fish and

Wildlife Research Unit, US Geological Survey. He has been active in national wild-trout circles for years, attending most of the Wild Trout Symposia in Yellowstone, and serving as editor of proceedings there for the past two. A biologist by training, he's also keenly interested in the social dimensions of trout fishing, and lately, has been involved in research that looks at national trends in the application of special regulations.

I asked Bob, over eggs, toast, and coffee, about Spring Creek's 1980s open-bait policy. The data clearly showed, he told me, that there could be a no-harvest fishery that allowed worm fishing. Spring Creek had high enough productivity (successful breeding) and recruitment (the survival of large numbers of young trout to breeding age). Combined with mandated catch and release and relatively low rates of natural mortality, hooking mortality wasn't having an appreciable impact on Spring Creek trout populations. This was against the conventional wisdom of the time. And it was a big job convincing people otherwise, Bob told me.

Why has hooking mortality been such a hot topic in trout management for so long? And what impacts has the research had on trout angler behavior? Fisheries managers, both marine and freshwater, looking to rebuild and sustain depleted wild sport fisheries in the face of increasing fishing pressure, considered the concept of recycling live fish (returning live caught fish to the water). They needed to understand the contributions that hooking mortality and sub-lethal injury made to natural mortality. With the data in hand, managers could then design fishing technologies, regulations, and a methodology for releasing fish that would optimize survival and minimize death and injury. One result of early hooking mortality studies of trout was that the reputation of the worm and other live bait, already low (see Lee Wulff's first quote at the beginning of this chapter), sank even lower.

In fact, when it comes to worms, the entire research enterprise of hooking mortality studies opened a can of them. Why? First, the worm in trout fishing has a cultural association; demonize the worm, and you demonize a certain kind of angler. Second, doing good hooking mortality studies is really difficult, because there are so many variables to fish survival. Factors like water temperature and quality come into play when considering fish survival rates. Species' differences—

cutthroat, brook, brown, and rainbow trout all exhibit different susceptibility to being caught and injured by hooks. Other factors need to be taken into account, too: the shape and size of the hook, the size of fish, the time of day, the natural history of species' eating manners and food types, hook barbs, fishing techniques, netting and releasing practices, and the investigation of sub-lethal injuries that could affect spawning success or behavior.

Deeply hooked or not, fish can be easily injured through the stress of capture, air exposure, and physical damage to eyes, gills, and the esophagus. Injured fish might survive, but injuries might hurt their long-term chances for reproduction, or could reduce growth and increase susceptibility to disease. That's why some rulebooks mandated barbless hooks (barbs are somewhat debunked now as an influence on mortality, and the requirement of barbless hooks is less seen in trout regulations). On top of the biological data and social biases, there is the humane realm. Americans increasingly view the wild world through the lens of humane attitudes and the ethical dimension. Why are we torturing fish simply to return them to the stream to be tortured again, many would ask? Today, some countries are banning catch and release altogether and instead instituting low bag limits that require anglers to stop fishing when they catch their limit, and to take and use the fish they catch.

In the case of the innocent earthworm's marriage to trout fishing, it's been a long, rocky one. How ironic that Lee Wulff, who would become the barbed-tongued chief spokesman for catch and release and against bait, was writing in the worm's favor in 1954. Or was he? Was that comment he made in *Collier's* back in 1954 accompanied by a wink and nod to his fly-fishing audience? He had certainly contributed to the whispering campaign himself.

But you have to go back to the nineteenth century to get a sense of how deeply ingrained urban myths about worms and rural anglers are. Stereotypes of rural fishers using bait as lazy, ignorant bumpkins poaching the nobleman's fish are sprinkled throughout the earliest trout-fishing literature in America. Even the first fish commissioners in New Hampshire worried that if rural people could live off fish and game, they would lose all ambition and set a bad example to youth; become burdens to the state. Worms became code for "backwards" among the urban fishers desperate to escape their own rural farming ancestries. In Norman Maclean's *A River Runs Through It and Other Stories*, this is the type of angler the brothers complain about: those anglers that moved from Montana to San Francisco, then boast to their new city friends of their fly-fishing prowess, only to resort to worms when they visit home. This is the central irony of Maclean's moving novel—the vast majority of anglers in Maclean's time in Montana were worm anglers. The Scotsman Protestant minister and his fly-fishing sons were classic snobs, a rare exception then, and don't we all wish we could have had the Blackfoot River to ourselves in the 1930s?

Early on, Bob told me, biologists conducted hooking mortality studies in hatcheries, in controlled, still-water environments. They *wanted* the fish to ingest the bait deeply. They changed hook extraction methods and bait types to study the survival rates of deeply hooked fish. In a study conducted in Wisconsin (Mason and Hunt 1967), the mortality rate of rainbow trout that were deeply hooked in a passive hatchery setting (after 120 days) was 34–95%. One 1977 study found a mean hooking mortality of fish caught by bait to be between 30% and 60%, with an average of 40%.

Eventually, hooking mortality studies moved out into the field and into moving water. Angling-based studies on rivers and creeks in Idaho, Montana, and Colorado showed a different picture, and much lower bait-fishing mortality rates—as low as 10%. An Ontario publication designed to offer state-of-the-art catch-and-release methods conducted a meta study of 118 hooking mortality experiments and found higher rates (17%) of hooking mortality. A recent study looking at the effect of actively fished circle hooks (hooks designed to minimize deep hooking) reduced bait hooking-mortality rates in rivers and streams to the dry-fly level—5% or lower.

Regardless of recent studies and new hook technologies, hooking mortality today is held up repeatedly as a reason for restricting bait fishing from blue-ribbon trout streams. Are some of these hooking mortality claims a red herring for a management rationale that has less to do with biology and more to do with reducing fishing pressure?

At Spring Creek anyway, biology, rather than culture, settled the argument. Managers knew from the data that water temperature and flow rates were the primary limiting factors to the trout population here, not angler predation. Besides, said Bob, brown trout can be damned hard to catch, even by very skilled anglers. Even if harvest were allowed, and a low bag limit, the majority of anglers out there are simply not catching many fish. Of those that do, the majority are voluntarily releasing them with or without a no-kill rule.

After breakfast, we went out for a look at Spring Creek. Driving a river is like living in time-lapse photography—you look at lots of small places, still shots that punctuate both the actual flow of water and the narrative flow of words. We found the river in the heart of one of its most developed sections in State College, and we stopped at a certain large spring near a tributary brook. Bob told me that Spring Creek becomes a proper river at that point. Until then, it's a skinny, green ribbon of a creek. We don't have any spring creeks in Vermont. The brooks are freestone and mostly nutrient poor. Our highland trout streams have clean gravel bottoms; water supply, temperature, and food availability are the limiting factors.

The springs I saw here, on the other hand, were covered by a green skin of floating duckweed and fringed with watercress. The creek channels supported flowing green beards of submerged vascular plants. Spring Creek flowed like a green dragon, winding behind garages, passing unseen under culverts, and flooding out into small, wet meadows next to parking lots.

Urban rivers have a lot to contend with. As we left State College, Bob told me that early studies had linked a city's water quality to the percentage of its total impervious surfaces. Total impervious surface has since become a standard indicator of an urbanizing coldwater fishery's chances of survival. Above 12%, and coldwater fisheries in urban areas are predicted to collapse. The upper half of Spring Creek runs through an area with over 19% impervious surfaces, so river restorers were faced with a serious challenge. In paved landscapes, Bob explained, stream flows during storm events tend to flash, increasing sedimentation. Also, asphalt, cement parking lots, roads, and steel roofs all heat water and contribute pollutants, including metals, solvents, and other chemicals used in industry, university, and the home. Urban storm-water runoff infrastructure is often old and unable to do a good job of trapping sediment. Silts smother gravel redds (spawning nests) and destroy the habitat for the insects trout feed on. Surprisingly, though, Spring Creek ultimately proved that the early models on impervious surfaces were flawed; urban rivers are more resilient than we initially thought. Still, to save an urban river, you have to deal with the crap flowing off pavement, including lots of sedimentation.

"To our credit, we had this great volume of spring water available," Bob said. Spring water flows fluctuate with changing precipitation levels and seasons, and the fortunes of trout rest in these fluctuations. Summer droughts, low flow, and warm waters, for example, reduce trout growth, or even kill trout if temperatures run too high. In winter, trout grow best when the water temperature and precipitation are above normal.

Negotiating the narrow neighborhood streets that the creek crosses, Bob described one of the chief challenges to stewardship of an urban river: dealing with wastewater. What to do with it all? State College's population quadrupled in the last hundred years, from 40,000 to 160,000, and that probably doesn't include seasonal Penn State students, who are famous for their beer consumption and attendant urine production. A bigger problem is phosphates from soaps and detergents used in the home and on campus. Phosphates stimulate plant growth in freshwater systems, and plants demand lots of oxygen for respiration. By 1958, Spring Creek was carrying an enormous load of green plant biomass, thanks to the phosphates from sewage treatment effluent. A large aquatic biomass has a high biological oxygen demand. Plants respire at night, using vast quantities of dissolved oxygen—oxygen that the trout also need for their respiration. Two thousand hatchery trout died of asphyxiation due to a lack of oxygen in 1958 at the Benner Springs Fish Hatchery. It wasn't the first time, and it wouldn't be the last.

"The upside of that fish kill," Bob said, "was that it led to a series of in-depth investigations of water quality, benthic macro-invertebrates, and fish at Spring Creek—a comprehensive and long-term look at an entire aquatic ecosystem."

Over-enrichment is much less of a problem today, Bob explained.

Phosphate-bearing effluent has been greatly reduced through spray-irrigation technologies and by the consolidation of five separate waste-water treatment plants into two. Effluent from the large wastewater treatment plant in College Township meets drinking water standards today; for safe measure, it's piped to a golf course for irrigation, a laundry service, and a constructed wetland. Overall acreage in buffer strips and conservation lands along the river has increased dramatically as well. But phosphates weren't the only pollution problem. Industrial chemical spills have plagued Spring Creek from the mid-1950s.

In 1956, a cyanide spill from a lab at Penn State entered the creek, killing fish all the way through. It was all hatchery fish back then; perhaps only 5% of native trout genetic strains were left. Spring Creek saw massive inputs of hatchery fish annually. Once the cyanide flushed out of the system, new hatchery fish went in.

The most significant pollution problem came from the Nease Chemical plant, which produced the pesticides Kepone and Mirex from the 1950s through the 1970s. It was this contamination that ultimately changed the management of Spring Creek trout for good.

The scene of the crime was a small culvert and ditch below the old Nease plant. Standing next to it in 1984, Bob said, you could smell the chemicals in the water: "They were that strong." In 1976, investigators from the Pennsylvania Department of Environmental Protection found high levels of both Kepone and Mirex in trout flesh. Both are considered carcinogens. To protect human health, stocking was eliminated in the reaches below the contamination source in 1978, and in 1981, the Pennsylvania Fish and Boat Commission created a no-kill zone from the contamination source down to the confluence with Bald Eagle Creek. By 1983, the Nease Chemical plant had come under the purview of the EPA's Superfund program. The cleanup continues to this day.

Kepone levels in fish declined rapidly, but Mirex was persistent through about 2000. Around that time, the catch-and-release emergency mandates of 1982 turned into permanent regulations under the Spring Creek Trout Management Area Plan.

Could you still have a quality fishery with some trout harvest? I asked.

Yes, absolutely. A regulation structure could be designed that allowed fishermen to keep a fish or two within certain size parameters and still meet fishing quality objectives, Bob told me. But politically, it was easier to keep the no-kill rule in place. This is an urban population, and the fishing public wants catch and release, including the bait fishermen; there's the perception that the river needs it. Catch rates have gone up, sometimes by a factor of 5x depending on the preiods being compared. But trout fishing for the ordinary urban angler is about something other than catching and keeping trout, Bob said.

An angler here can catch and keep memories of a fine day outdoors, a day immersed in the trivia of hunting without intent to kill, fishing with worms if he wants, or casting a fly of Joe Humphreys', design. On Spring Creek, no one is excluded if they prefer plunking worms to watching the natural drift of a fly. The rules appear to meet the needs of this meandering urban river, the people, and the fish. Somehow, that inclusion of bait—as small a concession as it might appear to many— makes the rules fit society better, as if an important social principle was adhered to.

Just as there are white hat, black hat, and yellow hat Amish around Bellefonte, each in their own private valley and with their own slightly different manner of worship, trout anglers of all stripes on Spring Creek do agree on the most fundamental matters—cold, clean water, wild fish, peace, beauty, and the land's health.

CHAPTER 4

The Pere Marquette River: Hooked on Dollars

Another hopper poked his face out of the bottle. His antennas wavered. He was getting his front legs out of the bottle to jump. Nick took him by the head and held him while he threaded the slim hook under his chin, down through his thorax and into the last segments of his abdomen. The grasshopper took hold of the hook with his front feet, spitting tobacco juice on it. Nick dropped him into the water. Holding the rod in his right hand he let out line against the pull of the grasshopper in the current. He stripped off line from the reel with his left hand and let it run free. He could see the hopper in the little waves of the current. It went out of sight.

— ERNEST HEMINGWAY, "Big Two-Hearted River," 1925

Somehow, over the years, the general populace has acquired the notion that trout are food fish in the same sense that perch, bluegill and crappies are food fish. . . . The most flagrant yet universally condoned abuse is bait fishing.

— ART NEUMANN, founder of Trout Unlimited,
The North Woods Call, 1959

The area's reforms [North Branch of the Au Sable River, northern Michigan],
largely created by outside urbanites, proposed to project a moral fishery that
favored aesthetics over subsistence.
> — BRYON BORGELT, "Flies Only: Early Sport Fishing
> Conservation on Michigan's Au Sable River,"
> PhD Dissertation, University of Toledo, 2009

Peyton and Gigliotti (1988) observed that the extreme levels of specializa-
tion, intense feelings about fishing, and associated ethics of trout anglers
on the Au Sable River cultivated an intolerance of alternative recreational
choices. . . . [They] suggest that as angling groups gain political influence, they
sometimes use that influence to gain regulations favoring their interests and
restricting entry of competing users. . . . On Michigan's Au Sable River,
extreme stereotypes were drawn yet the two groups of anglers were indistin-
guishable on all measured characteristics except two: where they lived, and
whether they placed a priority on the right to harvest a fish.
> — RUSSELL F. THUROW and DANIEL J. SCHILL,
> "Conflicts in Allocation of Wild Trout Resources:
> An Idaho Case History," Wild Trout Symposium V, 1994

Northern Michigan, justly famed for its trout fishing, is sort of on the way to Wisconsin, if you look at the map sideways. I had always wanted to visit there. Hemingway lived there and "Big Two-Hearted River" takes place in northern Michigan. The Great Lakes surround the mitt of it. I also had a worm fishing opportunity in Michigan with two guys, both named Ray. I wanted to meet them, fish with them, and listen in—no two ordinary guys from Michigan are more involved in the ongoing culture wars over trout.

Ray and Ray are not only fishing buddies, but fishing advocates; they've been shoulder to shoulder in a long and bitter campaign against the imposition of special regulations that limit tackle type and live bait on the best stretches of the Pere Marquette and many other prime rivers in northern Michigan, including the Au Sable. This is the part of Michigan best known to fly anglers for its "Holy Water," an eight-mile, flies-only, catch-and-release section of the Au Sable main stem championed by attorney Jim Schramm and businessman Rusty Gates, who took their gear-restriction fight to court and won in the 1980s. There is deeper trout fishing history in Michigan too. It was the birthplace of one of the first fly-fishing-only public waters in the country (1909) on the North Branch of the Au Sable. It's also home to the little town of Grayling, where Trout Unlimited came into being in 1959 when anglers fought the state of Michigan over its hatchery-trout practices and won. There are very strong feelings in northern Michigan to this day, where the fight for more gear-restricted water is alive and well. Anglers of the Au Sable, Michigan Trout Unlimited, Federation of Fly Fishers, Michigan United Conservation Clubs, Michigan River Guides, the Resource Stewards, and various watershed councils represent a veritable phalanx of enlightened self-interest with an unswerving focus on reforming coldwater regulations. On the other side of the table are Ray and Ray and their allies. Because the Rays prefer trout fishing methods that run to live bait—worms, crickets, and wax moths—and because they harvest trout for the table, they're pitted against these groups. From an organizational point of view, this is a David versus Goliath scenario. And yet Michigan, in many respects, has been resistant to special regulations limiting an angler's method. Ray and Ray represent a type of angler that is very likely in the majority.

Ray Richardson and Ray Danders are highly skilled trout, steelhead, and salmon anglers. Over the past forty years, each has logged thousands of hours on the Pere Marquette, and for twenty years, they've been a fishing duo. All that time together has merged their ideas, methods, easy manners, and even their looks—both are fair skinned, ruddy cheeked, of medium build, middle aged, and wear glasses. Ray R. works for a Ford parts company. He grew up on a family farm on White Lake, in Whitehall, Michigan. He recalled to me the alewife boom years, when as a boy, he filled wheelbarrow after wheelbarrow with dead alewives every morning to clean up the family beach. It was the explosion of these exotic, herring-like fish (*Alosa pseudoharengus*) in the Great Lakes that fattened the coho and king salmon introduced in the mid-1960s. Salmon wouldn't have thrived without the total suppression of the non-native lamprey eel. So what we have in the

Great Lakes is an artificial sport fishery of monumental proportions, including enormous economic value.

Ray D. grew up in Grand Rapids, and as a young boy, began making excursions with his family to fish in northern Michigan. He's semi-retired now and has returned to a home and life on the banks of the Little Manistee River, another fine northern Michigan trout and salmon stream. His stories of the state swapping away public lands to private fishing clubs read like a Stephen King novel.

In Michigan, as elsewhere, arguments for catch and release and gear restrictions are persuasively couched in biological, economic, and conservation terms, and the political, organizational roots of gear-restriction advocates run deep. The economic argument is perhaps the most persuasive, both on rural Midwestern main streets and in the state legislature, and fly-angling groups have recently taken a strategic turn in their fight to focus less on the biological impacts of bait fishing and more on the economic benefits of no-kill trout fisheries. Anglers from away have money to spend, and they can spend it in a grow-ing and competitive marketplace of destination trout fisheries from the coastal Pacific and Rocky Mountain West to Wisconsin, Pennsylva-nia, New York, and Alaska, among others. These anglers are the most likely to hire a guide; there are nearly seventy registered guides on the Pere Marquette alone. Angling businesses, including motels, restaurants, tackle shops, and guides, serve to benefit financially, and they have significant political clout. Trout fishing can be a major engine of the tourist economy.

Mostly, Ray R. told me, he, Ray D., and their loose-knit organization of traditional anglers have been dealt setbacks. Over the years, they've had to contend with a Michigan DNR Coldwater Resources Steering Committee that is stacked against them (my own conversations with state biologists in Michigan bore out their claim, though this appears to be changing). They've seen many of their favorite home waters closed to bait fishing, including places they fished as kids. The last big dust-up was during a regulatory review process in 2010, which included a rewrite of a ten-mile section on the Pere Marquette just below an eight-mile stretch made fly-fishing-only earlier. Fly anglers pushed hard for gear and bait restrictions year round, and the Rays pushed back with their band of supporters. Ultimately, there was a compromise that restricted bait from spring through August, then allowed bait for the rest of the year. Ray and Ray saw it as a loss.

"They propose to take it all away and then give a little back and that's called a compromise. We're not against conservation," Ray R. told me. "If I had to give up fishing for the betterment of trout, I would. But that's not the case here." Ray and Ray helped gather three thousand signatures against the bait ban and presented evidence that a bait ban was not necessary for a high quality fishery. But the director of the Michigan DNR had already made up his mind, and his directive to the staff was to get the job done.

"We're not making this up," Ray R. said. "We had a reliable back channel of our own—the retiring head of the trout program. We were out-organized. The director told us, 'they won't listen to you because they know you'll go away.' The fly-fishing clubs will never go away. And they're always at the table. You've got to organize politically or you'll keep losing ground.

"Bait fishermen are not dumb and not apathetic," he continued later. "We'd rather go fishing, but we did attend all hearings, many of which were a long drive, though we weren't always well received by the bulk of attendees. We expected the state to look after everyone's interests. That didn't happen. Special regulations up here could be such that bait, lure, and fly anglers can fish side by side and not impact the number and size of fish in these rivers, but that's not what they want."

Several fisheries biologists told me that the regulation ultimately put in force was utter nonsense from a biological perspective and far too confusing. It was a political solution that neither side liked. To Ray and Ray, the regulation wasn't about protecting fish; the industry simply wanted to clear the river of local riffraff, so well-to-do fly-fishing customers who hire guides could have more elbow room during the summer months, when floating these rivers—in the absence of the crush of steelhead and salmon fishers—can be a very pleasant experience.

The lure of fishing tourists can be difficult to ignore for states that are hard pressed to pay for resource management and conservation. There are strong economic arguments for the jobs created and dollars spent, which can manifest in rule changes that favor traveling anglers—their practices, habits, and desires—over traditional, local fishing customs. Michigan ranks eighth in the nation for attracting non-resident anglers

(Vermont is ranked forty-fourth; New Hampshire, thirty-first; Pennsylvania, sixteenth).

Earlier in the week, I had met with Mark Tonello, state fisheries biologist for the northwest region—including the Pere Marquette watershed—to get a better sense of the biological and social dimensions of trout fishing on these rivers.

Tonello grew up farther south in suburban Detroit, fishing Lake St. Clair—described by some as one of the best lake fisheries in the country. His home river was the urban Clinton, stocked with walleye and steelhead. He was hooked on fishing with his family from an early age. As a kid, he told me, he'd do anything to get to a wild place to fish. Getting to work for the DNR in northern Michigan was a dream come true.

On the topic of hooking mortality and conflicts between the desires of different angler groups, Tonello said that trout fishing pressure on the Pere Marquette is lowest in the summer. The biggest crowds turn out for salmon and steelhead in fall and winter. Most anglers are out in the Great Lakes salmon fishing in the summer, which leaves the Pere Marquette under-fished. "We'd like to see more fishers of all ages and origins enjoying the Pere Marquette in summer. You also have to consider," he added, "that Michigan trout anglers are releasing upwards of 85% of the trout they catch these days. And higher rates of hooking mortality can be offset by lower rates of natural mortality. No, hooking mortality is not a great concern."

Tonello went on to explain that in the sections of the Pere Marquette I'd be fishing with the Rays, brown trout populations run anywhere from 160 to 260 pounds per acre. Anything over 100 pounds is excellent. And of course, that abundance is all about water quality. The Pere Marquette is a low-gradient, groundwater-fed system. Glacial gravels and sands absorb rain like an enormous dry sponge, then slowly release ground-cooled water into the river. There's great spawning habitat and excellent cover in the form of downed woody vegetation. The river flows through shady sections of the Huron-Manistee National Forests, state forests and parks, and corridors of private easement land. Michigan has more miles of public-access land in proportion to total land area than any other state in the union. As for trout food, browns can feast on the eggs and fry of steelhead and salmon, and on the entire suite of insect hatches, including a tremendous *Hexagenia* hatch that brings a bump in angler interest in July. Farms in the watershed add nutrients, but apparently not too much to create the kind of problems we have in Vermont, with over-enrichment on Lake Champlain. The Pere Marquette is a seamless aquatic nation with plenty to explore for the fish and fishermen, and undammed throughout, so these highly migratory fish have the full run of the watershed.

Ray and Ray fish using eight- to ten-foot-long inflatable pontoon boats; they've tried every kind of floating vessel over the years, but pontoon boats seem to work best. We spent an hour assembling and inflating them at the put-in, provisioning them with rods, spare tackle, coolers of food and drink, and containers of baits: crawlers, crickets (grasshoppers), and "waxies" (the small, white, living larvae of the honey wax moth. You can buy them in blue plastic containers). Some trout anglers raise wax moths, and they may have grasshopper-rearing cages as well. If they catch a salmon, they may strip its eggs and make up their own spey bags. Everything on a small pontoon boat must be placed just so. Each boat had three rods, including a spey rod set up with a fly reel in case we decided to fish for Chinook salmon (in the river now, but not in great numbers). If there is an elite class of bait trout angler, it's the two Rays.

Fishing from pontoon boats, Ray R. instructed, is like wade fishing with a boat attached to your midsection. Anytime you decide to stand up, you can, allowing that there's ground to stand on. Standing up stops the downstream motion of the boat. You can beach the boat if you want and then simply wade up or down the bar to fish. Or you can drift and fish, the water's surface inches below your backside. These boats are not fast rowers, Ray added, but they turn on a dime; and on a bendy river running at six hundred cubic feet per second (cfs) and littered with fallen trees, that's helpful. Recent floods and plenty of rain meant the Pere Marquette was close to bank-full. Staying away from the clutching branches of deadfalls—where a swift current can easily pin you—was a skill I learned the hard way. "Keep your back to the outside corners and you'll be okay," Ray told me. But things can happen fast, especially when you've got a fish on.

The Rays told me they like to take their time. Fishing slow lets them cover the water. And the no-hurry approach keeps them out of trouble.

We hop-scotched downriver all morning, one or all of us stopping at long glides, where tea-colored water washed over sandbars and abruptly dropped into deeper pools. Here and there, we picked up small rainbows and browns, releasing them. In November, six-pound steelhead begin moving out of Lake Michigan and into the Pere Marquette, following the salmon runs. They'll stay the winter, then spawn in spring, many making the return trip to the lake. November is Ray's favorite time to fish for steelhead, but that wasn't our quarry now. Brown trout were.

The Pere Marquette received some of the very first German browns released in America, and the river's been good to them. They grow big here and the rules protect the larger fish. But we weren't catching them. It didn't matter. The sun was warm, and the mist had long burned off. I found myself comparing worm fishing techniques to my own fly fishing. From a distance, it's not much different. The Rays use a size twelve to fourteen conventional J-hook, baited; I was using live hoppers because, well, when in Rome. Besides, I was having my Hemingway moment (fictional Nick Adams is arguably Michigan's most famous grasshopper fishing artist). Anyway, fishing the way we were was anything but simple. The rigged line is more complex than a fly line (nothing could be simpler than rigging a fly—or more complex than casting one). Above the baited hook, the Rays use several feet of three- to four-pound tippet tied into a swivel, and just above that, they add some weight to get the bait down. The lighter tippet allows them to break off when they snag the bottom, without losing the weight and swivel. Above the weight is an orange bobber that they can easily move up or down, depending on how deep the water is. The analogy to fly fishing is obvious. I would be using a weighted nymph, probably a beadhead Prince Nymph or a Hare's Ear—whatever works. I might add a small bit of weight in deep holes like these. The nymph would be tied, using a loop knot, to a nine-foot knotless leader, and that would be tied to a sinking tip or floating line. I'd probably use a strike indicator—a bobber, essentially—attached somewhere along the leader, and I'd be watching it. The Rays can turn to a variety of baits and lures, though they don't have the dozens of fly patterns that a match-the-hatch fly fisherman might carry. This may seem like an essential difference. It isn't, considering that a fair number of fly fishermen fish with a very limited selection of flies. The presentation school: I count myself a member. A good friend of mine on the Yellowstone River fishes just one pattern all year.

The cast, of course, is different. And I can see advantages to each. What isn't different is managing the line once the bait is laid out across the water—mending is equally important to their method of fishing bait. They were as committed to a drag-free presentation of their bait as I would have been were I fishing with a fly rod and wet fly. From sandbars on the outside of the curve, I watched them manage long, natural drifts through pools and into tangled deadfall-covered holes on the inner corners of the river, the bobber taking a dip when a fish struck the bait. Those long, drag-free drifts are what caught most of the larger fish we saw, including Ray R.'s nineteen-inch fish just after lunch, one of the fattest, prettiest browns I'd seen in years (released).

We'd drifted into a sandbar at midday, still far from the midway point to our float, and dove into the lunches they'd packed—apples, a bag of doughnuts, ham and cheese sandwiches, cokes, and water.

"What burns me worst," said Ray R., "is that bait fishing gets labeled as primitive. Fly fishing is at the top for difficulty and skill and conservation, but bait fishing is child's play at the bottom. They talk like we're children." But drifting bait underwater, figuring out underwater currents, and holding places and depths is all knowledge gained over years. The two Rays were sure out-fishing me.

I've often heard the same idea repeated about the evolution of a fly fisherman. What Ray's talking about is found throughout the scientific literature too, and in popular fishing literature. It's often repeated in conversation: Worms are for children. Lee Wulff more than once referred to bait fishing for trout, and eating trout, as meat fishing—fine for children, but not for sportsmen. In his fishing hierarchy, he likened the urge to catch the most fish to children riding around a carousel and trying to grab the most golden rings, an instinctual urge similar to a carnivore's instinctual drive to stockpile meat; whereas chasing the most *challenging* fish represented a type of high dignity, reserved for the true sportsman. Wisconsin social psychologist Robert Jackson (former professor at the University of Wisconsin–La Crosse) looked at such a hierarchy of trout fishers' motivations in Wisconsin, invoking Maslow's hierarchy of needs. His paper, presented at the fourth Wild Trout Symposium in 1989, drew heavily on the stages of an angler's development. He also built on Dr. James Henshall's model from the century before, which described the angler's evolution from the desire to limit out, to the desire to catch a trophy, to a stage where catch method (the fly) mattered most. Jackson added an additional "transcendent stage," the sportsman's stage, where satisfaction lay not in catching fish, but in mentoring and coaching others. His studies found Wisconsin's northern brook trout anglers to be lower down on the spectrum than the brown trout anglers on Wisconsin's southern spring creeks; and TU members, in general, ranked highest in those most elevated categories of appreciating aesthetic beauty, releasing fish unharmed, and enjoying surrounding nature. In a 1988 study, Jackson found that 40% of TU members in Wisconsin valued trout fishing above *all* other activities. Trout fishing can seem like an evangelical calling, the "total angling experience" a path to personal integration and harmony . . . but, as Ray and Ray reminded me, sometimes a fishing rod is just a fishing rod, and a fish food for the belly.

Editorial note to self: If bait fishermen—or those fishers who keep and eat trout—are analogous to "children," and children analogous to the primitive mind, then that's where the analogy breaks down entirely. Indigenous fishing cultures—the Everglades' Calusa, for example—had sophisticated methods for capturing, preparing, and preserving fish. They were able to sustain their culture through low cycles, when fish were scarce. The Calusa built elaborate canals so they could paddle from the Gulf, through mangrove islands, to upland areas where their settlements grew large. Fish were part of complex religious rituals, language, and music, and were woven into the tribe's cosmology. Trout fishing behaviors today aren't nearly as complex. Maybe it's time to knock down the hierarchies? Fishing with an effective, legal method (not dynamite, for instance), however efficient, such as a baited hook, and then utilizing the fish caught as food for family and friends—as protein in the larder, preserved for leaner times—has a social dimension that sport fishing without killing, even with these overtones of spirit, beauty, meditation, and conservation, can't have. And let's be real, fly fishing itself does not equate to conservation—restoring and protecting water quality does. Who's to say what is higher, what is lower?

Both Ray and Ray don't trust social science, and frankly, it hasn't done them many favors. But it's less social science and more raw politics that inflames their ire.

As soon as the government starts giving special privileges to special groups, with no benefit to the general public, that trust is violated, the Rays told me—by flies-only laws, for example, or other rules that take the public's access away. Lately, the Rays have couched their fight in terms of the public trust doctrine to drive this point home.

This idea of fly fishing's superior conservation pedigree may have originated in Michigan back in the early 1900s, with William B. Mershon's successful efforts to make the North Branch of the Au Sable River fly-fishing only. The story is ably told by Bryon Borgelt in his unpublished University of Toledo PhD thesis. Mershon, a timber baron from Saginaw, Michigan, saw the end of virgin white-pine forests and the parallel extinction of grayling from Michigan waters, thanks in part to his participation in the industrial removal of the forest, overexploitation of grayling, and the introduction of brook trout. While he turned to brook trout conservation in his later years, his claims as a conservationist were confounded by a major conflict of interest: He and his business partners owned several thousand acres and planned to build a lodge on the North Branch of the Au Sable. Persuading the Michigan Legislature to make that stretch of river fly-fishing only in 1909 guaranteed that local bait anglers wouldn't be fishing his water. The fly-fishing only designation lasted off and on through 1928. Mershon, who fancied himself a progressive, hated bait fishermen and believed they were destroying his brook trout (a resource he needed for the urban clientele he wanted to attract).

Floating and casting on the Pere Marquette through the afternoon is a certain kind of bliss that all anglers, lucky for the privilege, know. It's flow time. Timeless time. That said, all can abruptly change; the sun can drop behind a cloud, the wind can shift and rise, and bliss can turn into shit incredibly fast on a river. As it did for me. Tracing it back, in that moment, I was thinking of the strange divide there is between anglers around secrets—as in, not naming the river, or the pools, or the general place where you had recent fishing success. The film that describes the formative years of the Federation of Fly Fishers is called *Never Name the River*. Not naming, I suppose, is meant to prevent overfishing, and it's part of the fly fisherman's unwritten code, the ethos of the morally conscious fly fisher—just as catch and release is, or the commitment to conserve clean water, or the unspoken ethic to give the other angler space on the river, or to volunteer to clean up a river, or to teach children. Self-containment. But naming places, and the passing along of names, had deep survival value for indigenous subsistence anglers. Many of the bait anglers I've gotten to know share their good fortune (name, date, place, time, all) out of deep loyalty to friends and family. Maybe this is a reflection of that old subsistence custom? David James Duncan's book *The River Why* brings up this disparity between fishing cultures and then reconciles it. (Duncan's entire book is a merging of opposites—worm, fly, and everything—into a divine union of love. Duncan wrote the only trout book needed.)

Never name the river. But why not? W.D. Wetherell's *Vermont River* never actually names the river, though those of us living in eastern Vermont and fishing that river know it by name. In the olden days, the successful hunter went home and told his band what he'd found and where. He brought his brothers back, spears and arrows at the ready. Indigenous hunters could be very effective with stone spearheads and wobbly arrows. It may be that, four hundred thousand years ago, telling the name and showing the place led both to the survival of the tribe and to massive species extinctions of animals—there is a tendency toward extinctions whenever humans show up—but today, in the age of social networking, not naming the river seems quaint at best. Trout fishing is a highly managed state of sociobiological affairs. The best fishing spots are generally well known, and the poor, adult trout in them—native, domestic, or wild—are hooked and caught more than once. A better fate may be the frying pan, at least for wild and domestic fish that are destined to die after four years anyway (and that, as exotics, some say never belonged there in the first place) and abundant native trout. Trout are food for much else. The mink, the otter, and the griz should be first at the table, but even they can eat only so many cutthrout. Nature herself, if left to her own devices, is cunning at creating abundance and, ultimately, balance. For the fisher who pushes off into the unknown, from the small upland streams of Vermont to the deep backcountries of the west, fishing pressure drops away; to a careworn and busy society, naming a place few will ever visit is a way of remembering it. A type of storytelling where naming matters. And eating a wild trout is a way of eating your way, figuratively speaking, back in time.

By the time I had worked out these deep philosophic thoughts about secrets, my boat had drifted over a black-water pool, and the current was pushing me toward a downed tree on an inside corner. The kind of place the Rays had warned me against. I did not want to drift into that tree. I set my anchor and assessed, then decided why not sink a grasshopper, like Nick Adams, into that underwater tree to see what I might catch. Thunk! I was onto a large fish. I tried to hold on but the fish seemed to be making a cat's cradle out of the underwater branches and my line down there. In the thick of it, I hadn't felt my anchor dragging. Soon, I was in the tree with the fish; then the fish was gone, and I was caught.

Pontoons don't slide off needle-like tree limbs the way they do off glacial boulders. Currents pin and deadfalls grab everything, including coolers, fishing rods, clothing, and a man's cool. I discovered, trying painstakingly to extract myself against a stiff current, that it had grabbed one of Ray R.'s fishing rods and plunked it over the side. Ray prides himself on his equipment. His rods are customized, built up from expensive G. Loomis blanks. Losing one was like not only getting drunk and puking at the palace ball, but also getting a massive DUI ticket on the way home.

No matter. When I caught up with them and broke the news, Ray was understanding, and he was catching fish. The other Ray had hooked and released a fat salmon. We'd work out the rod issue. Late in the day, they switched to waxies, and the fishing, with the dropping of the sun, picked up again. Ray R. caught a seventeen-incher and kept it for dinner, and I just simply stopped fishing. Fishing had become a disaster. We finished the last mile to Sulak in the gloaming, unloaded, and took the boats apart. In full darkness, the Rays left for the other car at the put-in, leaving me an hour to watch over the gear and ponder.

The dark is a good place to consider the mists of the past, including this quickly fading day—on balance, a very good one. Two guys who knew the place showed it to me. You can't get to know the heart of a river by phone, text, tweet, or Instagram. You need to get off your butt and away from your computer screen to go fish the place and meet the people who know how. That's the logic for hiring a guide, and I often have—but even better to get an insider's view from a local angler who doesn't guide for a living, and who grew up fishing the same water. The lack of commercial expectations means less angst. Since I wasn't paying the Rays anything to take me fishing, losing the rod—I was still kicking myself for it—could be considered a kind of disappointing guide fee. Replacing it would set my trip budget back and my teeth on edge. But what's money when you don't have much . . . besides everything? On the other hand, I felt like I'd glimpsed the heart of the Pere Marquette. And that was priceless.

Who owns a river? The better question is, who does the river own? Whether rural, indigenous food anglers or urban fly-fishing warriors, serious trout fishermen get deeply attached to their rivers. Rivers provide food, sport, and intangibles like peace of mind and a host of environmental services indispensible to life. In the case of Mershon—a profit-hungry timber baron who owned the banks of the North Branch—and others like him, the conflict of interest taints their conservation objective. It's understandable, I suppose, hating the native bait fisherman who slips in and takes your quarry handily, but it's serious business when you legislate a river away from locals, and it's even worse when you kill off the native fish. Mershon, through clear-cutting the forest and manipulating the Michigan Legislature, managed to accomplish both.

Money talks, and the touted economic benefit of destination fisheries has often clouded broad social and economic objectives. Take for example the paper that Richard W. Talleur presented at the fourth Wild Trout Symposium. He describes the economic effects of no-kill regulations on communities, including the Au Sable. According to Talleur, they were significant. The section he studied was the famed eight-mile Holy Water. Local fishing promoter Rusty Gates reported to Talleur that the local residents' resistance was "highly emotional," however, "fly fishing guides who cater to quality-oriented anglers are reporting a brisk business." What's clear from Talleur's paper is that local anglers were viewed as less important and needing to be reeducated. Chairman Mao's "reeducation camps" come to mind. In reality, as the locals pointed out, they were already releasing a very high percentage of the fish they were catching, and they were willing to support further conservation measures. They simply didn't want to be pushed out altogether because they didn't cast flies. They lost that water, while fly anglers from afar were invited in with open arms.

It was close to 10:00 p.m. when Ray dropped me back in Ludington and we said our goodbyes. Michigan trout rules come up for reconsideration every five years or so. Ray and Ray will have their work cut out for them into the foreseeable future; groups like the Anglers of the Au Sable are ready with their lists of rivers for tackle restrictions and other special regulations.

The good news for the Rays is that the Michigan Coldwater Resources Steering Committee seems to have a new makeup, with broader representation—and the DNR has been reaching out, genuinely interested in what the likes of Ray, Ray, and their organization have to say. The double-Rays could enter the rule-making process as full partners if they wanted to.

What would a hit out of the ballpark look like to them? No more lost rivers, the Rays told me, and the acknowledgement that how they fish is respected as equal—as no more damaging in highly productive trout rivers than a dry fly presented drag-free. They can live with very low bag limits, even catch and release if the science shows it's necessary for protecting a river and its trout. Just don't tell them that they can't drift a worm deep, unless that's a proven limiting factor to trout health, growth, and happiness (if a hooked trout can be happy being hooked and released, I don't know). What's abundantly clear is that there's room in Michigan for everyone who wants to go trout fishing. And there's a stewardship role to play for everyone. The world is a mess at least by half.

CHAPTER 5

The Last Great
Worm Fisherman

"Everybody in the state is familiar with him [Roger Kerr]," said Rick Kyte, a past president of the local Trout Unlimited chapter. "He was kind of a thorn in my side when I was president."
— LA CROSSE TRIBUNE, July 27, 2014

The problem . . . is convincing some anglers that it's fun and honorable to release fish after catching them. The kids aren't the problem, they learn what you teach them. . . . The problem is the old people who came out of the Depression and have always killed fish. Those people won't change. All you can do is wait for them to die.
— GENE VAN DYCK, Wisconsin Department of Natural
  Resources fisheries biologist, *Wisconsin State Journal*, 1990

The bottom line on all of this is that SW Wisconsin has become a playground for urban fly fishing, catch and release anglers at the expense of local anglers. The DNR and Trout Unlimited have no interest in liberalizing trout regulations because this might bring back some of the "dropouts."
— ROGER KERR, *The Dodgeville Chronicle*,
  December 28, 2006

There is no sign announcing you've entered the Driftless Area. It may be the most unheralded boundary anywhere. Off the interstate, a lost province of rural towns, some so small you don't notice them, the Driftless Area's claim to fame is that a glacier never sat on it. Sublime.

The first time I set eyes on one of its storied spring creeks—the Big Green River—I couldn't see it for the fog that hung over the corn. It was cold, and the coulees were filled with blinding mist and the dark of predawn. Coulees are narrow floodplain valleys lined by steep, highly erodible limestone and sandstone hills.

Rivers aren't rivers here, it seems, but skinny ribbons that catch the light before disappearing under their banks of tall grass. In this corner of Wisconsin, springs make rivers. They arise from fractures in limestone close to the base of the ridges, then run through the narrow valleys before joining the truly mighty waters of the Mississippi or Wisconsin Rivers. Above the coulees are broad hogback ridges—more like smooth pillows of windblown soil, cut by squiggles of streambeds heading down to the Mississippi. The ravaging forces here were not mile-deep ice sheets—the latest was the Wisconsin ice sheet ten thousand years ago—but humans in the form of nineteenth-century farmers, many from German and Scandinavian reaches of Europe, cutting off trees on steep slopes and plowing up bottom lands for animal feeds. They didn't know what to make of the land and the land didn't know what to make of them. The resulting massive erosion filled the coulees with as much as twenty feet of silt. The floods washed away whole towns.

Roger Kerr had loaded the truck the night before, so all I needed to do was sleepwalk into the kitchen, down a cup of coffee, eat a bowl of cereal, and grab the cooler, ice, and worms we'd purchased the night before at the local sporting goods store, where Roger's nephew works. Roger's wife Mary was up. She goes to work in a battery plant every day at 5:00 a.m. Still, she got up even earlier to fix the coffee and put out the cereal.

Our tackle for a day of fishing? We had a few plastic bags for fish and a small cooler with water frozen in soda bottles to keep the fish cold. For hooks and split-shot sinkers, Roger had an ancient, green metal box that fit in the palm of a hand. The rods were six-and-a-half-foot glass rods, 1970s vintage. The reels, old open-faced Mitchells, or some such thing, were also on the order of thirty years old, but they worked perfectly well.

Jumping a fence and walking to the river through scrub, we attracted a herd of skittish horses looking for a handout. They followed us in the dark, clear to the creek, then suddenly galloped away. Our wading gear consisted of mid-calf rubber boots. We weren't going to be wading really, but fishing along muddy banks from bubbling pool to bubbling pool.

The Big Green was ten to twenty feet wide. I didn't think the creek water, cloudy from a recent rain, was very deep, or that it could hold many fish. Not to worry, Roger told me, the Big Green was loaded with wild brown trout. The water was cold. He only wished he could electrofish this pool, like in the old days when he regularly conducted fishing censuses here, to show just how many fish there actually were. No need—we immediately started catching them.

For an hour or so, we drifted pieces of worms—with a split-shot sinker or two, set a foot above the hook to sink them—along banks and into the centers of pools. We only moved about a hundred feet for that hour, fishing just several small pools.

I found the split shot difficult to control—those worm pieces drifted invisibly willy nilly down there in the murk—and couldn't feel the strikes at all, so I kept missing fish. By the time the sun was full up over the east bluff and the fog had burned off, we had our limit of six wild brown trout between us, having released carefully the half dozen fish that didn't meet the ten- to thirteen-inch slot-limit requirement. Truthfully? Roger caught them all. Mixed in with the trout we caught was a creek chub (released unharmed). Roger seemed more pleased with that creek chub, as a small measure of the creek's biodiversity, than all the brown trout put together. Roger is part old-school recreational angler out to catch dinner, part scientist, and part, as he put it in one of the dozens of handwritten letters he sent me, Cesar Chavez. A populist, progressive in his politics, he views the growing body of regulations in fishing as an evil standing between a rural angler and his simple desire—to stalk wild trout for dinner. I don't know what Roger made of me. An effete eastern catch-and-release fly angler? The fact that I was interested in his story, that I had traveled out to meet him, and that I wanted to learn his ways of fishing seemed to matter. But, let's face it, it's odd just showing up on some stranger's doorstep in Wisconsin. Doesn't matter who you are. The Kerrs took me in. They might have felt obligated, or felt that I would work for their cause. There was no question in my mind that I would work to understand and write about their point of view. An article sometime. A piece for *Wisconsin Outdoor News*?

I do have the traveler's knack for showing up at dinnertime. The night before, within five minutes of arriving, I was sitting down to dinner with Roger and Mary Kerr. Dinner was ham salad, fried trout, coleslaw, bean salad, and juice glasses full of homemade elderberry wine. There was very little conversation. Sitting there with the two of them, quietly eating pan-fried brown trout, for whatever reason I felt more like an exchange student from China who didn't speak Wisconsin English (they say *warsh* up instead of wash up), than a New Englander with a fishing bug, a journalistic curiosity, and wanderlust for Wisconsin.

It's not that Boscobel's foreign. It's the self-professed turkey-hunting capital of Wisconsin. And it's a clean, prosperous-looking town with wide shady side streets and modest homes. Main Street features a nineteenth-century hotel (birthplace of the Gideons International Bible) and the Unique Café, housed in a turn-of-the-century brick bank building. If anything, Boscobel is the opposite of foreign, looking and feeling like the small white town where I grew up fifty years earlier. Except for the colossal supermax prison. (By some quirk of my GPS, I ended up at the gates of the prison on arrival in Boscobel. What was the universe telling me? That I was imprisoned, like any nonfiction writer, by screwy notions of what makes a story?)

There is also an M60A3 battle tank in Boscobel, parked across the street from the Ready Mix concrete plant. There is a place called Teddy's Auto Sales and a pristine A&W that appears not to notice that it's vintage. I'd forgotten how much I missed A&Ws. They pulled up stakes around us years ago. In Boscobel, there were kids zooming around on bikes and a muster of Civil War reenactors getting ready for events to come on the school playing fields. I saw a pair of women in old-style hoop dresses and parasols, walking down the middle of a road. I passed Tall Tails Sports & Spirits just off Main Street, not far from the bridge over the Wisconsin River. You can buy bait, bullets, and booze there. Essentials. (I noticed, as I explored other towns and intersections in the Driftless, a tendency to put liquor and bait together. Some of the names were humorous. My favorite was the Firm Worm Bait-n-Liquor . . . you'd never see that in prudish Vermont.) Boscobel was the town I left forty-four years ago.

In all respects, the Kerrs live a classic Middle American life. Theirs is a simple ranch house on a large lot, which backs onto a wooded hill with acres of forested land. They have bluebird boxes on their back deck—that's one of Roger's projects. He suspends bright, metal washers from fishing line around the birdhouses to keep the starlings and sparrows away. Roger had a long career with the Wisconsin DNR and lives on the pension he earned, along with Mary's wages. His marriage to Mary is his and her second one. His first wife, Carmen, a Vermonter, passed away from breast cancer nearly twenty years ago.

So what turns an otherwise normal manager of waters, fish, people, and land into a determined trout-regulations protester? What happens to any of us who follow an idea to its bloody end with a zeal usually associated with religious fundamentalism? I have no answers. But I think I know the cause, unrecognized by the media and unforgivable to the few who do go to battle: injustice, perceived or otherwise. There is a principle at stake.

Walking along the sunny, empty Big Green coulee with Roger, talking fish, I recognized him as one of those rare elites that some of the scientific papers about anglers mention. Few trout anglers, it turns out, are any good at fishing. Most of us catch very few fish. Managers conduct creel censuses from time to time, where they interview every angler on a particular creek, across all or part of a fishing season, to get at this kind of catch data. The typical hourly catch rate? As low as .5 fish per hour in many places, with most anglers dialing up zeroes. However, there is a much smaller group of highly successful anglers, like Roger, who catch most of the fish. It's these anglers that managers worry most about, or they used to. High-end exploiters have the power to decimate trout populations. Unless they release the fish they catch. Master anglers: we extol them. The fly-angling community has many such wizard anglers, and the literature is full of how-to secrets. We spend a lot of money trying to become them.

I wondered how many trout Roger had caught in his life. His was a professional trout life—trying to increase them, dealing with the issues of the people who fished for them, and now, in retirement, battling trout rules. I imagined he had caught thousands of brown trout in his life. Even if his catch were a conservative two hundred trout per year on average, that's twelve thousand trout across sixty years. But what if he made a concerted effort in retirement to fish every day of the season and keep the standard ten-fish daily bag limit? (Current regulations in Wisconsin allow an angler to catch and keep ten fish a day in most regions—but typically only three to five can come from any particular creek. Bag limits on many of the creeks in the Driftless are three fish, or two. Some creeks are catch and release using artificial baits only.) The trout season in Wisconsin runs from the first of May to the fifteenth of September. Roger could harvest about 1,200 fish in a typical season, but since there are possession limits in the home, he'd have to either eat those fish as the season progressed or give them away—or risk a serious fine.

At some point in our ramblings, Roger described the first big brown trout he caught—a six-pounder on Spring Creek in Pennsylvania—as life changing. He grew up in Ossining, New York, and fished on Spring Creek as a boy with his uncle. He went to Penn State in State College to study forestry, then, after participating in a fish-shocking survey on Spring Creek, switched to biology. With the help of Robert Butler, head of the Cooperative Fish and Wildlife Research Unit there, he got a summer internship in Vermont (not far from where I live), working on the federal salmon reintroduction in the White River watershed. Co-incidently, I too had worked indirectly on Atlantic salmon reintroduction, though on the hatchery side (I spent two summers at the Berlin National Fish Hatchery in Milan, New Hampshire). After a brief stint in graduate school, Roger was then hired by the Wisconsin DNR to manage trout creeks in the Driftless Area—that was forty-five years ago.

After catching our limit on the Big Green, we got back in the truck and drove up the valley. Roger wanted to show me Crooked Creek. It was a Saturday morning in July, and there was no sign of another angler on the Big Green. We stopped briefly on the Little Green so Roger could give me a lesson in catching a trout with a full-length nightcrawler. The water in the Little Green was crystal clear and pouring through a culvert into a caterwauling pool. We stood on a heap of branches downstream and cast carefully up into the fray, letting the worm drift down through the white-water tumult. The hits were obvious and we let the trout swallow the worm before setting the hook. Four casts and four ten-inch brown trout. Each went onto the soda bottle ice in the cooler. In that harvest of trout, we had turned scofflaws; since we had in our possession more than double the bag limit allowed on the Little Green, we were in violation, even though we'd caught six of those trout on the Big Green. Technically, we were required to go back to Roger's house and leave the Big Green fish there before keeping any fish on the Little Green. It's a fair enough rule, designed to keep people honest and harvests moderate.

Back in the truck, after talking to a fly angler from Chicago (while he went fishing, his two boys played video games in the minivan parked in front of us), we turned off onto a dirt county road, marked by a pair of letters. Soon, we were careening up out of the watershed of the Big Green and sailing across the top of the world in the middle of ethanol corn, with views of twenty miles and better. It was like dolphins coming up for air. Then we were down into a different, tiny coulee with an overflowing creek bubbling through it, undoubtedly filled with trout. Where had the sky gone? Roger talked rattlesnakes while I marveled at how utterly confounding the compass points of this landscape were. The Driftless is crenulated. The roads wander like the pattern of squiggly lines on the backs of brook trout. Imagine a round, flattish dome of land, 24,000 square miles of it, cut in two by the Mississippi River. Rain falls. For thousands of years, rain falls, and the rivulets cut through limestone, leaving behind bluffs, sandstone outcrops, and these narrow valleys. The land is zipped tight by a covering of prairie grasses, sunflowers, and oak and pine savannah. Rain percolates through in trillion-gallon measure and slowly discharges at 50° F into the numerous springs that formed these creeks. Before European settlement, these creeks grew large eastern brook trout, while the big, warm mama Mississippi River and papa Wisconsin River grew a hundred types of other native fish, from fifty-pound channel cats and enormous sturgeon, to ten-pound, needle-toothed bowfins. The spring creeks we saw—Roger knew them all—wound through farmland and disappeared into oak and walnut; the landscape bore little in the way of suburban sprawl or commercial development. A long driveway to a fancy house here and there, a church, a German Bohemian eating place, a Finnish graveyard, Amish farmyards, and commercial-scale corn plantations; sprawl was nearly absent. My basic thought was: Where the hell have I been all these years? Hiding out in the provincial backwaters of New England.

Soon, we were back on a paved road, cutting through the coulees of Crooked Creek. Crooked Creek is important in the annals of Roger's work with trout in the Driftless, because back in the 1980s Crooked Creek was the starting point for Roger's experiments with moving wild trout. (It's also where he first tried to get cited by wardens for intentionally and wantonly breaking the rules.) At a certain bridge, Roger pulled off and we crept up for a look—we stopped at a lot of bridges that day. Peering up and downstream, we could see brown trout hiding and darting everywhere. Dozens of ten-inch fish were breaking for the cover of deep green emergent and floating vegetation.

In the 1970s, Crooked Creek, Roger told me, was one of the few in the Driftless with a healthy population of wild, reproducing brown trout. There were a few others: Trout Creek, Black Earth, Timber Coulee, Iowa, and Coon. But most of the hundreds of other creeks in his counties and across the Driftless were put-and-take fisheries. That means the brown trout in them were grown in hatcheries to catchable size and delivered by hatchery truck to be caught and removed in their first year. The typical trout population was made up of these domesticated fish, whose physiology and behavior had been shaped by hatchery life. Most creeks in Roger's territory back then held a few hundred hatchery trout per mile. Domesticated, hatchery-reared trout were easier to catch than fish born and reared in a creek. Survival and reproduction were poor. If hatchery fish managed to spawn, they spawned too early and their eggs hatched too early. If winter's low water, ice, and cold didn't kill them, spring floods did. The few larger holdovers that survived the winter bottleneck were caught by early-season anglers and eaten.

Regulations back then had no upper size limit like the slot limits of today, so most of the bigger fish were taken by May. No matter. A new generation of hatchery stock would be ready by opening day, and the cycle would start all over again. Those 1970s anglers hit opening day with a vengeance, fished for a few weeks until the fish were gone and the weeds got tall, then leaned their rods against the garage wall until the fall rolled around. According to Roger, fish shocking in the Big Green from the 1960s through the 1980s showed fewer than several hundred fish and no fingerlings in most of his creeks. Neither reproduction nor stream restoration were occurring on a widespread scale. But Crooked Creek, with its population of wild, reproducing brown trout, was different. Conditions were right for a natural fishery there: Sedimentation rates were low, water was cold year round, and water levels stayed up year round.

"A few of us area managers—Dave Vetrano up north and me down here—noticed these wild stocks and began moving them around," Roger told me. The first transfer happened in 1987. He, Mary, and Mary's son shocked fish on five or six different occasions in Crooked Creek and moved them to the Big Green. A few years later, they electrofished the planted areas on the Big Green and found surprisingly high levels of year-one fish. Catchable-sized wild trout had increased as well. At one prime site on the Big Green, Roger found nearly 2,000 catchable wild fish. By 2001, they had 2,851 wild fish in the same study area. "We knew we were onto something big," Roger said.

In this wild fish genetics game, Roger and the Wisconsin DNR were part of a national trend toward wild trout and away from fisheries reliant on domestic hatchery fish.

The wild trout movement was at the very heart of the formation of the Wild Trout Symposia that began in Yellowstone in 1974. Roger's work moving wild trout was the simplest way to spread wild genes. The Wisconsin DNR formalized a hatchery-based wild trout stocking program in 1995. The aim, according to Wisconsin DNR trout researcher Matt Mitro, who presented a study on the impacts of the program at Wild Trout VIII in 2004, was to increase the survival and longevity of stocked trout and build self-sustaining populations. He found survival rates of genetically wild strains two to four times greater than domestic strains (wild trout were taken from creeks and spawned in hatcheries with minimal human contact, and then fingerlings and yearling trout were planted back into promising creeks). Going wild ultimately transformed the Driftless fishery. Since Wisconsin's experiments with wild trout stocking, the numbers of wild trout have increased fifteen-fold in the Driftless Area, by Roger's estimate. The trout fishing has never been better.

For his work with wild trout at Crooked Creek, Roger received Wisconsin Trout Unlimited's highest conservation award in 2000, the year Roger retired. Ironically, his career as a law-breaking trout regulations protester began at Crooked Creek around then too. Roger had been unhappy with the impact that a new system of trout fishing regulations, put in place in 1990, was having on anglers. In 1968, Wisconsin's trout regulations were two pages long, he explained. They specified a general limit of ten trout and a six-inch minimum size. By the mid-1970s, the state added a single class system for wild trout creeks. The 1990 regulations represented a major break from the minimalist trout rules tradition. They created three classes of trout stream and five categories. Class 1 streams (37% of 9,560 total miles in 1994) would not be stocked with domestic trout. Class 2 streams, 44%, received some hatchery trout (today, mostly fingerlings from wild genetic stock) where some carryover survival was expected. The remaining 19% were Class 3, with only marginal conditions for trout reproduction and survival. These were stocked with catchable-sized hatchery trout. Within this three-tier framework, a five-category system of regulations was established. Category 5 was deemed "special opportunity waters." In 1990, thirty waters in Category 5 were made catch and release and thirty-four were managed with slot limits and lower daily bag limits. The 1990 regulation was a thirty-two-page book hard for some to fathom, claimed Kerr. By his count, the book contained one thousand special regulations. Today, fifteen years later, though there have been several changes and some simplification, the 1990 template is still intact.

What was the 1990 regulation trying to accomplish? Robert Hunt, head of the fisheries research division at the Wisconsin DNR for years and chief architect of the 1990 regulation, described the rule-book change at the fifth Wild Trout Symposium in 1994 as "the most site-specific, biologically based set of trout-fishing regulations in the nation." He went on to add that "for some anglers, their recreational satisfaction was also projected to grow by providing an 8-fold increase in the number of special opportunity fisheries where all or nearly all trout caught must be released." For the manager, the new regulations were meant to give flexibility to manage creeks according to their unique biological character. The 1990 regulations were also designed to curb overharvest, and that may have been their primary aim. Hunt, also architect of Wisconsin's trout stream restoration program, outlined his views on overharvest at the Trout and the Trout Angler II conference in 2000. "Excessive angler harvest can override any and *all* other positive fisheries management initiatives." He added that "a regional shift to more restrictive harvest regulations [the 1990 rules] has reduced this threat in the past decade, but managers must remain vigilant to maintain this trend and encourage vigorous enforcement." With so much money and effort going into trout creek restoration in Wisconsin, the threat of overharvest, no matter how remote, had to be eliminated, Hunt felt. But according to Roger, the fears of overharvest of brown trout are blown out of proportion in southwestern Wisconsin today. The new rules were overly complex and overly restrictive, he felt. By 2005, Roger was in full-blown revolt. The regulations had not grown more wild trout, he said—wild trout transplants and the restoration of trout streams had. But the regulations had scared off anglers.

So, at Crooked Creek, Roger made his first attempt to break trout fishing rules. It was to draw attention.

"We trout-regs. protesters got nowhere trying to do things

properly," Roger said. He and his friends had already tried putting res-
olutions through the Conservation Congress and failed, despite strong
local support. Roger saw breaking the law as a way to get around
what he saw as TU's stranglehold on the Conservation Congress's
Trout Committee. In 2005, he sent a letter to Grant County's warden
Martin Stone indicating that he planned to harvest a nine-inch trout
from Crooked Creek. At that time, Crooked Creek was a Category 5
creek with a ten- to thirteen-inch slot limit. Nine inches could get you
a hefty fine. Martin Stone's polite letter refused to rise to Roger's bait.
A court of law, Martin chided, was not the right venue for such an
argument. Come back to the spring hearings of the Conservation
Congress, he urged. But Roger had already spent plenty of time working through the spring hearings. He wasn't going back to the Congress.

What was the gist of Roger's protest? First, there was the biological question: Did Wisconsin's Driftless Area spring creeks have an abundance
problem, as in hordes of trout but not hordes of anglers keeping trout?
Had special rules driven off local bait anglers? If so, where did they
go? What could social science tell us about why it is that these anglers
stop fishing? If not the rules, then what pushed local angler numbers
downwards here? Finally, a political question. Was there a powerful
fly-fishing minority, aka Trout Unlimited (roughly 5% of Wisconsin's
trout anglers belong to Trout Unlimited), keeping overlying, complex, restrictive rules in place? Roger once told me that when a trout
biologist says his prayers at night, a TU member is on the other side of
the bed saying his: Please God, more catch-and-release waters.

After the forays at Crooked Creek, we headed across the Wisconsin
River to visit some of the area's better-known spring creeks. Roger
fumed a bit at the absence of anglers. "TU and the department claim
there's heavy fishing pressure in the Driftless today," he said. "That's a
fat lie. While there's heavy fishing pressure on a few creeks, hundreds
of others are rarely visited. Only a few talk about it, but everyone
knows."

Not until we got to Big Spring Branch did we find more anglers. They
were an octogenarian pair from Illinois. We stopped to talk and had

a pleasant chat. Then Roger asked did they eat trout? That's another pet peeve of his—people who don't eat trout. Roger, with his propensity for numbers—a main job of a trout-fishing manager, after all, is keeping track of numbers, weights, and lengths of fish—had been keeping an informal running tally of anglers who dined on their catch. No, they didn't. "Trout aren't much good to eat," one added.

"Trout, no good to eat?" Roger said, smacking the steering wheel and looking heavenward. "The locals are gone," he lamented. "The trout fryers are extinct. The kids are locked in minivans for 'safety,' playing video games. And the trout fishing has never been better! I'm glad I'm old and won't live to see what this world is coming to."

I felt his pain. The real question mark is less whether us old guys eat trout and more what those kids will come to know and love.

We parked at a small, mowed grass lot on the upper reaches of the popular Big Spring Branch of the Blue River. At the upper bridge that marks the beginning of a catch-and-release section on Big Spring, we could see the real-time results of better genetics, improved water quality, and in-stream restoration. Peering over the railing into a clear pool with bright-green mats of algae and pondweed on the edges, we saw a school of skittish brown trout, mostly in the eight- to ten-inch range. A catch-and-release rule protects wild brook trout too. Big Spring Branch's quarter-mile stretch of headwaters is close enough to the spring source to create a barrier of colder water that has kept brown trout out.

That, Roger said, leaning on the rail of the bridge and gazing down, is a lot of fish. But if your objective is to produce large trout, he continued, you'd have to cut down the number of fish in this creek by half. Impossible, if your mindset is that trout are scarce and too valuable to catch only once. Then, the biological facts don't really matter; any harvest of trout is bad. The simple idea is that if you throw the fish back, it survives and gets bigger. But not here. Here, it gets only so big because the stream's food supply is used up. And then, after three to four years of small, incremental growth, the skinny brown stops growing and it dies. But does size matter? Probably less to the traditional trout angler, Roger's people, who liked fishing when there was still an early season that allowed the harvest of trout. Modern rules, Roger believes, conspire against these anglers.

We walked back to the parking lot and ran into a young fly angler rigging up. He lived in Madison. "I used to go to Montana to fish," he told us, "passing through here, but then I discovered the Driftless and I haven't been West since." We talked about flies and tackle, and then I watched him walk to the creek and begin working his way up into brook trout land. Eventually, all we could see above the bank were the loops of his fly line catching the sun and shedding drops of silver water. "He's got a perfect morning," I said. And a spring creek full of fish, all to himself.

Back in Roger's truck and driving over to the Fennimore Branch of the Blue River (Castle Rock Creek), we talked about that fly fisher and fishing pressure. Like every aspect of sport fishing, fishing pressure has a social values dimension. One man's friend is another's crowd. Most fly anglers value their solitude and plenty of elbow room for casting on a creek. I do. They tend not to stand in one place long. They move, sometimes rapidly, so they cherish open space and room for a back cast. Just seeing another angler can be a downer, unless it's their friend working in the opposite direction. But they are also attracted to bait-restricted special-regulations water, catch-and-release areas, and fly-fishing-only water—this puts them at odds with each other and increases fishing pressure on a few select waters. Their tendency to crowd together into these specially regulated areas is the single most powerful argument for why more such areas are needed. Bait and lure-using anglers aren't so different. The rural angler fishing home water may have a more deliberately social tendency. They may prefer their home water and go back to it over and over again. But they love solitude and good fishing too, as much as anyone. After all, all who fish are hunters hoping for success.

Fishing pressure, as measured by the human predator's impact on the trout population, is another matter altogether. You would expect the size and number of catchable trout to go down directly as the number of anglers increases, but in a very productive wild brown-trout fishery like this one, you may not see any impact at all until the amount of fishing effort gets outrageous. Roger loved talking about fishing pressure. (We were once again speeding across the top of the world, now on our way to Livingston). You would also expect special regulations to produce more and larger trout, he said, as is usually their purpose. In some cases, they do. But many anglers believe they *always* do. And that is simply not the case. They often do not. Trout and their rules in Wisconsin have become strange in this one way, he continued: Outside of trout fishing, when the numbers of fish go up dramatically and stay up year after year, bag-limit increases are soon to follow. That doesn't happen in the trout world. Once special rules or low bag limits are put in place, they are likely to stick. (Although Roger has pointed out in numerous letters that the count of special rules in Wisconsin was cut in half in rule-book changes made in 2002, though bag limits and size limits generally stayed low.)

In 1989, Robert Behnke, writing for TU's *Trout Magazine*, attempted to clarify for TU members the conditions under which dramatically low bag limits and catch-and-release fishing make biological sense. "Special regulations work," he wrote, "but only in the right places for the right reasons. . . . Very few streams have the optimal combination of habitat and food supply to allow continued growth and survival of a significant proportion of a population to attain an older age (5 or 6 or older) and large size (more than 14 inches). . . . No angling rule can modify nature's elimination of older fish by natural mortality once their growth ceases due to inadequate food supply. . . . Terminal size and age is determined by environmental conditions and cannot be changed by special regulations." Behnke's golden ring isn't catch-and-release fishing after all; it's a natural fishery where there are large, elusive, native trout. There are precious few such potential places in the world, he tells us, where the art and science of fisheries management and political support come together to restore and protect them.

One of Roger's trout-regs protest sympathizers is Jimmy Knutson. He read one of Roger's letters to the editor a few years ago and contacted him. We met Knutson at a mini-mart in the small agricultural town of Livingston and sat down in a booth by the checkout counter for some squeaky cheese curds, "so fresh they moo," the package said. This was my first taste of a Wisconsin specialty. They actually do squeak when you chew them. I was served up a tall glass of Coke to moderate all that squeaking.

Knutson is a round guy with a fantastic southern Wisconsin drawl. Wisconsinites, like other midwesterners, speak such that the middle of the word sounds a bit like stone going through a crusher. And like any other region of the country, they have their expressions unique to Wisconsin. Vermonters—woodchucks as opposed to badgers— soften their T's and convert their E's, so that "Vermont" sounds like "Vamaunt." We don't say "you betcha." We say "yup."

Knutson used to work for John Deere. He grew up fishing on Martinville Creek, the Newell, and the Crow. In 1990, all three went to Category 3 water, with a three-trout creel limit and nine-inch minimum size—a virtual catch-and-release rule and a game changer for keep-and-eat anglers. (Fly-fishing writer Ted Williams, in a witty turn of phrase, once described this type of rule as a workaround for the "hobgoblin of catch and release," a reference to Ralph Waldo Emerson's "a foolish consistency is the hobgoblin of little minds"—suggesting that a bait fisher's opposition to a catch-and-release rule could be met by simply changing out the language. He was wrong about that. Someone who's fishing for dinner isn't fooled when the creel is empty; he's just pissed off.) When the new regulations went into effect, Knutson said that he hung up his rod. The wounds, even after twenty years, evidently had not healed.

I asked Knutson if some of his friends gave up on bait fishing and turned to fly fishing, so they could fish no-kill water and catch as many trout as they wanted? I'd read that part of the drop in bait fishing could be explained by locals taking up fly fishing.

"Why would they?" Knutson asked. "Not any I know. Fishing with a worm is better if you really want to catch fish."

Knutson said he first went fishing in Martinville Creek at the age of five with his grandfather. He told me his mother had made him a sleeping bag from his father's Korean War blanket. They would all go down to the creek together when he was young, and they'd set up camp for a family holiday. On opening day, all their neighbors were out, and they might have to walk a quarter mile to find a place to fish. The roads along creeks were lined with cars, he said. Trout fishing, it seems, was ritualized back then as more of a holiday with culinary benefits. Trout fishing for some number of generations was as much social gathering, with a combination of fishing, eating, and gabbing. Roger had reported the same phenomenon on the Big Green.

"We'd catch some trout and fry them right there on the bank," Knutson said. When he got older, he'd go down to the creek after school with his friends, and he'd camp on the creek on weekends. "Now there's lots of no-kill waters around here. And the bag limits are too low. It's not worth it. There were a dozen or so trout anglers around here in the 1990s," he said. "Most quit because of the rules."

"What changes would you like to see now?" I asked.

"Why are there bait restrictions at all? Why should there be? How is that fair? I'd like to see at least a five-fish bag limit—five even smaller fish make a meal—and no size limit, even in the early season. Not that I'd catch five fish every time, but at least we'd have something to aim for."

"Would anglers who have quit come back if the bag limits increased?"

"People are bitter. Maybe. Maybe not."

"Would you?"

"I might," he said.

On our way back to Boscobel, Roger and I talked about the 1970s and 1980s. There were big social and economic changes going on then. It was a tough time for midwestern agricultural communities (the farm crisis years of the 1980s; bank deregulation under Ronald Reagan and the failure of savings and loan institutions). Was that where all of Knutson's bitterness was coming from? A creel shrinking from ten fish to three? No big deal, right? Who cares?

But maybe the change in trout rules contributed to a sense of loss of local control, of big government or a bureaucratic scientific elite imposing its will in ways that hurt the middle class just a little bit more. An economic downturn in rural areas hurts, but rural people have their standby workarounds. They can grow their own food. They can raise and sell fishing worms. They may still have family nearby that can provide support during lean times. And they can catch dinner out of a creek if they need to. They can hunt deer. They can jack deer, for that matter.

Bitterness is like a botfly. It burrows as a tiny worm, a seemingly unimportant thing, when a bit of personal power—an avenue to survival, if not prosperity—is taken away. It grows as more and more is taken away. Creel limits trended downwards in the 1990s, paralleling a drop in local trout anglers, as Roger has claimed. In fact, the numbers of anglers had been dropping significantly before 1990, but jumped down dramatically after 1990. There were some ups and downs, but numbers never recovered to early 1970s levels. There was a lot more going on in the 1970s and 80s in the regulatory world. New rules sought to improve water and air quality and protect rare species. In the trout world, the fight was on over trout hatcheries and stocking. The decade of the 1970s marked the rise of a new, conservation-conscious angler and the pushing out of a certain type of angler from the country's most iconic fishing destination, Yellowstone National Park. A different culture became dominant with the closures, and the marginalization of rural anglers may have accelerated the general public's flight from trout fishing.

Wisconsin's 1990 regulations were entirely in keeping with the times. Nationally speaking, Wisconsin had been deliberate in adopting new regulations and was coming late to the table. Roger's argument, his thousand letters, his charts and numbers going back to angler surveys and trout censuses from the 1970s all focus on the one claim that the regulatory tightening was not biologically defensible. Not in the Driftless Area. The regulations ignored the astronomical growth in the numbers of brown trout. Unrelated to the down-trending bag limits, said Roger. The drop in anglers? Directly related to special regulations that favored urban anglers.

Almost no one in the trout management establishment believed him. Or if they did, they weren't saying so publicly. Was all his protesting just a fish dream in Roger's mind, a tilting at water weirs? Or was his

CHAPTER 6

The Best Way to Fix
Wild Trout

protest fundamentally about the growing lack of public trust in small towns. The sense of being unfairly looked over—ignored.

I fell in love with a ninety-year-old woman named Madeline. As for the best way to fix wild brown trout . . . but let's start with the wine. When it's a Saturday night fish fry at the Kerr house, the homemade bottles of fruit wine are recommended. If not with Madeline, I did have a serious affair with a bottle of elderberry wine. When I returned to Vermont, I thought, I would convert a section of my yard to an elderberry plantation as soon as I had the time and money.

When cooking trout, you only need Fryin' Magic, Mary Kerr assured me. Joining us for a dinner of fried walleye, trout, and bluegills—along with a plate of fried morels, all dredged in Fryin' Magic, and assorted ham salads and eggs—were Fred and Madeline, good friends of the Kerrs' who lived a few blocks west. Larry, an antiquities dealer from the town of Wauzeka on the banks of the Kickapoo River, was there too.

Fred was in his nineties and took very good care of his wife, ninety-year-old Madeline, who was succumbing to a memory loss that was leaving room only, it seemed, for song. They drove up in an antique, orange convertible Triumph Spitfire that Fred had rebuilt himself.

They brought the banana wine, so we had a fruit compote of wine that included raspberry, blueberry, and elderberry, plus the plates piled with pan-fried fish.

It could be that, generally speaking, the fly-fishing community, according to the beloved fishing writer whose pen name was Robert Traver, lets loose with bourbon in tin cups and cigars, and hopes for a mermaid. And it may be that rural bait anglers sit around the table drinking homemade wine, eating trout, and hoping to hang onto a job or sell a knife. I have no idea. I sat next to Madeline with Alzheimer's, who, every few minutes, looked over with her girlish smile to ask, "Do I know you?" Then she would tell me her name and squeeze my hand. She liked to sing a little ditty, too: "Oh, I'm just a little girl from Memphis, I got my curly hair from Mom . . . who my dad is, I think his name was Tom . . . "

Fred, though he claimed to live in a brain fart, was sharp as a tack. He kept a hawkish eye on Madeline and would catch my eye briefly every so often and give the faintest menacing smile: *don't think you can move in on her*. Fred also entertained us with stories of their foray into the lobster fishing business in the Florida Keys. That was only one of a string of Fred and Madeline's adventurous business startups. During WWII, Fred flew in B-24s as part of a photo-documenting crew in the Pacific theater. After the war was over, they dropped him up in northern Japan where he wandered around taking pictures of a medieval, rural world remarkably intact. He was a trucker for twenty years after that; then he and Madeline started a pair of restaurants in Colorado; and then they bought a burger joint here in Boscobel, before buying the lobster boat and business in the Florida Keys; and then it was back to retire in Boscobel, where Fred now restores old cars. I guess if you live a long time you wear out a lot of pairs of pants. Madeline grew up in Memphis, working in beauty parlors before she and Fred got married. She still has those beauty-parlor good looks—haunting, dark eyes and a mischievous smile. By the end of the evening, I knew her songs and could sing along with her. And, Fred, I confess now, I squeezed her hand back. I didn't propose, but I think she got close to it.

Larry, one of the Kerrs' oldest friends—who wore cutoffs and what looked like a sleeveless sweatshirt over a white, sleeveless T-shirt—was also highly entertaining. He'd been in antiques for years, but that had never translated into much financial profit. Almost, though. One particular pocketknife, for example, he'd come so close to selling for something like five thousand dollars that he could taste the money. In the end, the Chicago buyer—a wealthy lawyer—had a flaw. It wasn't the knife. I felt genuinely bad for Larry and his knife. I'd been in his position, when our kids were in college, of feeling that if I could just sell something, a child perhaps, everything would work out. But children were going cheap back then.

"You know," said Mary, "who gets any real money these days for used stuff? Clothing? Toys? There's too much old stuff for sale."

"Yes, too much," agreed Fred, though he had a knack for buying old cars on eBay and reselling them for a profit. Madeline, as if to agree, sang, "In heaven they have no beer." Maybe we should be hawking beer to angels? Fred was clearly still fondly in love with Madeline, and everyone else was getting drunk.

"Did you know," I said, "about the last thing the human mind lets go of is music?" I told them a story of my father, who at ninety-three, confused about much else, could sing a complex harmony. Close to the end of his life, he sat down at the piano one night after dinner and belted out his old song list—including show tunes from the 1940s—as if there were no tomorrow. He hadn't played music or spoken clearly for weeks, but that night he straight-out played for forty-five minutes. It was his last time playing, I told them. Three nights later he died.

"It's hard losing your dad," said Mary. Madeline reached for my hand and then broke into, "You married a girl from Memphis . . . now take me far from here." Fred had gone and done that. Taken her far.

Of course, there's loss full-round every table. That's the nature of things. Roger had told me at some point about his first wife, Carmen, who after twenty years of marriage had died of breast cancer. They'd met on a street corner in Montpelier, Vermont, where Roger was spending the summer working for the Atlantic Salmon Recovery Program. Within three weeks, they were married. I'd told them about my daughter, fighting ovarian cancer at the age of twenty-nine. Mary, I learned later, had had her brush with breast cancer too. Deathly ill once, now five years in remission.

But the conversation over fried fish always turns back to the hopeful, and at some point, after the knife-that-almost-sold-for-five-grand story,

Mary regaled us with a tale of her first husband, who had a problem with drink. "I suppose," she said, "if not the drink, something else would have wrecked it." The last straw was his mule. Mary grew up on a farm in Crawford County. Married and with little money, she'd been selling heifers that she raised in the backyard, and he had a mule that he'd tied up on a post nearby the heifers. "And didn't that horny mule bother my young cows with all them antics of his?" Around that time, her husband had gone off with Mary's paycheck in hand and come home drunk, having spent her entire paycheck on a motorcycle. That day, with the mule bothering her heifers, she thought she could settle him down with a blast of saltpeter to the rump. But it wasn't saltpeter in the shells, and it wasn't his rump either. "Then that mule was up on his toes, hopping around, mewling, barking, dancing, making a *warse* racket than before, bothering my heifers," she said, sighing. "I never could quiet him." That night, the mule broke loose and ate the seat off her husband's new motorcycle. It was the end of that mule and the end of the marriage.

"Good riddance," said Roger. "And look who you got instead, Mary." There sat pariah Roger, beaming at the end of the table.

"I know, I know," Mary said, chuckling. "Are you done so I can bring on some dessert?"

I suppose trout fishing was once much more like digging potatoes, making potato salad, and having a party over it, rather than sporting after some biodiversity to catch and release the poor animals over and over again, though Nature would always have, slyly, her due in fish flesh, while the country people continued to bleed and starve.

CHAPTER 7

The Trout Explosion in Southwestern Wisconsin

But pastoral poems had no place in the competitive industrialization of pre-war America, least of all in Coon Valley with its thrifty and ambitious Norse farmers. More cows, more silos to feed them, then machines to milk them, and then more pasture to graze them—this is the epic cycle which tells in one sentence the history of the modern Wisconsin dairy farm. More pasture was obtained only on the steep upper slopes, which were timber to begin with, and should have remained so. But pasture they are now, and gone is the humus of the old prairie which until recently enabled the upland ridges to take on the rains as they came. Result: Every rain pours off the ridges as from a roof. The ravines of the grazed slopes are the gutters. . . . The Coon Valley Erosion Project is an attempt to combat these national evils at their source.

— ALDO LEOPOLD, "Coon Valley: An Adventure in Cooperative Conservation," 1935, *The River of the Mother of God: and Other Essays*

Hundreds of southerly [Wisconsin] trout streams which once produced brook trout are stepping down the ladder of productivity to artificial brown trout, and finally to carp. As the fish resource dwindles, the flood and erosion losses grow. Both are expressions of a single deterioration. Both are not so much the exhaustion of a resource as the sickening of a resource. . . . The future farmer would no more mutilate his creek than his own face.

— ALDO LEOPOLD, "The Farmer as a Conservationist,"
1939, *The River of the Mother of God: and Other Essays*

Almost every one of Roger Kerr's arguments against Wisconsin's trout regulations handbook, with its "thousand special regulations," is based on the idea that Wisconsin's Driftless Area has a trout overpopulation problem. Is this so? Do these creeks have some crazy bunch of trout that need more harvest? Why so? And how to reduce their numbers and improve their condition, when most anglers are releasing virtually all the trout they catch voluntarily? Should we be reducing their numbers by gillnet or electrofishing for food for orphanages? If Roger is right, how the hell are we going to deal with all these damn brown trout that are so frickin' (Vermont expression meaning "very") populous, but hard to catch? It's possible there can be too much of a good thing when it comes to creeks and trout. Famed Montanan trout researcher Dick Vincent, best known in the trout world for ending hatchery trout stocking in Montana in the early 1970s, wrote an interesting piece about the Madison River many years later that may be germane to the Driftless brown trout story (*Billings Gazette* 1982). He thought brown trout populations for twenty miles above Ennis Lake were becoming overpopulated due in part to catch-and-release fishing. With both good reproduction and excellent brushy edge habitat for young fish, more were surviving into adulthood, and the size and condition of the trout were diminishing. Harvesting browns out of that system, he suggested, would have improved the health of the fishery that remained. Was that southwestern Wisconsin's problem, too, in some super productive creeks?

I was in Coon Valley for a day, up in the northern reaches of Wisconsin's Driftless counties, a landscape of national importance in the history of land restoration. In 1933, four hundred farmers, most of German or Scandinavian descent, enrolled over forty thousand acres of land in the first year and a half of a cooperative restoration effort managed by the new US Soil Conservation Service (a precursor to the Natural Resources Conservation Service, NRCS). Agronomists, foresters, wildlife ecologists, and farm technicians all worked together with these farmers to reduce soil erosion. Over two hundred Civilian Conservation Corps volunteers signed on to help. Aldo Leopold served as a wildlife advisor. They went about restoring watersheds; trout and anglers were a few of the lucky beneficiaries. Without land restored to health and water quality returned to pristine, regulating harvests is merely regulating ruin. I was hoping to look at a thriving wild trout population with the two fisheries biologists who knew it best.

Jordan Weeks is the senior fisheries biologist in Monroe, Vernon, La Crosse, and Crawford counties. He wore a soul patch, dark glasses, and a video cam strapped around his head when he was sampling trout in the stream. Who says it isn't cool to work with nature? Monroe (eighty trout streams, 250+ miles of classified water), he said, is a bit out of the Driftless sweet spot in terms of fishing quality. But otherwise, his region contains nearly a thousand miles of classified trout water and several dozen creeks that hold upwards of five thousand wild brown trout per creek mile, including parts of Timber Coulee Creek and Coon Creek in Vernon County. Weeks's assistant Jake Schweitzer had gone to UW–La Crosse—younger, bigger, a limited-term employee at the time, nearly as smart, arguably underpaid—and got his degree in biology with an aquatic science concentration. He wore a Milwaukee Brewers T-shirt, so it was redundant when I asked him if he was a Brewers fan. Yes, he said unsanctimoniously, he is a fan (what you have to put up with when a reporter shows up). On his time off, Jake goes hunting for large brown trout closer to Stoddard, near the warmer waters of the Mississippi, where brown trout are fewer and, with less competition, can grow ungodly large. I described to him my days on the Mississippi, fishing for bluegills. At Wyalusing, site of the last passenger pigeon in Wisconsin, we caught them so fast it began to seem like the bottom was paved with fish. That afternoon, we had all kinds of fish—native and exotic—on the ends of our lines, including the snappy dogfish. I described one I'd caught that nearly took my finger off. "Bowfin [dogfish] is a true native," Jake told me.

"Toothy and an excellent fish," added Weeks. I mentioned that I'd been wanting to catch a sheepshead but hadn't. Jake frowned, "If you can't catch a sheepshead with a bobber and worm on the Mississippi, there's something wrong with you." Weeks agreed and seemed to take a step away. Weeks is a muskellunge man. It's his dream to catch a satisfactory musky, he told me. I didn't ask how he defined satisfactory, but I did take it to mean very large. He also said a satisfactory musky is a fish worthy of a tattoo. I didn't inquire further. He may daydream of tattoo-worthy musky, but I'm guessing his actual dreams are filled with small creeks choked with brown trout. "Brown trout are our 'carp' up here," he quipped, "and when they finish eating all the bugs, they eat their young. They aren't Christians in that sense," he added.

"Of course, they're fair, they eat other fish too," Jake said. Jake likened young white suckers to a brown trout's Vienna sausages. "There are just too many mouths to feed down there," he said. Both Jake and Jordan liked seeing white suckers, creek chub, sculpin, and other species in their surveys. These coldwater fisheries aren't especially diverse, so a measure of diversity is a healthy sign. Coon Creek and Timber Coulee tend toward brown trout monocultures; not exactly the most interesting fish community from an ecologist's standpoint, but a challenge to manage, biologically and socially.

By 9:30 a.m., we were on Timber Coulee Creek pulling on our waders, when the landowner and his family came up in an orange ATV. Weeks chatted with them. The family had restored a few old log cabins to pristine quality across the creek, and they come up on weekends and holidays from the city. They don't fish, but they're interested in the history of the creek and in the work Jake and Weeks are doing. Soon they were opening gates for us, and they stayed for the counting up of the first run of fish. Also there to help was Mike Juran from La Crosse. This was Mike's fifth trip as a volunteer. He's a TU member and an avid fly fisherman with a serious fishing addiction going, and Weeks had him trained up good.

Once in the creek, Weeks and Jake moved fast. Jake, the mule, had clipped into the two-hundred-pound boat and followed Weeks upstream, taking netted fish from him and transferring them into the tank. He also netted fish that Weeks missed. They get about 85% of the fish in the creek, on average; fewer when they hit a honey hole and closer to 100% when the picking is thin.

It was interesting to see where the trout were—often where you'd expect them to be, in the deeper holes and under ledges and fallen trunks, but not always in the obvious places. This, though, was an unnatural roundup, and the trout fled upstream as if cattle-prodded, flashing forward and ducking into the luxuriant growth of curly pond-weed and watercress to hide. They can't hide for long. A fish's body is like a battery, Weeks explained. Head positive, tail negative. The probe is positively charged, and it runs one to three amps—enough to stop a human heart, so you don't put your hand in the water unless you want to risk a trip to the ER. Stunned brown trout rise from the dark depths like a fish rapture, and the two biologists deftly net them.

Weeks and Jake moved a hundred meters upstream, then pulled over to refresh the tank water and count the fish. The numbers were astounding: Over three hundred browns were netted out of the hundred-meter section they surveyed. If they'd surveyed the deep pool sections downstream, they said, they could have doubled the count, so thick are the brown trout there. They quickly ran through length and weight, laying out each fish on a scaled trough. Juran read out the lengths, Jake weighed, and Weeks recorded the data. It was quick and efficient, and the fish were soon back in the creek.

The results didn't surprise them. Average size was 10.6 inches. They had five fish over 12 inches, which represents a maximum legal size limit in this part of Timber Coulee Creek, and only one fish over 13 inches. The angler's chances of catching a 12-inch-plus fish here are remote, but his chances of catching a 10-inch fish are high. And 10 inches is decent. A trophy trout by industry standards? No. That would be on the order of 14 inches or so. The angling public, already releasing voluntarily most of the fish they catch, has little chance of impacting the trout population here. It's the ever-present specter of corn prices shooting through the roof—as they have in the past—that threatens these fish more than anglers or the floods and droughts of past years. When corn prices go up in response to rising ethanol demand, marginal croplands flow out of the Conservation Reserve Program. This may translate into more siltation, warmer water temperatures from tiling, and lower base flows in Driftless creeks. It also means less riparian wildlife cover. The impacts extend to invertebrate species on land, like monarch butterflies, since the supply of their food—milkweed, typically growing on uncut hedgerows and marginal crop and pastureland—disappears.

Back to brown trout: I saw one white sucker that had thus far escaped the sausage mill, and several lucky, two-inch young-of-year. I asked why there weren't more young-of-year fish if the creek is so productive, though I couldn't imagine how any young-of-year survive predation by mom and dad.

"Most do not," said Weeks. Seventy to ninety-nine percent die before age one. Bigger trout eat them, kingfishers eat them, and so do great blue herons and mink. Still, natural reproduction in Coon Valley is high enough to replace the loss, including the adult fish loss—and at four years of age or so, there's high mortality at that end too, Weeks explained. In fact—and this is a generalization—every year class of trout in most trout streams in America experiences high mortality, with an average that can approach 60%. Much of first-year production goes on further up in the watershed and in smaller feeder streams, Weeks said. More small trout survive in these places because there are fewer larger fish and more escape cover.

The fish they were measuring were between three and four years old, Weeks continued. Ten and a half inches is not such an exceptional growth rate for a four-year-old brown trout. And the condition of these fish isn't optimal either. At a minimum, Weeks's creeks run 1,000 catchable fish per mile, but many support over 2,500 and the best support 5,000 and up. That is one mother lode of trout density and biomass, being fed in creeks that are only five to ten meters wide. Is density impacting trout growth? Or, to ask it another way, is it food supply here that limits growth? It would seem so. Most anglers fishing here, though, are very happy with the high densities and medium size, Jake said. The average fisherman is catching fewer than one fish per hour of effort, even in places like this. But the chance to fish over a lot of wild fish is appealing and anglers travel from afar for it.

How would one go about growing bigger trout here? With difficulty.

Weeks described an experiment on Spring Coulee, in which they captured and removed eight hundred catchable trout from a few hundred meters of stream, leaving the "big boys" (the largest size class they left in the stream). Their experiment was designed to determine if they might grow larger fish by reducing trout competition for food in the stream. The eight hundred captures were sent to a section of creek miles downstream. His educated guess was that, when he surveyed again in a year, he'd find eight hundred nine- to eleven-inch fish again—the same density they'd started with. Nature abhors a vacuum. And recruitment here is excellent. His hunch is entirely in keeping with research over the years showing how hard it can be for anglers to influence a well-established, high-density brown trout population with good recruitment.

The challenge Weeks faces—to skew his trout to larger, older fish—was echoed in studies by Wisconsin trout researchers Ed L. Avery and Robert Hunt in the late 1970s. They looked at four productive brown trout creeks in central Wisconsin, where, they concluded, heavy fishing pressure (on average, 373 hours per acre, or between 2 and 3.5 trips per mile, per day) and no size class protection for larger fish had skewed the trout population to younger, smaller fish. Trout that were at least four years of age in these creeks represented only 1% of the population and averaged 12.3 inches. Avery postulated that this was due in part to greater angling pressure on older, larger fish (an average of 52% of year-two fish and 37% of year-three fish were harvested). On average, creeled fish were about nine inches long. Only 4% of the harvest was of fish greater than twelve inches. "The frustrating reality," Avery wrote, "[is that] it is unlikely that Class 1 water [wild, naturally reproducing trout; no stocking] in this region of the state ever held significant numbers of resident trout larger than 13 or 14 inches because of the small size of the water and a food base dependent on aquatic invertebrates." With heavy fishing pressure, if Avery had been able to protect the biggest fish in his creeks, say with a slot limit that allowed the harvest of no larger than nine- to ten-inch fish, he might have been able to bump up the percentage of thirteen- and fourteen-inch four-year-old fish—but his were different times. The general regulation back then was ten fish in aggregate, with a six-inch minimum size. Sixty-nine percent of Avery's anglers lived within fifty miles of the creek, and 60% to 70% were using worms and harvesting fish. He was studying what amounted to highly sustainable fisheries, with lots of recruitment and lots of cropping of larger, older fish. Anglers back then weren't complaining about the lack of large fish. A nine- to ten-inch fish fits the frying pan perfectly, and there appeared to be an inexhaustible supply. With similar harvest rates and a regulation that protected fish of twelve inches and up, could Coon Creek sustain higher harvest rates, and would that result in larger fish? That's what slot limits attempt to do. "Maybe," Weeks said. "If anglers actually harvested fish. But nobody is keeping fish these days; it's a cultural thing, and it's been that way for years."

"We saw a man with an antique creel walking down the road last week," Jake added. "We had to laugh out loud. You just don't see that anymore. Most of those guys quit over the age of sixty. And nobody my age is fishing. The majority of anglers are not young." (I shifted uncomfortably.)

"It's unfortunate," Weeks said. "Fish management is paid for by license sales, and creek restoration by trout stamp sales. Who is going to be trout fishing ten years from now?" (Not Weeks. He'll be musky fishing.)

When I think about the difficulty Weeks and Jake might have mustering up more harvest in their fisheries today, if that's what they truly think is needed (Roger thinks that's what's needed, but for different reasons that have to do with attracting more local anglers), it's like they've lost a tool that earlier researchers had use of: anglers opting to keep fish. Anglers catch fish and can, regulations permitting, remove them from the stream, but many today do not.

Harvesting fish can be what is needed most. In reading about managing New York state's brown trout fisheries, I learned that researchers often had to ease off no-kill or virtual no-kill rules, increasingly popular in the 1970s, to improve the growth and condition of fish, especially in those year-two and year-three classes—protecting fish that might live to four or five years and grow large if the food supply is there. Today's widespread culture of catching and releasing trout regardless of the rules means less flexibility to manage abundance through harvest.

There is another reason Weeks might want to consider encouraging more bait anglers and more harvests on his creeks. As Thurow and Schill (1994) put it, allowing bait fishing and limited harvests can broaden the base of support for conservation measures. They were analyzing conflicts between different camps in trout fishing on the Big Wood River in Idaho. "The successful use of restrictive regulations *with bait* would have widespread application to restoring wild-trout fisheries. Such regulations might increase angler acceptance of restrictive regulations and could build support for wild-trout management." Another way to look at it is to allow that in some cases, an increase in hooking mortality is justifiable if it helps you unify the fishing community around a broad, landscape-scale conservation agenda.

In fact, Weeks already knows this stuff. He had recently recommended opening the Bohemian, Little La Crosse, Mormon Coulee, and South Fork Bad Axe creeks to a creel limit of ten fish with no size limit. These creeks have very high density (2,500+ per mile), though the condition of the fish (fatness of a fish relative to its length) is below one hundred, the bar set to delineate thin from fat. It can be very tricky politically, opening a closed creek back up to bait fishing and harvest. A lot of trout anglers are simply opposed to killing fish, so opening up harvests looks like moving backwards, or a slippery downward slope, even if more harvest is what the manager recommends.

We drove down Coon Valley to their next survey site, not far upstream from the point where Timber Coulee Creek becomes Coon Creek. The creek flows through open meadows there, and the valley is broader. It's a telling thing about the hydrology of a place when you pull off the road, park in a random spot, and there's a spring bubbling up beside you. You get the feeling in these coulees that you're walking on water. We netted 164 fish at this second site, none of which were larger than twelve inches. The average length was just over ten inches. That's a decent catchable trout for every square meter of the creek! You can keep five fish of that size here. Almost no one does.

It would be challenging fishing here. The river is narrow, and it flows through tall grasslands. Mike Juran has it wired, though. He's a guy who's spent considerable energy learning to stalk these fish. He told me he'd caught thirty-five in a recent five-hour outing. That's a remarkable hourly catch rate. The average angler is catching less than one per hour. Many put up zeros. Mike is an example of a fishing elite that's head and shoulders above the crowd in sheer fishing skill. Anglers like Mike, the scientific literature shows, are often more supportive of stricter limits on harvest. Mike, though, has been vocally supportive of Roger Kerr's push to increase harvests and extend the fishing season.

Open grasslands seem to be the ecotype favored by managers in Coon Valley. The Wisconsin DNR, working through leases on state lands and through conservation easements on private lands, aims to keep land open if it can. Grazing plays a role in that. Weeks pointed out a thirty-seven-acre, state-owned plot, where cows were busy stripping off willow leaves. Whereas back in Aldo Leopold's day they were planting trees, now they're cutting them down. Weeks mentioned a two-hundred-acre, state-owned property where the trees, planted years ago to stabilize slopes, had been cut down and the hillsides reseeded with a conservation mix of grasses. Grasslands are more productive than forests; they can turn more sunlight and CO_2 into storable calories and at a faster rate. Grasslands grow communities of invertebrates that trout live on. So trout productivity here is sun driven, Weeks explained. Adding sunlight by opening up scrub and forestland warms the land and optimizes plant and insect growth—and that's good for trout. Back home in Vermont, it's reversed. A solid canopy overhead helps keep trout streams cool in the summer. Here in Wisconsin, trout biologists destroy beaver ponds to reduce warm water sinks; that would be unheard of back home (unless beaver dams were flooding roads), where the goal is more often than not to preserve the wetland qualities and habitat diversity that beaver create. In Vermont, remote beaver ponds also have some of the best brook trout fishing.

Sun or shade? Food or cold water? What matters most? Before white settlement, the prevailing cover in western Wisconsin was open prairie and oak savannah. Native Americans and early settlers used fire to keep the land open. Later, it was grazing and timbering. There was pine and some limited mixed hardwoods on the cooler north-facing slopes that missed out on fire. Coon Creek restorers in the 1930s were looking not at prairie, but at a failed industrial farming system. Early restorers fenced in cattle, bulldozed terraces, planted perennial grains, and reorganized cropping systems. Farmers were encouraged to contour plow, rotate crops, strip crop, and keep creek buffers free of animals. These conservation-minded farmers stabilized creek banks by planting willows, and they planted pine and oak on steep slopes.

Were these early erosion-control methods successful? Stanley Trimble, a UCLA hydrologist who studied seventy-five years' worth of historical erosion and sedimentation rates in Coon Valley, found much higher rates of erosion between 1900 and 1940, compared to 1940 to 1975. In places, he measured sediment layers of thirteen feet or more, completely covering over earlier water-control structures like levees and ponds. Erosion was literally overwhelming farm society during the first half of the twentieth century, the Dust Bowl years. Studies by Warren Gebert and William Krug found that low spring flow rates increased significantly throughout the Driftless during the period of active restoration, while flood peaks significantly decreased. Erosion control worked here, not only to keep soil in place, but also to recharge springs and stabilize water flows.

New ways of farming introduced during the Coon Valley Demonstration Project integrated soil conservation with water management and forest and wildlife concerns, across a wide spectrum of disciplines. Many of the ideas being tried in 1930 went back to lessons Aldo Leopold had learned working in the Blue Mountains of New Mexico in his early years with the Forest Service. Coon Valley was the first of 175 similar projects designed to restore farm communities of land and people across the country. According to the archive at UW Madison, restoration ecologists made lots of mistakes back then; but because they valued good science, they learned from their mistakes. Today, some 94% of all runoff-related erosion has been curtailed throughout the Driftless. Water, instead of cutting gullies as surface flow and carrying massive sediment loads, soaks into the earth through root systems and duff. It recharges groundwater reserves and flows out at a measured pace through discharging springs downslope and in the valleys. In recent times, Coon Valley has withstood the test of several thousand-year storms.

After another transect and trout count on the grassy banks of Timber Coulee, where I was employed as fish measurer, we headed to the truck for a drive to the Westby Rod & Gun Club—a tavern and banquet and dance hall in nearby Westby—for lunch. Badgers love their taverns, and rod and gun clubs do some stream stocking throughout Wisconsin so the DNR can focus on wild trout. Walking into Westby Rod & Gun felt a bit like entering the mythical Sidetrack Tap in

Garrison Keillor's Lake Wobegon. I made the comparison out loud and maybe should not have. Regulars were schooling in there, and the waiter said "you betcha" when I asked for some hot sauce. Had he heard my Lake Wobegon comment and was he mocking me? Or did he think hot sauce was a bad idea? That's my paranoid tendency. I never heard irony used around the Driftless—outside of Madison, for that matter—and never heard the word "*uff-da*" (like "rats!" or "oh well" in Scandi-speak), but I'm an outsider. What do I know? Wisconsinites could be the most ironic people around. Look who they elected governor. Somewhere out in the Driftless maze of narrow roads and coulees, there are pristine little towns, uff-da stores, Lutheran churches, a Norwegian cultural center, cleanliness, godliness, polka bands, the schottish dance, and Finnish food, all locally grown for rural consumption. And beside them, whiskey and worm establishments that are covers for underground whorehouses and meth labs. Uff-da!

"Look," said Weeks, over an enormous hamburger that he wolfed down between gulps on a super-sized Coke, "we have to be customer focused at the department. The bottom line is, we do what people want. There are maybe five thousand citizens who get actively involved in this work as volunteers in the regulations process, and a hundred thousand or more who don't. It's that involved and vocal minority that shapes rules. The largest complaints are in regard to catch-and-release regulations associated with a live-bait restriction. These streams are few in number statewide. There are many more stream miles that have simple rules with no bait restriction."

But why should a vocal minority shape the rules? I asked. A better question would have been, how do you increase public participation in decision making? Or, how do you build back public trust in towns judged too small to host a forum? I guess I'd be pissed off too if the creek I fished with worms suddenly said "no worms," and there was no reason other than some vocal minority thinking it's better. I'd be out of sorts and out of a local creek. Would the argument that I could just go somewhere else make me feel any better? Maybe not.

I asked Weeks, if he were a dictator and controlled fishing regulations, what would he put in place?

He said, "We know there is little difference in populations in

Timber Coulee between a catch-and-release section and the portion that allows harvest of five fish under twelve inches in length. Personal opinion only? I'd have year-round fishing *and* year-round harvesting of trout in the Driftless. We have a surplus. I'd keep the 10% special-regulations waters around here. They are attractive to a very important constituency that rolls up its sleeves and pays more than its way to fish. The other 90%, I'd open to all comers, all tackle, bait is fine, with a reasonable bag limit—say five fish—and maybe keep the slot limit, to see if we can tweak to larger older fish.

"Fisheries here can support more harvest. Maybe liberalizing rules will serve to satisfy more anglers. Of course, if the harvest ethic changes, we would need to react quickly to amend the harvest rules. I firmly believe that having closed the early fishing seasons is wrong . . . but that it is okay to have portions of time [and places] when harvest may not be allowed. . . .We work too hard to provide excellent fishing to tell our anglers they cannot enjoy at least a catch-and-release experience."

Can't his anglers have a catch-and-release experience whenever and wherever they want? I wonder. And how does Weeks answer Roger Kerr's contention that there were terrific brown trout populations in some creeks (Black Earth, Mount Vernon, and Trout Creek near Madison, Iowa Creek) in the 1970s, with a ten bag limit, no special rules, and mostly keep-and-eat anglers fishing them? Why quibble over bait bans and catch-and-release miles that are not needed? Why not promote more harvests?

Vernon County today still has a thriving agricultural economy. There are slightly fewer farms and these are slightly larger, but Vernon County can boast the greatest number of organic farms in Wisconsin. Everyone benefits, farmers and anglers both, from clean water. Driving down Coon Valley, with its bucolic farms and steep green slopes, the angler gets to see what decades of conservation work can bring to a whole watershed, including its fish. If all we did these days, Weeks explained, was to slope banks back, we'd be way ahead of the game. Regrading banks—pulling eroded soils out of creek beds—

dissipates flow and reduces in-stream erosion. We may deepen and narrow channels, and add limestone riprap to stabilize them. That's all. Nature does the rest.

Restoring trout creeks, it seems, is like composing music. You lay down a riff and repeat it, and nature improvises from there. Weeks pointed to a small tributary. The four-year project there included building scrapes for bird and amphibian habitat, and hibernacula for snakes and turtles. Trout stream restoration is a natural ally to the restoration of entire natural ecosystems. Grassland birds benefit. Native plants support native bees and butterflies, all under assault in this development age. Networking and partnering with like-minded groups is on the rise in trout restoration circles. That's very attractive.

"The old guys," said Weeks, "did the best they could with the conditions they had back then. They had more damaged habitat, more pollution, a greater dependence on catchable trout stocking, and greater fishing pressure. They accomplished a lot with what they had. The challenges we've got today are different. Harder in some ways."

And when it comes to squabbling over trout regulations, that's still going on in America with a remarkable durability, perhaps reflecting deeper issues (social justice, divides between the rich and the rest of us, the clash between urban and rural culture). Culture is in a constant crush to replace itself. But the heat may be dissipating from the rules debate. There are other concerns. In the mad push toward wild fish and healthy aquatic ecosystems that began in the early 1970s—part of the noble effort to deal with the widespread abuse of wildlife, land, and water—special regulations for wild fish and wild fly anglers were over-applied. Good data and thoughtful, objective planning eventually corrected some of that, but not all. Poor approaches to citizen engagement can still rule the day. And sometimes the best science is too easily swept aside by the political process.

Having penned that just now, I realize "the king is dead, long live the king." It's the likes of Jake and Weeks and their generation who will soon have the reins. They'll have a lot to reconcile, and, I hope, the resources and support they need to make things right. They may be contending with worsening fiscal realities, growing climate change impacts (less a water temperature problem in spring creeks, but possible greater frequency and intensity of storms, and the constant specter of drought), and issues no one has glimpsed yet. But they'll have tools and intelligence in the fields of social media, big data sets, genetics, geolocating and tracking, and crowdsourcing that we never dreamed of. Social science will be more finely tuned.

Other changes will be purely social. The demographic face of America is changing. Transportation and housing sectors will be entirely transformed, obscuring old boundaries between city and country. The folks with lots of money will have increasing mobility and spare time to live and play where they want, whereas the shrinking middle class, including families that used to farm, will move to cities where the work is, and many will have to keep working until they die.

Meantime, the brown trout crowd each other in Coon Creek, and itty-bitty little brown-trout babies and creek chub Vienna sausages will flee hungry momma and poppa with little hope for growing to their full potential. If they make it to year two, their salvation may be catch and release. No one is evangelizing fish—yet. The best a passionate old angler can do is, in the words of a wise ex–trout chief I know, *get the hell out of the way.*

A few years ago, trout researchers in Wisconsin went back through all available data to the 1950s to assess the current state of trout population statistics. Lead researcher Nancy Nate's written conclusion was that there have probably never been more trout in Wisconsin than there are today. As to why? Regulations, she concluded, haven't *hurt* trout populations, though it's not clear that they have helped. What is clear, regardless of the regulations, is that there is one hell of a load of wild trout in Wisconsin. Something on the order of thirty million. If they ever decide to rise up and rebel, pity the people who try to catch and release them . . . or try to eat them for that matter.

CHAPTER 8

The Best and Worst of a Destination Fishery

The theory is that if the fish are released, their populations will not decline in the face of fishing pressure, as had been the case; in addition, many writers argued in favor of C&R on the basis of "sportsmanship" (Schullery 1987; Radonski 2002). To a large degree—especially for trout—the theory has been borne out in practice (Barnhart and Roelofs 1977, 1987; Radonski 2002). In some cases, the hooking mortality is less than 1% (Schill et al. 1986).... Catch and Release has allowed or helped in the development of tourism . . . and arguably has helped to spread a conservation ethic (Schullery 1987). . . . In my judgement, the worst aspects of C&R—and they can be truly ugly—are those involving practitioners of C&R who believe their way is the only moral or ethical way to fish, or who do not recognize that their approach violates the cultural mores of the people in the region they are fishing in. Fishing tourists typically are wealthier than the people where they fish . . . and there is a risk that the tourists will trample on the cultures of the locals.

— DAVID POLICANSKY, "The Good, Bad, and Truly Ugly
of Catch and Release: What Have We Learned?"
Wild Trout Symposium IX, 2007

The people who scheme about such things (planners, entrepreneurs, movers and shakers, economic development experts, politicians, etc.) would love it if the Driftless Area were a thriving destination fishery. The contemporary urban trout angler is apt to be a traveler, too. He or she has excess income enough to travel and, in some cases, travels great distances in search of good trout fishing. For me, that's part of the allure of fishing. Seeing a new place from streamside. States lucky enough to have strong coldwater fisheries, particularly the Rocky Mountain states and the Pacific West, vie aggressively for the attention and dollars of these anglers. Entire trout-fishing retirement and recreational communities have arisen in such places as Livingston and Bozeman, Montana; Buena Vista, Colorado; and the western shores of Yellowstone National Park, including Jackson Hole and West Yellowstone.

What makes a destination trout fishery different from a non-destination trout fishery? It's not all about the size of the fish or the number of fish, though those are major factors. Traveling anglers are looking for a culture of fishing that is as agreeable and civil, from a lifestyle standpoint, as it is adventurous. Does the Driftless qualify as a destination fishery? What demographic changes have to occur if a trout place is to fit the description?

I had intended to camp in Avalanche after the day on Timber Coulee, but it was raining, so I got a clean, cheap room at the Adriatic in La Crosse. La Crosse, like Dubuque, Iowa, and other towns I've seen along the Mississippi, is appealing (all across the Midwest I found cheap, hyperclean mom-and-pop motels close to historic city centers). When you get through the blight of gas stations and other new urban sprawl around La Crosse, into the heart of the old city, you find yourself on what feels like a 1940s Jimmy Stewart movie set. Stone and brick buildings—old union halls, corn exchanges, Beaux-Arts bank buildings—rise to modest heights. Fading Rexall ads stare out at you from the sides of some of these—all suggesting an earlier prosperity, hard work, and a widespread farm economy that linked small towns to market towns like these. I noticed not a few brewpubs, another sign of change. Wisconsin has always boasted decent beer, including "the beer that made Milwaukee famous" and probably shouldn't have. These days, it's all about craft and micro. You can drink a throat-numbing American IPA flavored with jalapeños if you've got the nerve. The light lagers flow freely, too. If I were going to move to the Midwest—and I might if my wife makes a run for it—I'd move to a place like La Crosse on the Mississippi. Get a room downtown above a brewpub and set it up as a beer camp for further fishing and birding explorations afield.

Quality fishing is, as so many presenters at the Wild Trout Symposia in Yellowstone have observed over the years, in the eye of the beholder. Willis King, a grand old man of trout science in the Smoky Mountains and moderator of the first Symposium in 1974, may have been the first to speak that observation in a public forum about trout fishing. As for angler desire for large fish—if the words and deeds of the fly-fishing clubs that pushed so effectively for changes in trout management are any indication—it's bottomless in the trout fishing world. Destination fisheries can develop wherever desire and the dream fish come together.

There is no question that promoters are working to develop the Driftless into such a place, oriented toward people traveling to it from outside the region. It is well known that the fishing here, thanks to watershed-restoration science and genetics, has vastly improved. And there is an attractive rural character hard to define but still in place, the bucolic beauty of open spaces, woodlands, farmlands, and small towns with honesty and history. Combine that with a critical mass of angler amenities, like fly shops, friendly guides, and places to stay that cater to anglers, and there's much to recommend the Driftless.

But how successful is the Driftless as a destination fishery? Are those skinny creeks crowded with skinny trout (Kerr's claim) enough of a draw to divert a branch of that westward flow of fly anglers seeking the dream fish and fly-fishing nirvana that they know they can find on the Snake, the Madison, the Colorado, the Yellowstone, and the Bighorn?

A study published a few years ago by Wisconsin DNR research-ers Matthew Mitro, Jordan Weeks, and Dave Vetrano shows the extent to which fishing in the Driftless has shifted from local anglers to anglers visiting from afar. Whether you view this as progress or as a disaster depends on your values and, quite literally, your point of view (in an Idaho study that attempted to distinguish various troutfishing cultures, the greatest predictor of opinions on catch-and-release fishing was geographic location—the home of the angler).

The study compared two sets of creel census data taken from Timber Coulee Creek. The early set was data that Wisconsin trout researcher Robert Hunt collected in 1984. The later set was from 2008.

Creel censuses are in-depth studies of angler success and behavior. The idea is to interact with every angler spending time on the stream across a season. Creel census work is more rarely undertaken than trout census work, and more expensive. Creel census data gives an accurate snapshot of the anglers and their fishing experience.

By 1984, the fishing had improved dramatically on Timber Coulee Creek. It's safe to assume that much good restoration work had already occurred. Major changes in farming practices in the valley began in 1933. By 1940, there was reduced sedimentation in streams, and increased base flows. The Soil Conservation Service (now called the Natural Resources Conservation Service) had erected dry floodwa-ter-retarding structures on some creeks (under Public Law 566, the Watershed Protection and Flood Prevention Act). Trout research-ers Cliff and Oscar Brynildson studied the impacts of the structures on trout populations in the 1950s. They found that the dams helped reproducing, wild brown-trout populations above the structures by removing predation by northern pike trapped below them. They removed food competition by introducing hatchery trout lower in the watershed as well. The Brynildsons' electrofishing surveys showed increased production of wild fish above and below such structures, some of which were built in the upper reaches of the Coon Creek watershed. All the while, the department was putting its stream restoration ideas to test throughout the region.

The Mitro-Weeks-Vetrano study noted that in 2008, as in 1984, Timber Coulee provided a high-quality brown trout fishery, in terms of catch rates and average size. Trout size structure at the end of the regular open season included more eleven-inch-plus trout in 2008, but the average size of fish caught in 1984 was larger (10.6 inches to 2008's 10.0 inches).

What's significantly different between these two years are angler demographics, attitudes, and fishing practices. The regulations in 1984 were much less restrictive. There was an early season (January to April), when two trout could be harvested with a size limit of six inches. In 1984, the regular season allowed a five-trout bag limit, with a six-inch minimum size. In 2008, legal fishing began in April, with a month of catch-and-release fishing using only artificial baits with barbless hooks. During the regular season (May through September), it was catch-and-release only, with artificial flies and lures, on roughly 2.5 miles of Timber Coulee, and a five-fish bag limit on the remaining 5.7 miles, with a size limit of less than twelve inches—virtual catch and release, even today.

Trout anglers in 1984 kept more fish, obviously; 1,859 fish were harvested from 1.6 miles of creek. In 2008, anglers harvested a grand total of 119 fish from 4.1 miles of creek. How many fishing trips are we talking about? In 2008, anglers made 61% fewer trips to Timber Coulee (arguably one of the most productive trout streams in America) than in 1984. In 1984, anglers made nearly 2,000 trips to the 1.6-mile study section; in 2008, anglers made 752 trips to the same area.

The graph of number of visits across the season is telling. In 1984, trips spiked in May, then quickly leveled back to 2008 levels, then spiked again in the fall. There was a different seasonality to fishing in 1984. The other significant difference is that 2008 anglers spent more time per trip on the water. This is a consistent trend across the country. Trout catch rates were lower in 2008, but anglers spent more time trying. The catch rate was 1.25 trout per hour in 2008, versus 1.5 fish per hour in 1984. (In Avery's 1980 Wild Trout Symposium presentation, he wrote: "Logic dictates the farther one travels to fish, the longer he is likely to stay to make his trip worthwhile.")

Where do Timber Coulee Creek anglers come from? In 1984, nearly 90% lived within twenty-five miles of the creek. In 2008, 15% lived within twenty-five miles and 79% came from more than fifty miles away. How do they fish? In 1984, 51% used bait, 24% used flies, and 14% used lures or other means. In 2008, 85% were fly anglers.

Timber Coulee by 2008 had become one of those creeks that, by regulation and reputation, concentrated fly anglers and was discouraging to bait anglers. Just a footnote here on Wisconsin trout anglers statewide today: 55% often use or only use live bait when they fish (a nearly evenly divided electorate when it comes to artificial versus live baits, but somewhat skewed to bait use). Most studies I looked at show that between 70-85% of anglers in the Driftless today—the most rural part of the state—are fly fishing. While 90% of Wisconsin's trout stream miles statewide will have no bait restrictions under the most recently proposed rule changes, nearly 25% of the Driftless Area's creeks will have special rules, gear and tackle limits, and/or areas closed to bait anglers. Bait anglers, since they are more likely to harvest trout, are not as attracted to catch-and-release areas. Fly anglers prefer them, but also fish where harvesting of fish is allowed (by wide majority this includes most creek miles in Wisconsin).

In 1984, under less restrictive rules, over a thousand more people had a fishing experience on Timber Coulee. By 2008, bait anglers had opted out. Many more fly anglers in 2008 were willing to travel long distances to fish, and they stayed longer on the stream and spent more money on lodging, food, gas, and fishing equipment. Their visits provided some jobs and extra money for existing businesses, though the drop in local angling may have hurt businesses in the worm, hook, bullet, bread, and booze markets (underground meth labs and whorehouses probably still going strong). Next year, all of Timber Coulee will be catch and release.

How beneficial is the Driftless destination fishery to the region from an economic standpoint? That is less well known. An economic analysis underwritten by TU several years ago projected nearly a billion dollars of economic benefit to the rural counties of the Driftless Area, across parts of Minnesota, Wisconsin, Iowa, and Illinois (the bulk of Driftless Area trout fishing is in Wisconsin; less than 1% of Minnesota's creeks can be considered blue ribbon; and Iowa, with about a hundred spring creeks in the Driftless Area, has only several miles of catch-and-release water). These included direct expenditures for gear and travel, and an indirect multiplier. Average annual expenditures by fishermen traveling to the region to fish were estimated at $6,000 per person. (These are not mom-and-pop type anglers, who spend money on gas, ice, beer, and worms, and that's about it.)

But the TU numbers seem hopeful at best. The US Fish and Wildlife Service's 2011 angler survey pegged *all* of Wisconsin's direct, fishing-related economic activity at $1.5 billion. Wisconsin's roughly 140,000 trout-stamp purchasers that year, both resident and non-resident, represented only about 12% of all resident and non-resident fishers in Wisconsin (out of 1.12 million total fishing licenses sold). The sample size was very limited and based on a county-by-county analysis that was then generalized. In several cases there were only a few data points per county.

More work is needed. If there are future studies showing economic benefit, they should try to assess the cost of lost anglers to local communities, and at least attempt to find out why the disparity today, when in the Driftless there are ample opportunities to harvest trout and the fishing is better than ever. While bag limits everywhere are down, and arguably lower than they need to be, opportunity to fish for trout is up. It's up all across Wisconsin. Angler numbers, by rights, should be up as well.

CHAPTER 9

Lawrence Creek
and the Lost Anglers

Bait fishing is now prohibited in all but the two front ponds: the ones you can drive to and fish from lawn furniture within earshot of the car radio. It's been said they had to sacrifice these two ponds to the idiots to avoid too much squawking of the "I've-been-doing-it-like-this-all-my-life" variety. . . . I now and then miss talking to the[se] businesslike, straw-hatted fish killers who remind me of my childhood. These were the guys with perspective and patience to watch a bobber; people who fished ten-dollar glass rods and who dug their own bait because then the fish were virtually free. I don't know where they went. They're illegal out here now, and all but extinct.
    — JOHN GIERACH, *Sex, Death, and Fly-Fishing*, 1990

When the catch and release restriction first became effective [at Fishing Bridge in Yellowstone National Park during Jack Anderson's tenure as superintendent] angling pressure dropped to half. . . . There is serious consideration being given to eliminating the bait fishing areas for youngsters in 1978. . . . There is the feeling in the park's management that discouraging meat gathering among the young will pay great dividends.
    — LEE WULFF, "The Bright Future of Trout Fishing,"
    1978, *The Compleat Lee Wulff*

If you find yourself in the Unique Café in Boscobel, Wisconsin, around breakfast time, you will see a group of quiet old men sitting around a large wooden table toward the back of the café, where the booths end but the long lunch counter continues. Whenever I came in for breakfast, they were there. They may still be there. Order the blueberry pancakes. Doyle and Nancy Lewis will serve you up the cakers, top off your coffee, and they may stay on to chat.

Aside from hubcap-sized pancakes, the Unique Café is wall to wall with antiques and memorabilia, displayed in every manner of case you can imagine. Doyle took me on a tour of the entire building once, three floors of a remarkable collection, from an attic full of large stoves and other heavy objects, to a basement man-cave shrine to the Green Bay Packers. He explained to me in somewhat apologetic tones that he is only a reluctant collector. I don't believe him. He loves his stash, including: Sinclair Dino Gasoline signs, Sun Drop Golden Cola ads and ads for Grapette soda, a sturgeon-spearing registry sign, foam Cheeseheads and bobbleheads, biscuit advertising, metal toys, rock-and-roll paraphernalia, silver spoons, buck knives, clocks, wind-up birds, cook stoves, steel pennies, plastic hats, political campaign buttons, sleds, hand-forged tools, plastic Jesus bric-a-brac, and everything in between. All this wasn't his fault, he said. People he didn't know got to sending him items from the homes of deceased hording aunts when they found out he accepted a wide range of classifiably old items. In fact, his café is more museum to cultural drift—the flotsam and jetsam of an old agricultural society—than pancake palace. No real glacial till, but plenty of the human drift variety. How he fits all of it in is a Midwest miracle; not a week goes by that more doesn't arrive. Where are the American Pickers when you need them? "I've been trying to get them here," he complained.

This is one of the pleasures of traveling to fish the Midwest, I note in my notebook: the local rod and gun shop, the tavern, the native white people you meet on the water. Sure, who wouldn't want to fly into a fancy resort in Alaska for world-class fishing at $3,000 a day? But you'd miss out on Doyle and Nancy. In the maze of the Driftless region of Wisconsin, you can't avoid the people who live and work there, all too willing to share the places they inhabit. That's what makes the Driftless better by half than a destination at the end of a long plane ride, sitting behind someone who's farting up a storm. In the Driftless, you travel by car, by hunch and GPS, and you end up drinking coffee and eating mammoth pancakes in the Unique Café. Lingering over Nancy's coffee, I thumbed back through a 1970s-era technical brief by Robert Hunt, chief architect of the modern Wisconsin trout regulations.

As we know, in 1968, Wisconsin's trout regulations were two pages long, specifying a general limit of ten trout and a six-inch minimum size. Bob Hunt's 1990 regulations were a thirty-two-page book containing, by Roger Kerr's count, a thousand special regulations—rules for creek sections, including tackle restrictions, that departed from the generalized statewide daily bag by creek and overall possession limit (to be fair, Hunt's 1990 regulation has been modified significantly since then, including being simplified, but the template remains).

Bob Hunt was a giant in the field. It's hard not to think of him when you think about wild trout in Wisconsin—in America. He believed strongly that the regulations were needed in an age of restoration and environmental protection, and that they were needed because angler demands were shifting (Bob was a charter member of Trout Unlimited in Wisconsin, as well). Hunt was born near Madison and spent his entire professional life in Wisconsin working for the DNR, much of it as head of the coldwater fisheries research group. As his friend and colleague Bob Carline wrote, "Bob Hunt produced some of the very best publications on the biology and management of wild trout. His paper on the response of brook trout to habitat improvement in

Lawrence Creek is an exceptional example of how to design a study to measure the effects of habitat manipulation. His publication on the production of brook trout is one of the very best papers on the subject. . . . His compilation of evaluations of angling regulations remains a most valuable addition to the fishing literature." (This is the publication I was scanning yet again at the Unique Café.)

Why did Hunt feel the heavy hand of environmental regulation was needed? (His regulation included three classes of trout stream and five categories. Category 5 was deemed "special opportunity waters"; thirty creeks in Category 5 were made catch and release, and thirty-four were managed with slot size limits and lower daily bag limits.) Because Hunt was fundamentally a trout creek restorationist—he literally wrote a book on it (*Trout Stream Therapy*). And he was a serious angler. As noted earlier, overharvest was a constant concern of Hunt's. In his view, once a wild trout stream was restored and base flows were running well, there was too much at stake, too much invested to risk any chance of overharvest. So went the thinking in many departments across the country beginning in the early 1970s—the beginning of the environmental decade, with the birth of the Endangered Species Act; the Clean Water and Clean Air Acts; the beginning of the National Environmental Policy Act, of the Environmental Protection Agency, of Superfund sites; the battles over snail darters and the Tellico dam on the Little Tennessee River. This was the environmental warrior decade, and battles were being won.

Hunt had presented the study I was reading at the Unique Café at the very first Wild Trout Symposium in 1974. His paper was built on work James McFadden began in 1955 (McFadden was the moderator of the panel presentation at the first Wild Trout Symposium on special regulations).

In a gross oversimplification, I'll summarize to say that the Lawrence Creek study compared different regulatory approaches and their impacts on wild brook-trout populations across thirteen years. Some of the findings were surprising. It turns out that at Lawrence Creek, despite high harvests, thanks to strong food supplies, natural reproduction, and the recruitment of trout into the legal six-inch class over the summer, there was an equal number of catchable trout at the end of the season as there was at the beginning. Was there overfishing on Lawrence Creek in 1955? Not by most biological measures, even with very heavy fishing pressure. Was Lawrence Creek growing a stockpile of trophy-sized trout? Definitely not. Most larger trout in the system were being caught and harvested out of the pool.

Hunt also found that lowering bag limits was not as effective as increasing size limits when it came to protecting trout populations. To see any real reduction in harvest through bag limits, Hunt concluded, you'd have to shrink bag limits down to two or three fish, from the statewide rule of ten (on many creeks in the Driftless, that's basically what came to be). Hunt also noticed that if you shrink the bag, you disincentivize trout anglers.

And here's the rub. Disincentivizing trout anglers at Lawrence Creek led to a major exodus of anglers away from the creek. Anglers in the 1960s hated the decreased bag limits and higher minimum-size limits, Hunt reported. The old trout-fishing economy, after all, was based on a dual benefit. Anglers, noted Hunt, reacted "very negatively." Angler flight seemed to catch Hunt off guard. In a section of his 1970 report called "Catch and Release Fishing," he wrote that when the size limit was increased to nine inches between 1958 and 1960, a virtual catch-and-release situation was created, and annual angler harvests were equivalent to 4%, 8%, and 1% of the preseason trout population. These compared to exploitation rates of 32%, 59%, and 65% during the previous three years. Anglers voted with their feet. Between 1958 and 1960, three quarters of the anglers who historically fished Lawrence Creek left. Interestingly, in 1959, when regulations were re-liberalized, anglers began coming back; but in 1967, they were still 30% lower than the 1955 levels. This is at a time when trout fishing across the state and country was growing in popularity.

You would think that the behavior of anglers at Lawrence Creek would have been major news in the trout fishing world. It was not. Not in 1974 and not for many years following. Few at the Wild Trout Symposia mentioned this inverse relationship between the growth of restrictive regulations and the dropout of anglers on a creek. Pollution, overexploitation, crowding, the quality angling experience— these were the overriding concerns of the day.

Who were the lost anglers? Where did they go? Why did they go? These are rich, values-laden questions that few were asking at the time. They're anthropological questions, social queries, home economic questions, and there is an element of social justice embedded in them.

Back in the 1970s and 1980s, many, if not most, participants at the Wild Trout Symposia would have considered excluding access to trout-killing anglers and reducing the use of bait substantial progress, because it reduced fishing pressure and hooking mortality. Defending the lowly, less outspoken bait angler was left to state fisheries employees who were familiar with the local angler, his cheap gear, and his intent to harvest, and who cast a wary eye on the focus on special regulations. These lost anglers—Roger's people—were poorly represented at meetings and hearings. The ones who left creeks or hung up their trout rods were not likely to jump whole-heartedly onto the environmental bandwagon either.

If you want to understand cultural divides today, it's worthwhile to look at the rules, who makes them, and who benefits. The prevailing belief in trout management circles in the heady early days of the environmental movement was that progress—moving forward—meant buying into the necessity of no kill, or low kill. Who benefited? The anglers at the pulpit whose methods were gentler on the tongue. Nathaniel Reed, then assistant secretary of the Department of the Interior, suggests managers zone bait anglers out of the best blue-ribbon waters. Lee Wulff quips that these anglers can confine their catching and eating to domestic hatchery fish manufactured to taste like strawberries if they want. Trout Unlimited's president Bill Luch, in his wrap-up remarks, is heard hectoring state fisheries managers for all the damage hatcheries have done. He lays blame and he draws lines in the sand. Gardner Grant is another voice without compromise to it. "Economics," he says, "makes it increasingly clear that trout fishing can ONLY [his caps] be regarded by ALL its adherents as a sport and not as food supply, and that sport will be increasingly defined as the catching and not the killing of trout." Some pushback comes from state fisheries managers like Delano Graff from Pennsylvania, who forcefully argues for the broad spectrum of fishing public that science, not emotion, should rule the day.

Sitting in a booth at the Unique Café on a third cup of Nancy's coffee, thinking about Bob Hunt and his work at Lawrence Creek, I conjure up an image once again of the ghost angling men of old—most of whom only fished a few times in a season, early and late, because there was ice fishing in winter and deer hunting in the fall, and bluegills and perch, and a pike and walleye trip up north. They were not experts, and they weren't overharvesting. Small trout fit the frying pan better than large, and most of the brook trout at Lawrence Creek— a very healthy mixed-age population—were weenies.

Bob Hunt came up in the ranks during the environmental decade. He was devoted to public service and rebuilding fisheries. Whether or not his regulatory framework has been successful at preserving and improving trout populations in Wisconsin still depends some on whom you ask. He thought it was needed. So did the new class of trout angler specialists coming from growing urban areas to fish Wisconsin. While there is still an urge to create special rules for special folks, the reality is that few spring creeks in the Driftless are actually tackle restricted or catch-and-release fishing today. Managers do remain wise to political factions and their power, but in an age of declining revenues for stewardship, it's hard. Factors other than special rules seem to control the quality and quantity of brown trout in spring creeks, and brown trout remain devilishly hard to catch for most of us.

The significant angler dropout that Roger Kerr saw in the 1980s and 1990s and tried to confront can't be blamed only on changes in Wisconsin's trout rulebook. The rules, the culture, the beliefs, new emerging environmental concerns, and values held by a dominant, politically connected trout-fishing minority had all begun to broadly reshape trout fishing in America. Not just in Wisconsin. The great irony is—and Kerr understands this, and Detar and Carline's study acknowledges this, and many social researchers have pointed to it— that the old culture of trout as food and family weekend recreation lives on in the countryside. The older culture never died. It's in private dining rooms, tall-tales bait shops, and local papers, but rarely on the national stage. You can find the old culture at the Unique Café too, where talk often goes to rule changes proposed at the Conservation Congress, or to turkey hunting, or to muskrat trapping. While such a place like the Unique Café is frequented by old fishing and hunting men caught in the slipstream of dissolving time, it's also there for the fishing tourist like me, with an interest in the drift and artifacts of culture, and the fishing and the eating. And the fishing's good here in Wisconsin, no matter where you come from.

CHAPTER 10

A Bluegill Insight

As expected, advanced anglers were less interested in relaxing the more restrictive harvest restrictions currently in place that produce the fishing quality they enjoyed. Casual anglers showed a strong preference for catching more fish by relaxing current harvest restrictions. Each specialization group showed a notably different pattern of preference.
— CHI-OK OH and ROBERT DITTON,
"Using Recreation Specialization to Understand
Multi-Attribute Management Preferences," 2005

We live in an increasingly specialized world. You need look no further than increasing specializations in science and medicine. Politics today is by identity group. According to Robert Ditton, who applied specialization theory to how we recreate, trout-fishing fly anglers are among the most highly specialized. They have the greatest willingness to pay for their sport of choice and the greatest interest in restrictive harvest rules that they believe improve the fishing. In contrast, Roger Kerr is quite unspecialized in his fishing interests. He's as much interested in the mighty bluegill as he is in trout. Crabbing is worthwhile as long as it yields dinner, and so is fishing for walleye or pike. According to Ditton, this question of how specialized a person is in his fishing habits is critical when it comes to understanding values.

Bluegill fishing is a great antidote to the highbrow trout fishing and conspiracy thinking I had gotten myself mixed up in. A reminder to me to stop thinking and go catch dinner.

Roger had borrowed Fred's forty-year-old Lund, with a ten-horsepower engine on the stern. Richard Seibert, a Boscobel native who'd moved away to Michigan years ago, had popped in on Roger during the days I'd spent in Madison. They'd gone trout fishing the night before on Saunders Creek, just up the road, and caught a twenty-inch and then a fifteen-inch brown. Each was beheaded and frozen now in its plastic soda bottle full of water in Mary's freezer, awaiting the baking dish. The twenty-inch brown stuck out of its container like a giant troutsicle. I took a photo and threatened to put it on a Driftless Area trout fishing website (a website Roger helped finance and get off the ground), just to make more people pissed off at him. Roger thought that was a grand idea. Offending no-kill anglers is one of his favorite hobbies. We launched at a state access point near Prairie du Chien. At nearby Wyalusing State Park, the last wild passenger pigeon in Wisconsin was shot. Years later, Aldo Leopold spoke at a ceremony commemorating the event with a stone marker.

Roger operated the boat, I sat in the middle, and Richard, with a good-sized joey on him, wisely wearing his orange life jacket, gingerly took the bow. There were ice coolers and bait boxes between us. It was a gray day with a smattering of rain now and again as we motored upstream. The river there had meandered far and wide, leaving phantom channels, abandoned side channels, and dark islands of floodplain forest. The forests had a desolate air about them because their lower portions had been stripped of leaves by recent floods. A mile to the west lay the navigable channel of the Mississippi and the Iowa border. Only once, through an opening in the canopy, we caught a glimpse of a string of ghostly white barges moving downstream; otherwise, we were lost in the gloom of a Mississippi floodplain forest.

Roger's destination was a side channel off a side channel. He and Mary had discovered it and had had good luck a few weeks earlier, limiting out on bluegills in an hour or two. Getting in there was a bit tricky, since the flood had washed whole trees into the slough and one of them all but blocked the entrance. We motored to the far end of the old channel and we anchored in this littoral backwater. We would have it all to ourselves.

Bluegill fishing, I thought, was only what little kids do with their parents from the end of boat launch docks. I had that wrong. Like mushrooming, bluegill fishing is good old-fashioned family hunting and gathering.

Suffice it to say, I enjoyed bluegill fishing. Partly, it was where we were, there in the belly of the country's greatest river, Huckleberry Finn country. Gray, drab, mucky, musty smelling, the slough had the feel of a dank basement where you might spin a stack of 45s, kiss a girl by the point of a bottle, and smoke cigarettes at the age of fourteen. Casting toward half-sunken stumps and boat wreckage, through duckweed-covered scum, felt like Cro-Magnon activity: instinctual, primal. I felt on a par with bluegill—a hungry animal in a wild place full of food, where everyone preys on someone and is torn apart and consumed by someone else. We didn't catch only bluegills, but also toothy dogfish, yellow perch, crappy, and black bass. And my companions proved companionable. Initially, I'd thought I might be bored around these older guys (eleven and fourteen years my elders) all afternoon in a small boat, but they proved entertaining and knowledgeable. For the entire trip over in Roger's truck, Richard said not a word. I was afraid I'd be in a boat with one of those famously taciturn Midwesterners and end up talking to myself. But on the boat, Richard opened up. He discoursed on everything from welded train track and oil fracking to Ernest Hemingway and Indian mounds. He never stopped talking. And the fishing was awesome! Roger moved the boat into the branches of downed trees, for the bluegills apparently favor that kind of habitat, and they were thick there, popping up out of the water like fish-sparrows on string, through the branches after the frantic struggle, and into the boat. Two piles of bluegills, fore and aft, grew and grew, and I had fully entered the fray of gathering them.

After fishing, we went for a ride north upriver past Prairie du Chien.

By the end of the day, retired to a small tavern full of locals for some *Totally Naked* beer, brewed in New Glarus, Wisconsin, I had moved beyond trout science, politics, and culture, to thoughts of the beauty of this place. The late afternoon sun had come out and illuminated a family, all in bright-colored bathing suits and lounging on rocks in golden light above a pond that their home seemed to grow out of. Water people. We had found an enormous gray mayfly, a holdover *Hexagenia*. These, Roger said, can darken the sky in early July. We had driven past acres of wild rice, past the watery habitats where the reintroduced trumpeter swan sits, and past the place, Richard explained in detail, where Black Hawk crossed the Mississippi in his flight from pursuing soldiers. There was talk of fish and fishing, places and fishing flavors, favorite catches and famous spots. The good news for the unspecialized angler—the person who is open to trying for anything, even if it can't be caught and shouldn't be eaten—is that there is always quarry. The unspecialized angler always has a door open, even as he perceives that one shuts. Though that same lack of a specialty may put him at a distinct disadvantage when up against an organized, highly motivated, politically connected fishing cartel like several that exist in the world of trout fishing, there is always a quarry and that matters.

Fishing, it turns out, is a portal back to the happy days of youth. Richard Brautigan, author of *Trout Fishing in America*—a thinly veiled autobiography—needed trout fishing as a kid to survive a brutal childhood, and trout fishing as an adult to survive success, alcoholism, and depression. Often enough he and his sister went hungry in a fatherless family that hardly kept track of the children's whereabouts. He learned at an early age that he could go catch fish from a flooded local quarry. He and his sister could get there on bikes, find water, and catch food. Brautigan found his adult salvation by remembering those salvation fish. Memories of them sustained him, inspired his art, even as hard drinking did him in.

If there is a positive memory of fishing at an early age, fish can become that original joy we go looking for no matter the turns life takes in adulthood. For Kerr, it began with a brown trout, and that led to forays on a bike to all the fishing spots he could reach in a day around his hometown. There's nothing like that passionate, obsessive first quest we find ourselves on. It can become a touchstone to every-thing else we do. For Brautigan, memories of youth fishing fueled his art; for Kerr, they fueled his professional life, his recreation, his trout-regulations protest mission. There is something hard at work inside, deeply embedded, moving us, something that has the dark shape of a fish circling round and round. Kerr is protesting something bigger—I'm not sure I know what it is, or that he does either. We fear loss. We fear that, little by little, all that we value will be taken away. High praise then for the little bluegill!

Driving back to Boscobel, to our east was Crawford County, the heart of the Driftless. Not a few of its prime trout streams empty into the Mississippi, entering marshlands and sloughs first, so they're warm water by then: Picatee Creek, Du Charme, Leitner, Cold Spring Hollow, and many others. Some of the monster-brown-trout hunters frequent these lower watersheds in the fall.

Secretly, the trout regulations book that Roger hated, I had grown to appreciate. If not for the regulations themselves, which are straight-forward enough, then for the maps, with their squiggly red, green, and pale-yellow lines denoting the various spring creeks—representing several lifetimes' worth of exploration. But I do love information, digital and otherwise. Roger doesn't use email, or a typewriter for that matter. He prefers the pen and paper, and he'll write your letter and sign it for you and send it under your name, or an alias, if you'll let him, so long as it promotes his vision of trout fishing in America. But zipping along the Mississippi, right here, right now, through a landscape arranged as a puzzle of small, hidden creeks and cloud-filled coulees, midsummer in the Driftless felt full of endless possibility.

CHAPTER 11

Melancthon Creek, Fishing Rules, and the Psychology of Social Change

This is the idea which in primitive society lends sanctity to the bond produced by eating together; by participating in the food two men give, as it were, hostages for their good behaviour; each guarantees the other that he will devise no mischief against him, since, [he is] physically united with him by the common food.

— SIR JAMES GEORGE FRAZER, *The Golden Bough*, 1922

[There is] a large group of anglers who would like to fish for trout but feel intimidated by the complexity of the rules . . . the father or mother who wants to take their children fishing, perhaps just on opening day. . . . They don't keep up to date of recent rule changes designed to maximize the production of trophy fish. They simply want to have fun one day of the year and have the chance to catch enough fish for a meal for the family. These are the people we are losing. There are also multicultural issues to consider. Newer citizens, such as some among the Hmong population, don't even try to fish for trout in this part of the state because they find the rules too intimidating.

— STEVE DEWALD, "Enforcing and Communicating
    Fishery Regulations in Wisconsin: A Conservation
    Warden's Perspective," Trout and the Trout Angler II
    workshop, 2000

E ast of Yuba and north of Hub City, Melancthon Creek begins its twenty-five-mile journey south to the Wisconsin River. Grinsell Creek joins, and then Hanzel (both from the Grimm brothers' fairy tale names; this part of the Driftless was settled in the mid-1800s by a community of German Bohemians). When Pine Creek joins at Rockbridge, the Melancthon becomes Pine Creek, and it's the Pine that empties into the Wisconsin River.

The upper corner of Richland County is broken up by bluffs, cut with narrow coulees, and spread across by farms that fold over gently sloping ridges. The farmers fill the coulees with corn. It's classic Driftless landscape. The creeks are narrow and they run cold. Some 237 miles of Class 1 and 2 trout creeks are found in Richland County that run a thousand to five thousand trout per mile and, as TU Ocooch Chapter member (this chapter is now closed) Steve Nockerts noted, "If you're looking for a place with a lot of streams and trout, where you won't see another fisherman, Richland County is the place for you." For Roger Kerr, Richland County, the heart of his old territory, epitomizes what has gone wrong in trout management in the Driftless. "What a shame! I repeat, what a shame," he wrote me. "Eighty-five trout streams, 110 Class 1 miles and very few local folks fishing there." He made a kind of stand in Richland back in 2005, putting together a proposal to the Conservation Congress. His proposal, among other things, sought to simplify trout rules. He told me his entire rationale for the effort was to get locals fishing again. While, by a vote of sixty-two in favor and five opposed, his proposal won approval in Richland County, when he brought it to the annual Conservation Congress meeting in Green Bay, he writes that he was "severely ridiculed" and that TU people with "TU shirts and hats on" voted him down. His proposal was quite simple, actually, and supported by the biological data. In fact, most of Richland County's special regulations had been removed in 2002 after it was shown that they had been ineffective (in 2002, Richland County had eighty-five trout streams, thirty-four covered by special regulation). But recent proposals by the Wisconsin DNR would increase them again. Kerr's proposal sought to increase bag limits from two and three fish to five fish with a seven-inch limit—a modest change that he felt would provide a psychological incentive for locals to get up and go fishing. After he lost his bid to boost bag limits and reduce minimum-size limits to encourage local fishermen, Roger did two things: He circulated a petition in Richland County to simplify trout rules—it garnered 2,135 signatures—and he wrote a detailed point-by-point letter to the Wisconsin Conservation Congress's trout committee. The letter outlined the changing situation in Wisconsin's trout, both the improvement of fisheries and the decline of anglers. It's a remarkably clear communication, both a complaint against the makeup of the WCC trout committee, populated by a majority of Trout Unlimited members at the time, and a careful documentation of the thinking behind his recommendations. The memo was ignored. When that failed, he resorted for the second time to civil disobedience. He wrote a letter to the local warden to give notice of his planned rule breaking and hoped-for arrest. This time he intended to fish with worms and artificial lures where they were not allowed. He also threatened to break the no-kill rules on the Blue River in Iowa County. Once again, he couldn't get the wardens to bite.

Recently, well-respected trout columnist Len Harris (long estranged from Roger Kerr by some earlier dispute or slight) asked essentially the same questions Roger asked back then and had been asking for years: Why are the 55% of Wisconsin's trout anglers who always or usually fish with bait (Petchenik 2012) being excluded (from the early and late seasons) and pushed off water by special regulations, and why are they so poorly represented on trout committees when it comes to discussing those regulations? And why, Roger Kerr posed in a recent letter, are many new special regulations going into effect in Richland County in 2016, when most of the prime creek miles in Richland are devoid of anglers? It's his old boss, he said, and nemesis Gene Van Dyck who has recommended the regulations.

I had to go to Richland County to see "ground zero" for myself. That would be John Slaney. Slaney, a farmer and retired teacher, grew up on the family farm in the upper reaches of Melancthon Creek. His family milked dairy cows and raised hogs on 120 acres, a third of which was tillable bottomland. There were seven children. The creek ran about ninety feet from the house. Fishing for trout was a multigenerational family tradition. Slaney remembers his grandfather fishing the creek. His mother, Agnes Slaney, and his uncle, Jim Kaderavek, both fished the creek when they were kids. Opening day was a big scene on the farm, with local anglers vying for a spot and families reacquainting after a long winter. The adults tended to hit opening day and then quit. The kids fished all summer. Slaney's mother kept the fishing tradition going with his children, taking them along with cane poles to fish brookies out with crawlers, just as she had done as a child.

In the 1970s, the state stocked the Pine, Hanzel, Grinsell, and Melanchthon Creeks with rainbows and brown trout. They also identified these as some of the most productive brook trout waters in the Driftless. In the late 1980s, during Larry Claggett's term as the trout specialist for the central region, the Wisconsin DNR began taking brook trout eggs to the hatchery and restocking fish throughout the upper watershed. Those wild fish genes, combined with reduced siltation and improvements in water flow and temperature, aided the native brook trout population. In 2003, Melancthon Creek and Pine Creek were changed by emergency rule to Category 5 waters: no kill, with artificial lures and flies only. With the stroke of a pen, miles of creeks flowing through farm country were made off limits to locals like Slaney's mother, who fished with night crawlers and fixed the trout she caught for dinner (John told me he preferred catching and frying up creek chub to brook trout). The sting of the new regulations was most painful to the Slaney family because, suddenly, they couldn't fish their own property the way they had for the past fifty years—property they'd kept unposted, with open hunting and fishing access to all comers, locals and foreigners alike. Private lands kept open for hunting and fishing has long been a rural tradition, from Vermont to Wisconsin, but as the colonization of rural America by urbanites has grown—in the form of second homes and wealthy weekend warriors in SUVs—more and more lands once open are posted, and walking through property boundaries is increasingly framed as trespassing.

Until Roger Kerr met John Slaney and began working with him, Roger was really kind of a lone soldier. And, he told me, he had become demoralized. He'd already written hundreds of letters and dozens of op-ed pieces, and had begun gathering together a mixed assemblage of allies among disgruntled anglers, mostly seniors, who saw change and weren't happy about it. But nothing was happening. One of his strong allies was Lee Fahrney, outdoors writer for *The Monroe Times*. Lee wrote about an informal survey he and Roger had undertaken of fishing spots on opening day in 2007. Lee, Roger, Iowa County board member Phil Roberts, and a newly elected delegate to the Wisconsin Conservation Congress who went by Lyle drove from creek to creek on opening day, checking for cars and anglers at favorite spots. Places like Trout Creek and Ley Creek along Hwy. 191, and the Pecatonica River west of Jonesdale. The idea was to compare opening-day anglers and car counts in 2007 to similar counts—a regular practice of the Wisconsin DNR dating back to 1970. Late in the morning, after checking the northern reaches of the Driftless, Roger went back home and checked his Grant County creeks, including the Big Green, Castle Rock, and Crooked. Meanwhile, his new trout-regulations protester friend Jimmy Knutson checked creeks in Lafayette County near his home in Livingston: Cannon Branch, Coppermine Creek, Gravel Run Creek, and Lovett Creek.

Lee found the contrast between years surprisingly stark. Iowa County, for example, posted 773 anglers in 1970 and only 12 in 2007. In 1970, Lafayette County had 154 anglers on opening day, and in 2007, zero anglers. In his piece about the opening day survey, Lee wrote: "We shared tales of the good old days when trout fishing was on every sportsman's mind at this time of the year . . . of the bonfires built to keep warm and cook up freshly caught trout. . . . The moment seems to have passed for trout fishing as we knew it thirty or forty years ago." In classic Roger style, he wrote up the data from that informal opening day survey, compared it to 1970 in a handwritten chart, and sent the analysis to everyone he thought ought to know, in and outside of the Wisconsin DNR.

When Roger met John Slaney, he saw someone for whom the fight against the special rules was as personal and focused as his own. He also saw someone the department might actually listen to. Roger had stirred up the pot too long. He knew he was viewed as a radical crank with zero credibility. John, on the other hand, was a farmer, a teacher, and a landowner with a creek running across his property. And Slaney was seriously offended by the department's actions.

When they first met, Roger had been finishing up his career as a land agent for the department, and his job brought him in close contact with landowners like Slaney. Roger spent hours listening to their concerns. (Slaney told me he had been approached by the DNR for an easement, but was never very interested in selling. He still owns the farm in Richland Center, and it's gone way up in value—too expensive to farm and too precious to sell, as he put it.) Slaney wasn't the only one upset in Richland County.

"To begin with," Slaney said, "the DNR rarely asked for any input from any of us before new regulations went into effect." In his case at Melanchthon, it was an emergency rule, simply imposed by the department without input. These didn't go through the usual process of springtime public meetings; there were no meetings. "One day," said Slaney, "the notices went into the papers, and the signs went up along the creeks."

"It wasn't as though they had any actual recent data either," Slaney continued. The department did have some data on the trout populations in Melancthon, but it was twenty-five years old. In fact, fishing pressure on Melancthon, as Roger had noted and made his cause célèbre, had dropped way off by the late 1990s. It didn't seem as though this population of brook trout needed protection from anglers. John and other anglers living in Richland County had noticed the angler drop-off too.

With Roger's help, Slaney and a fellow farmer from Hillsboro, Maynard Hewuse, put together a public meeting in Yuba (a small farm community settled by Czech Bohemians in the 1850s) and from it, gathered several hundred signatures. Initially, they got strong pushback from department staff. Slaney was told that the department wouldn't likely modify the new rules. That the rules were needed to protect a rare brook trout population. Back then, anyway, during the height of the move away from hatchery-based trout and toward wild trout, Roger told me, trout chief Larry Claggett wasn't a big friend of bait anglers, nor was fish manager Gene Van Dyck. There was no love lost between Kerr and his ex-boss, and John Slaney and Van Dyck didn't get along either, according to Slaney.

Based on some backchannel advice in the department, Slaney went directly to the Natural Resources Board, circumventing the slow-moving process of the Conservation Congress. By then—after a meeting at Roger's and some good old-fashioned petition work that garnered over two thousand signatures—they had some steam behind them and some positive press.

They met with the Natural Resources Board several times, Slaney told me. It was the Board that asked the Wisconsin DNR for more data on current trout populations in the creeks here. The department's aim with the emergency rule was to grow trophy trout in these streams. The assumption was that all high-quality brook trout creeks needed protection from "consumptive" bait anglers, so trout could get big. By 2003, this was a given—whether these assumptions had any scientific grounding or not. Slaney and many others saw the department's rule as socially exclusive. Their creeks had been a local resource for kids and families for decades. Slaney didn't mind if out-of-staters came to fish on his land. But he wanted his mother and kids to be able to fish there too.

Sometime around then, Slaney ran into Larry Claggett on the farm. And he didn't take kindly to that. For decades, Slaney's family had kept their land unposted. Everyone and anyone was welcomed to fish and hunt. Larry Claggett's attitude, Slaney said, changed all that. At the height of the controversy, Slaney put up big signs that read: "No fishing, compliments WDNR."

Others in the department were more encouraging. Tim Larson and Scott Stewart came to Slaney's aid with a possible solution. They suggested pushing for a proposed seven-inch minimum harvest size and a three-fish limit. John thought that would be okay.

On the broader issues of angler decline and the impact of special regulations on the general population of trout fishers, there were other sympathetic voices in the department. Several wardens, who tend to hear complaints first, spoke up. Richland County Warden Mike Nice wrote a letter noting the need to bring back the local anglers. Warden Supervisor Steve Dewald of La Crosse, in a talk he gave at the Trout and the Trout Angler II workshop in La Crosse in 2000 and a TU conference in 2002, urged a conciliatory approach between trout cultures. Dewald spoke up for a kind of balancing act between simplifying regulations and maximizing opportunities to catch trophy trout. He spoke up for the agriculture community too—at the time trying to "dig its way out of a commodity recession" (which has reversed itself significantly since 2002). Dewald also spoke up for wardens, faced with enforcing rules that trout groups lobbied for but that, from the broader public's perspective, were off the mark; the criminalization of trout violations in the 1980s, for example, which gave a fisherman a criminal record for catching one fish over the limit. Judges, Dewald noted, were reluctant to enforce some of these laws, and wardens, understaffed and underfunded, were pulled away from the enforcement work most needing doing because they were "stalking anglers with illegal barbed hooks during the early season." In an interview in *Wisconsin Outdoor Journal*, Dewald noted that there is a general trend in hunting and fishing that emphasizes trophy animals, and that more regulations aren't necessarily what the Wisconsin DNR wants—"It's what [vocal, small groups of certain] anglers and hunters want."

There were other positive signs that Slaney's group had local and state officials on their side. They got the early backing of the Richland County Conservation Commission. "That gave us some hope," said Slaney. And then the Wisconsin DNR went ahead and conducted its study, finding that what controlled trout populations in Melancthon and Pine Creeks was habitat, not anglers. "That was a huge help," Slaney said, "having real data that supported our position that bait anglers harvesting trout were not harming the brook trout population."

All that Roger Kerr had claimed about changes in the broad region were found in Richland too, Slaney told me.

Slaney didn't get exactly what he asked for on the upper Melancthon, but he and Roger and their group of advocates won the day: a rare victory for a very local cause. The department ultimately reversed the no-kill rule on all of Pine Creek and on the lower Melancthon. The new rules allowed for a five-trout bag limit, only three of which could be brook trout (within a slot limit of six to nine inches), and a seven-inch size limit for rainbows and browns. In a bizarre twist, regulators left the upper Melancthon artificial baits only. This included Slaney's property: his mother's water. At ninety years old, she may have been the oldest trout fisherman in Wisconsin in 2011. And she preferred night crawlers.

"She'd be fishing today if she could fish with worms," Slaney told me. He kept fighting to have the artificial-only rule removed from the upper Melancthon. It may have been a simple oversight. The artificial-only rule still remains in effect. Roger thinks it's pure malice.

The reaction among fly-fishing groups to the rollback of Category 5 regulations on the Melancthon was, predictably, shock and surprise. The online chat groups lit up with their version of conspiracy thinking. The loss represented the first salvo. The enemies of sound trout-creek management, they were sure, had become emboldened and would soon push for a rollback of trout regulations statewide, then region-wide, then worldwide . . . then universe-wide. No more humongous-trout stories.

Getting ready to leave, I asked Slaney how he might explain the local angler drop-off seen so dramatically in his corner of the Midwest.

Isn't it strange, I said, that here you all live surrounded by great trout fishing water, in a countryside that has an old fishing tradition, in a state that is nearly the most fishing enthused of all the states, anywhere, and yet few children and few local adults fish for trout now. And by some measures, 95% don't keep and eat the trout they catch. Why?

"You know," he said, "the countryside *has* changed. Rules have something to do with it, but I think it's demographics too, as much as anything. Beginning in the 1970s and 1980s, people left family farms at an accelerated rate. The economics weren't there for small farms in our area. People had more work in the city. The whole herd buyout happened in 1986. A lot of farmers got out. We've lost farms, and the population of farmworkers is less. There were four farms on the upper Melancthon twenty years ago; now there's one. Fishing went with all that. On top of that, land prices began to rise in the 1980s. Locals can't afford to buy land here anymore. They move. Who's buying land here now is who has money. Many come from cities outside Wisconsin.

Unless you already own it and can pay the high taxes, you can't get started in farming."

✑

Slaney's victory may have had something to do with the effort to roll back special regulations on the Prairie River in Lincoln County several years later. A 2003 emergency rule there had put in place a "trophy regulation" that designated a five-mile stretch of river to size limits of twelve-inch brook trout and eighteen-inch brown trout, caught with artificial flies and lures only. The emergency rule was designed to create big fish in a trophy fishery. At the spring hearings in 2008, locals came out broadly in favor of letting the rule lapse and going back to a standard harvest fishery. Wisconsin DNR Bureau of Fisheries Management specialist Joe Hennessy said, "The brook trout population is secure, regardless of the regulations."

The question of which regulations were appropriate on the Prairie River boiled down not to biology but to social preferences and fishing philosophies. Locals wanted a return to traditional fishing, regardless of the impacts of the trophy rule and the size of the brown trout. Rich Ament of Wausau testified before the Natural Resources Board that the trophy rule was hurting kids; there's a Boy Scout camp on the banks of the Prairie. It also hurt anyone wanting to use bait to catch trout. "Name one section of the stream that is bait fishing only," Ament challenged.

Many others, including Natural Resources Board chairman John "Duke" Welter, spoke passionately for a continuation of the trophy rule. Welter now works for TU as head of their Driftless programs. The department, Welter said, had not provided data to the public on the rule's effects on the trout population, and that circumvented the public process. As for the exclusion of bait fishing, he testified that fishing with bait causes ten times the mortality of artificial baits. While Welter's comment on hooking mortality can be construed as technically accurate, given the very low mortality rates from proper release of fish caught on a dry fly, the real question is the impact of hooking mortality on the Prairie's brown trout population (see Robert Bachman's excellent summary of hooking mortality studies,

2002). Jonathan Ela, a board member from Madison, asked to what extent this was a discussion of the Prairie River, versus a "range war between two different philosophies of trout regulations."

Ultimately, the board ruled to discontinue the trophy rule. The locals won out. Once again, the nerves of dedicated catch-and-release fly anglers throughout the Midwest were severely rattled by the outcome. The chat-room venom fairly flew, and no one, Boy Scouts included, was immune.

If there is a lesson at Melancthon, it's that we need to listen to land-owners like Slaney, who found a real ally in Roger Kerr, and wardens like Dewald, who observes a "philosophical gap in the field between bait and catch and release anglers that must be bridged to ensure a high level of interest in trout angling in the future." Dewald observed not just regulatory barriers for this group of rural anglers—a more complex rule book, shorter seasons, and punitive (even criminal) measures for breaking seemingly trivial rules, such as barbless hook requirements—but also significant psychological barriers erected when new urban anglers began showing up in great numbers. These were wealthier, better-appointed anglers who at times aggressively exercised their new rights to enter private farmland to fish. Compared to the new angler, rural anglers, struggling to adjust to the new realities of farming in the 1980s, were made even more aware of economic disparity. Rather than adapt to the new paradigm, many of these anglers simply stopped fishing.

But if Slaney is the example, then Dewald's call for balance between the old and new fishing cultures and competing philosophies was start-ing to come about during the first decade of the new millennium. Slaney participated in a 2009 Richland County Land Conservation Depart-ment project to restore Melancthon Creek. His property was part of a larger effort, funded by a Targeted Runoff Management grant from the Wisconsin DNR, federal funds through the Wildlife Habitat Incentive Program, and a grant from Wisconsin TU. Contractors added riprap, reshaped the creek channel in places, and re-sloped 610 feet of eroding bank going through John's farm. Whatever grant money wasn't spent was sent back to the DNR.

Was he satisfied with TU's and the DNR's work?

"Yes," he told me. "The work was excellent."

CHAPTER 12

The Perfect
Crossover Angler

The values of wild trout, then, are the qualities that render them desirable or useful, either relative to human perceptions and judgements or as unique organisms unto themselves.

> — BARBARA A. KNUTH, "Beyond the Pocketbook:
> Held and Intrinsic Values Associated with Wild Trout,"
> Wild Trout Symposium V, 1994

Successful conservation of North America's wild trout and salmon resources today requires building constituencies outside the traditional and, still, rather small group devoted to fishing for wild salmonids. . . . It is quite another thing to be able to reach out to non-anglers and enlist their support by demonstrating that the future of a fishery resource is vitally linked to larger questions about how we manage our water, forest, and rangeland resources, or our native species gene pools.

> — CHARLES F. GAUVIN (former CEO, Trout Unlimited),
> "Meeting the Challenge of Trout and Salmon Conservation and Avoiding Gridlock in the 'Information Age,'
> Wild Trout V, 1994

Okay. Here's a hush-hush secret between fishing friends. You know those monster brown trout that occasionally get posted to sites like DriftlessAngler.com and Crazy4Trout.com? The Joe Humphreys money shot? Not a few of those from the Driftless came from the water under a certain bridge in Crawford County, Wisconsin.

I crouched, peeking over the edge at a school of two-foot trout. Hunched beside me was Mike Juran—the TU volunteer and avid fly fisherman from La Crosse—and a local named Trapper, who makes his living working outdoors. Trapper's the one who brought us here and let us in on these enormous trout. They washed out of a pond on a nearby private estate (Google money or some such); Trapper looks in on the place when the landowner is gone. Otherwise, he's fishing, trapping, hunting. Or he'll be working on firewood. "Do you ever catch them?" I whispered, watching the submarines scatter, run upstream, and drift back. "A few," he said, unable to take his eyes off the fish. He'll give one to a needy family. Then there was a baked almondine for a woman he dated. He's guided some, he said. But not anymore. It's amazing, he added, what great lengths some anglers will go to, to catch a trout this big. I nodded. At this point in the narrative, I should write that I began to drool big gobs of spit into the stream. But that's not me. I'm so used to catching small brook trout that these looked jacked on steroids.

Halls Creek and the secret bridge are part of the system of crooked creeks flowing into the famously crooked Kickapoo River, south of Avalanche. It's not a well-worn destination for tourists like me. We drove through the pretty town of Soldiers Grove—"America's First

Solar Village"—on the banks of the Kickapoo. Soldiers Grove witnessed multiple devastating floods in the early part of the century, Trapper told me, but changes in agricultural practices, particularly no-till agriculture and other erosion-stemming work in the upper watershed, have reduced flooding significantly. South of Gays Mills, we hit Bell Center—population 117—and turned off at a farmer's gate, parking in amongst a rusting fleet of tractors, used motor homes, and trucks. A gated community for retired machines. Trapper knows the family because he's helped the Gays Mills Rod & Gun Club raise and stock fish here. Jordan Weeks, fish manager in this county, permits and applauds the work they do. That's not all Trapper, who spends almost every day outdoors, does for trout. He teaches children to fish. As a guy of the land, who works with local groups, who's as happy baiting a hook with a worm as casting a long loop with a dry fly on the end, he's a perfect crossover angler. The kind, without a huge personal agenda, that we need more of. That's not to say rabble-rousers like Roger Kerr are not needed. They are.

Weeks told me that in the early 1990s, brookies were stocked in Halls Creek to reestablish a wild population. It worked, and the creek was soon reclassified as Class 2, with natural reproduction and multiple year classes that may need some stocking to maintain the fishery. Class 2 creeks cry out for a partnership with a rod and gun club that has a trout-rearing and stocking program, or a TU chapter. Both types of clubs work with kids. "I see a lot of kids out on the creeks," he told me. "Once kids feel the tug on the end of the line and they bring that fish in, they're hooked. Live bait or spin fishing is easier for beginners, and kids want to bring that fish home to cook it up. If you want to teach no-kill to them, wait for further down the road."

What makes Halls Creek suitable for brookies is constant cold water temperatures, below 60°F. That's on the cool side for browns, but perfect for brook trout. The eight hundred fish from wild stock that the club puts in annually probably don't add significantly to the total population of wild trout.

Mike Juran caught the first decent brook trout that morning. He is clearly one of Bob Hunt's highly skilled anglers. He doesn't catch many brook trout, he told me. Brookies are somewhat rare in the Driftless, mostly found in the upper reaches of watersheds now, where there might be some physical barrier—a dam or a temperature barrier—keeping browns at bay. Brook trout don't appear to bear up well against competing browns in many of these thin creeks, so wild brook trout often get a high level of department interest and protection. It was native brook trout, after all, that fed generations of Native Americans and early settlers in this part of the world.

Long casts upstream caught spooky fish in that clear, cold water, and flies had to land softly and in the right places. The ones we caught looked healthy and wild. The morning stretched into mid-afternoon— we could have fished until dark and probably caught one mess-load of fish.

At around 2:30, we broke down our rods and headed into a Gays Mills tavern for lunch. Taverns in the Wisconsin countryside are comfortable homes away from home, and groups frequent them for evening meetings and lunch gatherings. Over lunch specials and beer in the empty late afternoon, we talked more about trout. One of the last fish I'd caught was a four-inch brown trout. Can browns be excluded from Halls Creek permanently? Doubtful, thought Trapper, but maybe a barrier of very warm water below Gays Mills keeps browns from moving in. Once browns get into a fishery and begin reproducing, there is little to stop them from pushing the brook trout out.

Are the regulations right? Trapper said he'd had a lot of friends quit fishing because of the regulations. "Trout regulations need modifying," he said. "Let's go up to a five-fish limit, at least. Maybe if you relaxed the regulations, you might have more anglers."

Mike agreed. "We all release fish," he said. "Everyone today does. You have to, given slot limits and size limits; most fly anglers release all their fish by choice. That's the standard. Some guys would rather sacrifice their first-born son than kill a trout." Such certainty is imposing if it isn't a belief you share, he added. Mike, a TU member and a highly accomplished fly angler who travels widely across the Midwest, was adamant about bringing back year-round fishing to Wisconsin. The science and the trout densities support it, but his letters and calls have fallen on deaf ears, he told me. He uses Iowa's spring creeks as a prime example. Iowa has a much smaller corner of the Driftless Area and sells only about thirty thousand trout stamps a year, but it has excellent year-round spring-creek fishing that allows harvests and live bait and lures at the terminal end. According to Juran, the fishing pressure can get quite heavy in the fall, but the fish stocks remain very healthy. Mike is also a great example of a flaw in Roger Kerr's logic and rhetoric. It's a mistake to paint all Trout Unlimited club members with the same brush. Mike's La Crosse chapter of the Coulee Region TU organization puts out a welcome mat to harvest-oriented anglers, and increasingly de-emphasizes the no-kill dogma. At recent kids' fishing events, 175 children got excited about fishing, he told me. "And they were excited that they got to take their fish home for dinner." This is increasingly Wisconsin TU's prime message: all anglers welcomed; whether you fish with worms or flies, we want you. What may be a decisive dividing line between anglers is yet again psychological in nature, and that's an individual's perception of fishing pressure.

How much fishing pressure does Halls see? A lot, said Trapper. He estimated as much as one or two visits a week to the farm, in the early part of the season. "One or two parties a week? You're kidding!" I said. That sounds like virtually no fishing pressure at all. "If you don't want to see anyone, that's a lot," Trapper said. While for most, fishing over lots of large fish may trump the value of having the water to yourself, for a powerful subset of trout anglers, an uncrowded experience on the creek is tantamount to a successful outing.

We kept talking—not all about fishing. On Obamacare, no agreement. Mike Juran is a small business owner. It's likely he'll have to fork up a lot of dough to cover his workers' health plans. Government is the problem, he said. We need less, not more. As for trespassing, one of my favorite topics, it just isn't what it used to be. Trapper described the special-ops-like lengths to which poachers go these days. They wear black, blacken their faces, and connect with friends on cell phones for remote pickups. We weren't talking about someone's private pot plantation, or taking illegal trout in illegal numbers, or shooting pheasants—those old-fashioned joys of hunting on a nobleman's land and getting away with it—but poaching threatened American ginseng for the Chinese market. The poachers may walk twenty miles a night, Trapper said. Trail cams are employed now to catch them.

Back in Avalanche, we dropped off Trapper with a case of beer—meager pay for a day of streamside learning and fishing. Trapper's new house, built with a lot of help from friends, stands next to his old house: a log cabin, partially burned. It's a very fine mortise-and-tenon frame, worth restoring. Each of the ancient logs was carefully shaped with adze and broadaxe a hundred years earlier. Just like trout fishing in Wisconsin, the old stands next to the new. It's heartening to know that the old ways hang on. Maybe the old ways will serve again? Today they stand in stark contrast next to the new, but that you can still choose a life like Trapper's in this day and age is a hopeful thing.

CHAPTER 13

The Sand County

The ethics of sportsmanship is not a fixed code, but must be formulated and practiced by the individual, with no referee but the Almighty.
    — ALDO LEOPOLD, "Goose Music," 1922, *Round River: from the Journals of Aldo Leopold*

May I urge all of you who administer fisheries programs to assign a high priority to the study of watershed relationships to trout populations. . . . The protection of riparian vegetation from either grazing, logging, or other uses will yield additional benefits beyond fish.
    — STARKER LEOPOLD, Keynote Address,
    Wild Trout Symposium II, 1979

Roger and I drove up to Baraboo one day to pay homage to Aldo Leopold. His shack, unchanged since the days the Leopold family occupied it, is now managed by a private non-profit foundation, along with several hundred acres of preserved land. We took a roundabout way and stopped at Frank Lloyd Wright's homestead, Taliesin, an enormous and elaborate celebration of interior manmade space on the brow of a hill on the Wisconsin River. As fascinating as Taliesin is, I prefer Leopold's shack for its simplicity. Leopold was a complicated figure. His writings, dense with metaphor, irony, memory, passion, information, and a wandering, restless intelligence, reflect that. He was a seeker, a boundary-breaker-downer, a bridge maker with interests and projects in academia, government policy, teaching, wildlife research, and restoration work, and maybe that's why he endures. But the shack reflects a simpler picture of Leopold that may be more basic to understanding him and his legacy—a family man who cherished simple outdoor life.

We arrived at the Aldo Leopold Foundation in Baraboo in the pouring rain and had it entirely to ourselves. Kerr was quite familiar with Leopold's writings and both of us were captured by the new visitor center, state of the art in terms of energy efficiency and water conservation.

The shack, under pines that the Leopolds probably planted, was surprisingly small and locked up tight. We looked in windows, circled the hallowed place a few times, then wandered back into the wet sand plain and forest behind the house, finding an inviting pair of white plastic chairs under the big green umbrella of one of Leopold's pines. A perfect place to contemplate.

Aldo Leopold had very much to say about hunting and fishing, and their place both in the American conservation tradition and in the American psyche. "To kill a mess of game . . . and bring it home to the family," he wrote in his 1931 essay "Game Methods: The American Way" (*American Game* 20, no. 2), "is just about as necessary to most grown Americans as for their very young sons to go fishing in the family washtub. And that, in my opinion, is very necessary indeed."

But when it came to trout fishing, it was Starker Leopold (1913-1983), Aldo and Estella's oldest son, who had more to say. Starker attended the first Wild Trout Symposium in 1974, where he gave a radical talk challenging the prevailing multiple-use policy on public lands. In this view, he built on his father's thinking, then took it further to the next logical implementing step.

Starker was the moderator and keynote speaker at the second Wild Trout Symposium in 1979, where he gave a challenging presentation on the need for a watershed approach to wild trout management. His father would have been proud and strongly in agreement. The 1930s Coon Valley experiment was based on Aldo's ideas about watershed-scale planning and social collaboration. Coon Valley set the stage for the restoration of Wisconsin's wild trout fisheries fifty years later.

Not much real attention was paid to watershed-level trout stream management in those early years of the Wild Trout Symposia in Yellowstone. Starker was an outlier. The focus at the 1974 and 1979 meetings was on the need for special regulations that limited harvest and restricted terminal-tackle fishing methods; catch and release, bait restrictions, quality fishing, and management rules for wild trout, as opposed to the stocking of catchable-sized domesticated hatchery fish, dominated the conversation. But the Symposia rapidly evolved to catch up with Starker's whole-systems thinking. Starker died in 1983, but his ideas about watershed management were taken up and amplified at Wild Trout III in 1984 by keynote speaker Benjamin C. Dysart III, head of the National Wildlife Federation. "We are not talking about a fisheries problem, we are dealing with the problem of land management," Dysart said. "It's time," he urged.

Also, by 1984 the research on special regulations' effects on fish populations was finally coming in. The proceedings of Wild Trout III read like a report card on catch-and-release trout fishing. What had the states learned? Delano R. Graff (PA) reports that "a new state-wide trout management plan went into effect on January 1, 1983." The shift he describes is from a system based on stocking and the social preferences of fly anglers (fly-fishing only, catch-and-release waters), to an objective approach based on years of survey work and an inventory of both the physical properties of water resources and on the "social factors" of the broader trout-fishing public. It was an enlightened approach. He also reports having a drawer full of hate mail from fly anglers.

On the Au Sable in Michigan, we see evidence of failure on the part of a slot limit to grow large fish. Why? The real reason for fewer large fish in that system at that time was the removal of sewage inflows several years earlier.

In New York, we see success on the Beaverkill—where a catch-and-release rule grows more larger brown trout—and an increase in number of fish. We also see big increases in fly anglers. On the Amawalk Outlet, there is ambiguity. Catch-and-release rules did result in more brown trout, but fewer in the large size classes and slower growth and poorer condition in two- and three-year-old fish. When the no-kill rules were relaxed, there was a slight decrease in relative abundance, but better growth of two- and three-year-old fish, strong recruitment, and an increase in fish from 6.7 to 15 inches. Harvesting fish, in this case, improved the condition, recruitment, and number of larger fish (presumably by decreasing intraspecific competition). On the Batten-kill, catch-and-release rules designed to grow trophy-sized trout were put in place in 1971. The growth, abundance, and condition of both brook and brown trout declined. Fishing pressure and rules appeared to be trumped by poorly understood environmental factors there.

The West tells a different story. In Wyoming, managers developed an objectives-based policy governing the use of restrictive regulations, recognizing them as valid when properly used. "But they won't be used simply to discriminate against certain segments of the angling public." John Baughman goes on to say that "size limits will be favored over no-kill since the expectation and/or opportunity to keep some fish is an important part of the angling experience for many anglers."

At Yellowstone National Park, there is ample good biological news on catch-and-release rules put in place by Superintendent Jack Anderson in the early 1970s to protect spawning cutthroat populations. Ronald D. Jones reports from his study of three waters' landing rates ranging from modest decreases to 100% increases, while the size of fish landed has "demonstrated increases up to 15.9%."

Colorado? Extensive experimentation on seventeen streams began in 1979. In R. Barry Nehring and Richard Anderson's report on catch-and-release management, they report that 88% of anglers polled in favor of continuing catch and release, where the objective is "to maintain trout populations with a high density of quality sized trout that provide a catch rate of at least .7 trout per hour." Regulations in Colorado that allow "some minimal level of harvest" were also working well to maintain quality size. We find in Colorado and in many western states a call for more catch-and-release water by fly fishermen and the growth of an angling public releasing all the fish it catches.

The Montana experience is different yet again, with a decision in

1975 to stop stocking and manage strictly for wild trout statewide. Jerry Wells reports that Montana was "late" on entering the world of restrictive fishing regulations. The Madison's catch-and-release section increased the number of brown trout over thirteen inches by a factor of three (in sections about the lake, with strong reproduction and recruitment of brown trout, the size and condition of trout was suffering due, in part, to insufficient recreational harvests and catch-and-release rules [Vincent]). A slot limit on the Big Hole was equally successful, though a similar slot limit on the Gallatin failed to produce any change in rainbow populations. Winter conditions and growth rates were named as controlling those.

Moving away from the Mountain and Pacific West, to the southeastern US, the presenters mentioned that "special regulations, in the past, have been established through political pressure to a greater degree than through biological need." The South reported on the evolution of a much more nuanced system of special regulations, based on both clear biological and social objectives, with a general rollback of catch and release where it had been misapplied.

While there was mixed to good news on the biological side when it came to catch and release, there was a shadow on the social side. They saw early reporting on angler dropout and a shifting trout-fishing demographic. In one river in Yellowstone, there was a 92% decrease in angling pressure, and there were other examples of increased fishing pressure, but a replacement of the local rural angler who fished with bait by the urban fly angler traveling from afar.

At least this much is learned: When it comes to sustaining wild and native trout populations everywhere, environmental factors prove prime. That's the starting point: Anglers simply can't have quality fishing, however quality is defined, for stocked, native, or wild trout without ample, reliable, clean, and cold water supplies, food, and habitat. These are watershed/ecosystem issues. If those are in place, then the manager can use a wide variety of tools and rules—given clear objectives, the nature of the resource, and knowledge of the full range of angler values—to manage the fishery sustainably.

By 1984, state managers from California to New York had gotten a much better picture of the uses and misuses of special regulations. By then, as well, the movement for catch-and-release "quality" trout angling had grown. Catch-and-release panel moderator at Wild Trout IV, Gardner Grant (among his many accomplishments, he was a long-time national board member of Trout Unlimited and president of the Federation of Fly Fishers and the American Museum of Fly Fishing), noted that the popularity of catch and release was creating "an unanticipated people problem." He wrote, "We see evidence of a growing number of fly fishing enthusiasts, many of whom are particularly drawn to the rivers of the West, particularly those with outstanding fisheries values." For the traveling fly angler, there simply wasn't enough restricted water. For the worm angler who kept and ate some of his catch, what had been open was closing. We began to see the managed effects of zonation, of class distinction, of a hierarchy in the trout fishing world that continues to plague the sport.

The summer/fall 2013 edition (Volume 13, Issue 1) of *The Leopold Outlook*, a publication of the Aldo Leopold Foundation, is devoted to Leopold's take on the role of hunting and fishing in society. There is a cover photo of a woman fly fishing in a grassland setting. Below her, out of the frame, lies an invisible Wisconsin creek and an invisible population of brown trout in the creek. The rod is held at two o'clock, and a thin, blue fly line arcs straight off the upper right corner of the page and into the blue of the sky. We can imagine that fly line continuing its upward arc even to Heaven, connecting land, grass, creek, fish, angler, and sky to God. Many of the fly anglers I know would be comfortable with this rather simplistic metaphor. Even if they don't believe in God, they fish with a passionate religiosity. Why shouldn't they? For the highly practiced, dedicated fly angler who is as familiar with the patterns of the seasons as she is with fly patterns and invertebrate life histories, fly fishing—with its graceful lines and targets and moving waters—is about as sublime as a sport can get. Well-written trout literature reflects the sublime. It continues to contribute an imagery, an ideal, in poetic narrative that supports this view, and the fly-angling culture seizes on it. Fly fishing thus has a self-mirroring cache that puts it, for many, at the apex of the hunting and fishing world, admired even by the non-hunter as art form, hardly hunting since the fish are generally returned unharmed to the stream. But the art of technique and aesthetic mastery needs to make room for the art of community and cultural accommodation when it comes to trout fishing and conserving nature. What kind of diverse practices are welcomed in? There's no disputing that as a group, trout fly anglers work very hard for the sport, fish, and places they love. And through organization, they have improved their political standing. But ethics, Leopold wrote, is a personal matter between fishers and the Creator. For humans to accommodate the Creation, a different view, a fairer, wider view is needed.

Leopold believed in the transformative power of leisure time, of drifting the nets of the mind, of the connecting power of the hunt. He cherished books and the thinking person, but he was no big fan of "high brow" thinking, or thought unconnected to action. He was no armchair prognosticator either. He was an activist who used his knowledge of wildlife management to bridge to diverse audiences. What would Leopold have thought about the practice of catch and release? I don't think he'd have viewed it as a panacea. His middle-ground thinking about natural resources in general would have made a natural connection between the head, heart, and stomach. Letting a fish go would have made sense to him, but so would have eating it. He had a negative reaction against the trophy hunters, the dominionists, and he certainly opposed the market hunting crowds. For the angler set on catching and releasing fifty to a hundred fish a day, I think Leopold might have raised an eyebrow and wondered how that constituted sport.

CHAPTER 14

Lost
in the Driftless

Failing this, it seems to me we fail in the ultimate test of our vaunted superiority—the self-control of environment. We fall back into the biological category of the potato bug which exterminated the potato, and thereby exterminated itself.

> — ALDO LEOPOLD, "The River of the Mother of God,"
> 1924, *The River of the Mother of God: and Other Essays*

On my way out of Avalanche back to Boscobel, I passed through Viroqua. The unusually poetic name has Native American roots with a French variation meaning "maimed by a buffalo." Viroqua's got a broad main street lined with nineteenth-century storefronts and clean sidewalks. It's home to the Driftless Angler fly shop, a promising looking family-owned place. They'll take you fishing or give you a free map and mark it up so you can go exploring. I wanted to fish Reads Creek down Highway 14 on my way back to the Kerrs' in time for dinner. The shop in Viroqua had a fine selection of flies, including some regional favorites like Pink Squirrels, a pink nymph pattern, and pink Coulee Scuds. Armed with these pink flies and a circle on the map, I headed for Reads Creek.

Fly anglers like to have back and forward casting room; unless fishing must devolve to mere drifting flies downstream, open lands are far preferred, not required. Reads has long wide-open meadow sections, and these are a popular destination for guides and their clients. But where I ended up, at the wrong bridge somewhere other than an open meadow, was densely wooded. Forty-four percent of the Driftless now is wooded. One source says it's more wooded today than in the past ten thousand years.

What a delightful place to fish—to be—in spite and because of trees. I had some miles of creek to myself and could fish and walk under the happy illusion that I was truly alone, lost in a wilderness, though only a fool would try fishing here with an eight-foot fly rod. A spin caster, on the other hand, with, say, a five-foot piece, or a worm plunker with similar equipment could have had a field day. There were fish everywhere, holed up under overhanging brush, feeding with abandon on terrestrials and whatever else was floating in the film. A big trout was tailing under a log. At a large open pool above the bridge and next to someone's backyard, I was chased by a China goose and caught a pair of fish, released them, then entered a long tunnel overhung with alder and birch. From then on, I went cast-less, letting Reads Creek take me along to unknown places, letting the illusion of vastness and wildness overtake me.

Aldo Leopold extolled the unknown, the unmapped, the lost, even the little squiggles like Reads Creek. He believed these were necessary to the "spiritual and physical welfare of future Americans." Protecting blank spots on the map, the big rugged ones especially, that were quickly disappearing was at the center of his argument for federally designated wilderness, not only for the values of ecological goods and services such places provide, but for the human soul. The Driftless has such small bits of lost terrain; with a little effort, you can find them and you too can disappear.

One of my favorite writings of Leopold's, where far-ranging imagery seems to reflect exactly the way his mind worked, is an essay on the value of unknown places written for *The Yale Review* in 1924. "The River of the Mother of God" begins with a reverential listing of the many gifts, from rubber to rare woods and fruits, fertilizers, and medicines, that come to his life from South America, for which he is mindful of his obligation and his gratitude, the greatest of these being the idea of *el Rio Madre de Dios*. From there he takes us beyond the Andes to a story of a Spanish captain and his discovery of a river that drops into a rainforest from high in the Andes and disappears—a river with no beginning and no end. The captain, we learn, also disappears, as many a mythic hero does.

This *Rio Madre de Dios* is a place—an idea of a place that had been so long in Leopold's mind that he couldn't recall when it first entered. From that description of the River of the Mother of God and how it came to be discovered, and from the description of the Spanish captain who gave the river such a fine name (some of the last isolated tribes live along the Rio Madre de Dios to this day), Leopold's tone shifts entirely. He goes dark and bitterly ironic, to imagining a time nearly arrived when no such unknown places will remain unexploited. "The clank of steam hoists" will soon be heard in the "Mountain of the Sun."

The essay travels from a time when such unknown places defined us—from Sumerian tribes to Phoenician sailors, unknown seas, Hanno, Ulysses, Erik, and Columbus, and their voyages into the unknown—to the development of what is established, made into cities, commerce, civilization, settlement, and squalor. "And now the end of the unknown is at hand," Leopold writes.

Reading Leopold is to travel as readers, as partners to his wandering mind, to surprising places. The prose in this essay takes us across centuries, from the evolution of "the chase" as a fundamental fact of nomadic life—the Neolithic hunter and "his single combat with the Auroch bull"—to the recreational chase of the modern hunter with his setter, his rifle, and his back woodlot, his need for reconnection.

As a hunter/philosopher/scientist, wandering is Leopold's method of argument. In all of his ranging is an argument for wilderness, a known and familiar place to him. "The one thing needful is for the Government to draw a line around each one and say: 'This is wilderness, and wilderness it shall remain. A place where Americans may venture forth, as becometh men, into remote lands.'"

But that's not where his essay ends; Leopold, never satisfied to stray far from the particulars of life and a writing venture for long, launches into a full-blown attack on the automobile and the "good roads movement." He mocks the American style of progress, equating the motor tourist with Mammon. He derides the chambers of commerce and the "Greater Gopher Prairie Association with their chant of 'There is No God but Gasoline and Motor is his Prophet.'"

But still, that's not where all his wandering far and wide, from the Mother of the River of God to the most unholy of all roads that opens the last virgin wilderness, is going. That's not where he's taking us.

We journey with Leopold in this piece of writing not to some distant unknown place or protected wilderness, but to the center of our own being—to "self-control." Leopold—trustworthy and dependably loyal to his deepest values—takes us home to the hoped-for promise of self-mastery, of self-control. The journey into wilderness, into the unknown place, the roaming, reflecting modern mind, the angler in a meadow with a fly rod, or a worm—these are methods of travel. Each gets to choose their own method. Modern trout fishing—all manner of fishing—today, in a crowded, materialistic world, has to become an exercise of constraint, self-control in a world where self-control is too often absent. But what does self-control really mean? In trout fishing, under modern rules, is a man who harvests five fish for dinner guilty of lack of it? How about the man whose trout fishing flights take him to Iceland, Alaska, Quebec, Mongolia, Montana? Is he less guilty or more for lack of restraint? What about his appetite? Whose is greater? His or the rural angler who kills trout in a home country that has lots of them? From the TU angler in Wisconsin, we get the admonishment to harvest fish with a sense of restraint, of self-control; all the while, the disparity of material consumption between rich and poor grows wider. Those urban anglers, many of whom are well-to-do compared to the locals, can have everything they want, from empty private creeks in Montana, to salmon rivers in Alaska, to greater access to rule-making bodies close to home.

Back home in Boscobel, I met up with Roger and we stopped in on ninety-three-year-old Fred and his wife Madeline. We wanted to see Fred's photo albums from Japan, post-war, 1945. First, he led us through his garage to see his latest project, a 1968 black Buick Riviera. It's not clear how he fit the car in the garage with his failing eyesight.

There was not a quarter inch of clearance front to back. Did I want to buy the car? he asked. I have a Toyota Prius that gets fifty miles to the gallon, and it's paid for. I didn't think I wanted the Riviera. On the other hand, the Buick was classic shark/beast, all original parts down to the 430-horsepower engine, four-barrel carb, and all black leather interior. If I had to live in a sedan, I'd choose that one. A homeless family could sleep well in there, and evading police would not be a problem. "I'll make you a good deal," Fred said, as if reading my mind. "You can pay me over the next ten years." I was tempted, then exercised some self-control, combined with a *you've got to be dreaming* moment. And I wasn't about to bet on Fred not living another ten years.

Why was it I was so interested in Fred's photos of post-war Japan? It wasn't the cover photo of the mushroom cloud over Nagasaki taken from ten thousand feet. And there were no pictures of burned-in shadows, flattened cities, or piles of dead. His photos portrayed life in rural Japan as if rural life there ran uninterrupted during the war. Two weeks after Emperor Hirohito's surrender, Fred had been left to his own devices to travel into rural areas far off the beaten path, away from the seventy cities turned to ash, away from the 800,000 civilian dead. His photos of village life on Hokkaido, with men and women dressed in traditional garb, of animals pulling carts and children harvesting rice by hand in the fields, gave the impression that life in Japan's countryside had been frozen in the medieval. So wide sometimes, the gulf between urban and rural. I had read about early twentieth-century Japan. How quickly industrialized Japan became after its forced opening to the West in the mid-nineteenth century; how rapidly its imperial ambitions developed; how horrifyingly cruel the outcome of both. But in Fred's photos, I saw something else. The antidote to mass cruelty and war. Life in the countryside—the places soldiers had left behind, where, it seems, ancient traditions continued in spite of the war. Could peace have prevailed, and the war never happened, and the bombs never dropped if the countryside and country dwellers had been allowed to rule the nation? If the rural shogunates prevailed? We passed around pictures of Fred's planes and crews, and he talked about the many friends from the Hawaiian air station he'd lost during those years. He'd survived two crashes; he was lucky to have come back alive. I'm glad he did. Fred—a lapsed worm trout angler; once a professional lobster fisherman in the Keys; a restaurant owner in Colorado; a long-haul truck driver for twenty years; a US Air Force photographer during the war; the restorer of a 1968 black Buick Riviera, caring for his wife, a beauty parlor Memphis girl with Alzheimer's, who *must have been a beautiful baby/she must have been a beautiful doll*—had had a surprising life. An instructive life. Several, at least.

CHAPTER 15

The Ones that
Got Away

In a survey of Queensland recreational fishers, 70% reported experiencing constraints—predominantly lack of time, crowding, unavailability of facilities, and costs associated with fishing. Fishers with higher incomes, fishers with higher centrality of fishing to lifestyle, fishers who placed higher importance on motivations related to catching fish and relaxation, and fishers who were male were more likely to experience constraints.

      — STEPHEN G. SUTTON, "Constraints on Recreational
      Fishing Participation in Queensland, Australia,"
      Fisheries 32 (2), 2007

To get a better handle on trout angler declines in Wisconsin, I drove to Madison to meet with the Wisconsin DNR's chief social scientist, Jordan Petchenik. He'd just published the results of a major survey of lapsed trout anglers in Wisconsin. It was my first trip to Madison, the state capital. Madison, it turns out, is kind of a Midwestern Emerald City. My first glimpse was from the eastern promenade. On a midsummer evening, from a distance of a few miles, Madison appeared to be floating on water. A parade of bike riders and half-naked, bronzed runners made their way on the bike path between Lake Monona and Lake Mendota, whose shorelines were a green rim of forest dotted with bright lakeside cottages. There were fishing clans set up on lawn chairs, and out on the lake, the sails of a flotilla breaking the horizon—perhaps here to rescue a Midwestern Helen of Troy.

Looking toward the city center, I saw native son Frank Lloyd Wright's spaceship-like convention center coming into view. Above it, the tallest buildings of Madison were compressed on their hill, as if to hold up the gleaming dome of Wisconsin's Beaux-Arts capitol building; a potent symbol of the Wisconsin Idea from the first half of the nineteenth century—that government should serve the people, not a corporate elite class. Back then, it was a determined Republican majority that pushed progressive political, social, and economic change aimed at the material improvement of citizens' lives through science and democracy. Wisconsin's progressive movement became a model for national policy during the Roosevelt years between the Great Depression and the war. Division wasn't always the social norm. But what we read about Wisconsin these days is divided politics. Tea Party governor Scott Walker presides from the distant right, with the GOP controlling both houses. Far right Paul Ryan from Wisconsin is now House Speaker in DC. But Wisconsin voted for Obama in the last election and is also home to Russ Feingold: three-term, progressive Democratic senator, deposed by a Tea Party candidate and now running again. Tammy Baldwin, the US Senate's first openly gay member, is a Wisconsinite. Governor Walker, who came in on a recall vote and barely survived his own recall, has used his time in office to further divide and conquer, gerrymandering voting districts such that only about 10% now are in play (Pommer 2015), attempting to curb women's right to choose by trying to require ultrasounds before abortions, cutting taxes on the wealthy, curtailing state employee unions' collective bargaining power, rejecting federal healthcare dollars, limiting free speech in the state capital, and trying to cut funding for public schools. It's his war against unions that has gotten the most airtime. Ruth Conniff, writing for *The Progressive*, describes Walker as "pitting people against each other, so they tear down their neighbors who have union jobs and benefits rather than uniting to demand a better society for all." And yet . . . behold Madison, City on the Hill, and remember the Wisconsin Idea!

As I explored, Madison continued to amaze. I joined a musical spectacle on Capitol Square. Thirty thousand Badger State music lovers covered the lawn with folding chairs, wine, and picnic dinners for a free concert by the Wisconsin Chamber Orchestra and others. The music on that sun-drenched evening was three parts orchestral strings and two parts banjos (a tribute to the departed folkies John Denver and Dan Fogelberg). It was the perfect introduction to magical Madison. I found a seat on the grass and had my dinner of organic greens and a tofu burrito on a recyclable plate made from cornstarch that was apparently edible. The music transported me back to the peace and love of the early 1970s, where it seems part of Wisconsin still camps out . . . next to the survivalists' bunkers. And the lion shall lie down with the lamb!

I had studied Petchenik's survey of lapsed anglers after it was posted online, and I tried to keep up with the public response to it. His study has been widely praised, but the buzz about it from industry channels—the writers at *Wisconsin Outdoor News,* for instance— sounded to me like someone was trying to control the spin. Petchenik's study, among other things, set about trying to answer contentions like Kerr's concerning the trout regulations' impact on trout fishing dropouts, with social data from a group of recent dropouts.

The Wisconsin DNR building is downtown and secure. If you have an appointment, you're given a pass and directions. Petchenik met me at the elevator door, and because his small office was so cramped with ongoing work, we found coffee and a conference room. As we were getting settled, he told me that the department had just hired a second social scientist, and I said that he must have felt relieved to have a colleague on the way. He was.

Wiry, serious Petchenik loves his work. It's not only on trout issues; in fact, these days, it's proposed changes to the wolf hunt that are keeping him up at night. Wisconsin was an early adopter of the social science framework, the second state to hire social science expertise into its DNR, Petchenik told me. He was in college studying natural resource management at a time of transition from old management ideas to new. The old-timers—the target-species oriented and maximum-sustained-yield oriented—were retiring, and a new wave of thinkers was coming in, including social researchers like Stephen Kellert, the Yale professor whose early work uncovered a broad spectrum of social attitudes about wildlife. From the start of his career, Petchenik was on the cutting edge in a field that didn't have much of a published literature before 1970.

The ultimate goal of social science in the resource management field, Petchenik told me, is to bring the voice of the general public to the decision-making table, so decisions can be guided by scientific data, not anecdote only. That's not to say there isn't a role for anecdotal information; stories, observations, and recounted histories can be valuable, he added. But in the case of settling controversy and developing policy, survey data that captures a broad spectrum of the audience's attitudes and opinions is invaluable. The lapsed-angler study, he said, simply tried to determine what was causing anglers to stop trout fishing. If you identify the most important factors leading to angler dropout, then you may find that some can be influenced through management. That gives the department the opportunity to change its practices so that more anglers choose to keep trout fishing longer. If you fix problems that diverse stakeholders care about, the data indicate that a very high percentage of lapsed anglers will come back into the fold.

The irony of flat to declining numbers of trout fishers in Wisconsin is that trout fishing in the Badger State has never been better. A study conducted at UW–Stevens Point's Fisheries Analysis Center tracked an overall increase in the trout catch, number of trout per stream mile, and increases in all size ranges. The study considered all available Wisconsin fish surveys, going back to the 1950s. Trout fishing, by the numbers of stream miles and trout, is better than ever. Public access has greatly improved, and creek restoration efforts have boosted total miles of trout creeks from nine thousand in the early 1990s to thirteen thousand miles today. So, given that Wisconsin loves to fish, why would traditional Wisconsinite trout anglers—generally, the 55% using bait and lures and eating some of the trout they catch—abandon their own blue-ribbon brown trout waters, particularly in the Driftless region?

Wisconsin has a robust and proud trout fishing history. From the local perspective, what's eroding it?

Petchenik's study gathered data from a group of 800 lapsed anglers (those who did not buy trout stamps for three years in a row, beginning in 2009). He got replies from 498, a robust 61% response rate. The survey sought information on twenty-seven potential causes for lapsing, organized under seven broad themes: time constraints, fish preferences, access to and conditions of trout streams, expenses, regulations, and quality of the trout fishery. The study also captured demographic information from the responders.

A few observations to make before looking at some of the major findings. First, the study was conducted during a period of relative stability in trout fishing numbers. The big declines had occurred decades earlier (in the period between 1981 and 2001, stamp sales went from 194,000 to 135,000). Also, the trout anglers at the time that Petchenik was collecting his data in 2011 were quite different, in terms of values and attitudes, from the trout fishers of 1990.

What were the principle findings of Petchenik's study? First, it needs to be noted that researchers have found that in all recreational activity there is a relatively high level of dropping out annually. We try new things, then quit when they don't meet our expectations or we lose interest. Background dropout rates have been found to be as high as 25% annually for a range of leisure activities, including fishing. The first major finding of the Wisconsin study, Petchenik told me, is that "time constraints" are the primary reason trout anglers quit in Wisconsin today. Thirty-five percent of the respondents cited time constraints as their primary reason for quitting (in studies conducted elsewhere, researchers have found time constraints to be the prime cause for as high as 60% of respondents). In comparison, regulations were cited as the primary reason by 12% of the respondents. In fact, regulations came in fourth in a ranking of overall dropout themes. Age and health were ranked as the second most important factor, with 21% of respondents ranking it first. Next, the quality of the fishery on their favorite water was ranked third, at 13%.

After the study was published, the press quickly picked up on the time-allocation theme, perhaps partly in response to Kerr's barrage of anti-regulation materials, with his claims that regulations were too restrictive, too complex, and not bait-fishing friendly.

Yet, there needs to be an asterisk next to the time constraint finding. As Petchenik explained in the report and then to me again in his office, time allocation doesn't really tell the whole story or even the central point of the dropout study. The entire study is a look at time allocation. Every lapsed angler, by definition, made the decision to allocate his or her time away from trout fishing. That's a given. Fishing competes with a whole range of other activities, from kids' soccer games and computer gaming, to complicated two-parent or single-parent work schedules. Americans these days have less leisure time and more choices to fill it. How we spend time is ultimately a measure of what we value most, what floats our boat—and that, according to researchers like Fedler, Ditton, Sutton, and Petchenik, is a function of our perception of benefits and constraints, including internal rewards and external social support.

On this theme of time, and to nitpick just a bit on Petchenik's major finding, I asked him if claiming that it's time issues that cause people to quit isn't a tautology; it's like saying trout fishers allocated their time differently (opting out in this case), because they decided to allocate their time differently. The constraint of limited time, in other words, is a constant; it's other variables affecting the desirability of trout fishing, as measured against other competing activities that matter to trout anglers, that he's trying to get at. Petchenik's report would seem to agree. "The question which must be addressed is what, if anything, can be done to foster a re-allocation of time; that is, what can be done to facilitate trout fishing becoming (or remaining) a recreation priority?"

Petchenik pushed back on the idea that time itself isn't a variable, too. Time availability *is* broadly significant, he said, with changing gender roles in the family, more involved fathers, and working mothers; the pressures from inside the family are great. But managers can't change what is essentially an internal conflict around limits on time, nor can they change an angler's age or gender or socioeconomic circumstance. Ironically, time availability is less important to anglers over retirement age, and that's the majority of lapsed anglers (health issues as a constraint came in second). For the middle-aged-with-children lapsed angler, Petchenik said, time availability is a major blockage. Unfortunately, when parents stop taking the kids fishing, it's not like just losing a year class of fish, it's like losing multiple generations of anglers—and the potential of those future generations to join a culture of conservation.

That's not to say we should abandon families. Middle-aged-with-children is a vital demographic when it comes to recruiting young anglers, Petchenik said. When you don't have fathers or mothers taking children fishing, you don't have children fishing into the teen years and beyond. And the angler who's initiated into fishing by his family at a young age tends to stay with fishing the longest, often becoming the grandfather who initiates grandchildren into fishing. Family-initiated trout fishers appear to have the strongest commitment to the sport and keep at it longest, even as old joints give and balance on slippery rocks becomes precarious. Trout fishing carries deep, positive memories of childhood, family, and nature. The vast majority of lapsed anglers were not short-timers, said Petchenik, but older, long-timer anglers, many of whom learned in childhood. So children are the key demographic, he concluded.

He directed my attention to an illustration in the report that elegantly shows the relationship between addressable problems in a trout fishery. It's a simple flowchart that has, at its foundation, three circles of influence where management action can potentially change angler behavior. The department can improve fishing quality or change regulations, for instance, to improve angler satisfaction, Petchenik said. The three circles at the base of Petchenik's flowchart are "poor access and fishing conditions," "poor fishing quality," and "regulations (too many, too confusing, too restrictive)." Improvements to access, regulations, and fishing quality may fix poor values relative to the experience of lapsed trout anglers in Wisconsin.

Petchenik's report could and should drive policy change, as much as the data that biologists are generating in the field about the health and welfare of trout. As the study shows, trout regulations connect to each of the three fundamentally actionable areas. For instance, access has a regulatory component for worm anglers when regulations call for artificial baits only. That's closing off access to an important group, since children generally get initiated to trout fishing using worms as bait. And since trout fishing is still such a local enterprise in the countryside, if a fisher's favorite home waters are suddenly reclassified as catch and release or artificial baits only, these changes, on a very local level, matter.

There are psychological costs for bait anglers when their creek is transformed by regulation to "trophy water." And psychology, with its perceptions of success, plays an important role in time allocation decisions—we go where we are welcomed, whether it's a bowling alley or a bar. Positive reinforcement and friendships rule. Regulations that segment a stream, providing for some catch-and-release fishing, can feel like a put-down, psychologically barring some from accessing the whole stream. Or constant marketing to a type of angler demographic that doesn't include you. We all get the subtle message, who is valued and who is not.

Or consider fishing quality, another of Petchenik's three fundamentally actionable areas. Very low bag limits and high minimum-size limits (virtual catch and release), for many of the respondents, affected fishing quality. It's not just about confusing or complex rules; for many anglers, it's a question of a bag limit on opening day, even if a vanishingly small percentage of harvest-oriented anglers manage to catch the bag limit.

Quality, Petchenik told me, is an attempt at a general measure of everything that impacts the fisherman's experience. So quality *is* partly a measure of the size and number of trout you can catch, the number you can keep (if that matters to you), and the number of wild trout versus hatchery fish available (if that's what's important). The size of a trout is important to some. It's about being able to fish where you want, how you want, within sustainable biological limits.

But here, we get into the reality of culture shift. We live in an age of specialization. This is true in all manner of recreational activities and in trout fishing, where the most advanced, passionate, enthusiastic individuals are highly specialized—focused on narrower and narrower bands of activity. Fly anglers for trout are a good example. They spend more money and more time on their passion than most other passionate weekend warriors.

For the modern urban angler, we know that the size of the fish matters—at least a fighting chance to catch a brown trout over fifteen inches long—and so does the size of the catch. How many times do you hear the brag of the twenty-fish or thirty-five-fish morning? But a lot of other things matter equally to the modern urban trout angler. Cities batter the spirit. Anglers seek rejuvenation. Simply seeing a fish, observing hatches, being outdoors in a beautiful place, and practicing a method of fishing that, for many of us, reaches a high art form, rank high on the values scale. These anglers, too, are influenced by regulations and other management practices. They need more room on the stream. More miles of access and fewer competing anglers may matter. Change that is so focused can delight and motivate a growing audience, possibly a youthful one, that's curious about the game of trout fishing with a fly, and looking for new ways to connect and play with nature. Just as more diversified, small family farms have given way to large specialized operations (though there is a resurgence of local agriculture going on), the rural angler who followed the seasons of various fish, the way hunter-gatherers followed the ways of game, is giving way to the highly specialized urban affinity group.

Not surprisingly, it's this emerging group of enthusiastic anglers that also interests Petchenik. While the department is interested in learning what can be done to bring lapsed anglers back into the fold, of even greater interest is marketing to new recruits and active anglers to keep them fishing. I asked him what study he'd design to get at their interests, values, and desires. He smiled and pointed again to the flowchart in his report. He would develop a study based on that same chart, except it would be a study of angler recruitment. He'd get data from licensing on five hundred current trout anglers. What keeps people in? Where do they live? Specifically, where do they fish? What influences—socio-economic, cultural, biological, psychological—keep people involved in the sport? He'd create an umbrella of influences by asking specific questions about access, conditions, and demographics. Once he had identified the umbrella of influences—that set of qualities that defines a high level of satisfaction—he'd do an analysis of best management practices in terms of dealing effectively with the threats to those umbrella issues. He'd figure out what things really matter to trout anglers of all types and ages who are recent recruits or potential recruits, and then manage to those.

Listening to Jordan describe his ideal study, I thought about all the information we have not collected over the years about the people who fish. There were very few self-proclaimed trained social scientists working in trout management in the early 1970s, and there are still few today. Social research was conducted by biologists. Some of it was good, but much was driven by the new environmental agenda, and so it missed the essential connection between culture, conservation, and regulations in terms of whose interests were being served and whose were not. The quality of social science began to improve rapidly by the mid-1980s, but still, studies were not finely tuned.

One would think that the social science has progressed far since the late 1980s. Not so. By the time of the Trout and the Trout Angler II conference on the confluence of biological and human dimensions in 2000, social scientist Robert Ditton, the key presenter, complained that there just wasn't that much data out there when it comes to really understanding the motivations and attitudes of trout anglers. Highly respected trout biologist Robert Bachman, also at the 2000 conference in La Crosse, wrote, "Scientific inquiry into the human dimensions of trout management is still in its infancy and, in my opinion, much less well-understood [than the science of restoring trout populations]." When Petchenik, a bona fide social scientist, traveled to Yellowstone to present his lapsed angler study at the 2014 Wild Trout Symposium, he led with the statement, to paraphrase, "this is what a social scientist looks like," as if the biologists in the room had never seen one.

While progress has been made, social science lingers far behind biology. Yet at almost every scientific gathering, and in numerous papers, someone makes the statement that good social data as much as biological data are needed to drive the future enterprise of trout fishing in America. I would submit that we know far more about the urban angler today, and his or her interests and needs, than the rural angler. We spend far too much time following the money. Urbanites leave a much bigger paper trail. They participate, they travel, they buy. We also know that rural anglers are less specialized, often interested in other freshwater species than trout, and that women and families in these fisheries play a far more important role.

I wondered what would happen if Petchenik geolocated his data points and linked them to local regulations on local streams. Could that tell him about how local, how sensitive to management changes anglers are? To me, as much as I love the romance of travel, it's my home water that matters most. I've lived on a river of north central New England for the better part of forty years. The same may not be true for an urban angler who has less cold water close to home.

Why not a hierarchy that favors the local fishers? A catch-and-release rule may be entirely justified from a biological standpoint, but you'd have a tough time convincing the local that he can't fish while the out-of-towner can catch as many trout as he cares to and is able to. As one Midwestern social scientist noted at the 2000 conference in La Crosse, leave out one key stakeholder and "all hell can break loose." Look no further than Roger Kerr.

Data on trout fishing, gathered and viewed through an anthropological lens, might be more useful than social research. The close observance of customs, language, tools, rules, clothing, certain cooking and eating habits, and streamside manners vary across fishing communities, allowing us to identify each other and our affinity group quickly. They shape our identities. Thus, the fishing vest as an identifier for the fly angler, or the Simms wader. Social science alone may not be able to capture relationships at the local level. Maybe anthropology, with its subjective analyses, is a better frame. What holds a rural bait fishing community together? What breaks it apart? How is a rural fishing tradition like a language: once lost, difficult to recover?

The most interesting part of Petchenik's study is the profile we get of the average lapsed angler in Wisconsin. He's a white man, at least fifty years old, but more than likely over sixty. His household income is slightly skewed to lower income groups (below $50,000), and he is a rural person, but not poor. He's thrifty and doesn't like to waste a fish that's swallowed a hook by putting the fish back. The last time he went fishing, he was sixty or older. He uses worms or other live bait (57% say they rarely or never fish using artificial flies and lures), he releases some fish he catches because the regulations require it, but he tends to keep and eat fish he catches, and he fishes only a few creeks and close to home. He fishes mostly early in the season and late. Trout fishing is important, but so is gardening, home brewing, deer hunting, cutting corn, feeding hogs, bowling, going to church, or splitting wood. There's little boundary between food getting and recreation.

This year, US Fish and Wildlife demographer Edward Maillett came out with a detailed analysis of data related to trout fishing—from the much broader national fishing and hunting survey that came out in 2011. He found that even though 65% of all trout anglers live in urban areas (75% of the US population lives in urban areas today), trout fishing and all freshwater fishing are still more important to rural populations. A greater percentage of rural populations fishes for trout. Rural areas now contain 25% of the US population, but 35% of trout anglers and 45% of freshwater anglers who do not fish for trout live in rural areas.

When looking at the impact of rules on communities, generalized national trends might have easily missed his point. Rural communities, with a greater percentage of anglers, probably experience a greater impact when the fishing rules change.

Petchcnik walked me to the elevator and mused some in the doorway before saying goodbye. Though regulations appear to be a minor concern for most people who trout fish today, for a significant number of folks, the impact is substantial, he said. Those folks are rarely at the decision-making table and may be poorly represented. He shook his head, as if remembering something about his own childhood and learning to fish. Maybe he was remembering his father? Then the elevator door closed.

All this work designed to understand the mind of lapsed anglers, after all, begs the question, what doors could we open that children might want to walk through? Since childhood's exploration of the world begins in the backyard, how can we help families with children guide those first steps to the closest pond or creek where many a fish and bug certainly live? The chain is breaking and DNR fishing programs around the country are not proving super effective. Fishing, to endure, like language or love of books, almost always requires a mentor from home. Someone has to teach you to read by reading to you. Someone in the family who holds fishing knowledge, who themselves was taught—mine was my grandmother on my mother's side—has to speak and teach fishing. My grandmother took us trout fishing, and after she moved to Florida, she kept us supplied with live shrimp to fish from her dock on Tampa Bay, where I spent entire weeks catching and not catching fish. She grew up on a farm in Virginia, where hunting and fishing, crabbing and oystering were a way of life. When my mother, who grew up on that farm, fixed the eels I caught and brought home, she was connecting to her childhood with grandparents and uncles who fished and hunted. For every single older trout angler who walks away and hangs up his or her rod, you lose a link to the past and future both. It's a bit like the loss of Atlantic Salmon runs in New England—most are extinct, it turns out, not because of dams, which can be removed, but because the genetic material is gone. It's devilishly hard to reestablish genetic memory. Genes and trout streams are passed down.

On Petchenik's advice, when I left the Wisconsin DNR's offices, I cut through the capitol building to get to downtown Madison and the UW libraries. Everyone cuts through the capitol, he told me straight-faced. Was this his devilish Wisconsonian sense of humor coming out, a way to get back at a smug New Englander who drives a Prius? When I entered the building, I began to hear singing coming from the center of the rotunda, that great vaulted space in the heart of Wisconsin's center of government. This singing turned out to be the now-infamous singing protesters, who had been gathering each day at noon to sing against Governor Walker's positions on everything from collective bargaining by civil service unions to his choice of neckties. This disruption was, they claimed, an artistic exercising of their free speech rights. I came upon them and stood marveling at how loudly they could sing, and how out of key—the notes reverberated in that perfect domed hall like the bleatings of an insane-asylum choir of sheep. Governor Walker didn't think it was good singing either. As I stood mingling with the group and taking photos, black-uniformed policemen materialized from the shadows and began handcuffing people. The singing got louder, crazier. The governor had passed a rule requiring groups of twenty or more to have a permit to do such protest singing, or at least take singing lessons.

"You better go," one of the about-to-be arrestees whispered, "or you'll be arrested." I scampered away. In fact, a sign out the backside of the capitol, where I made my escape, said that the police had been arresting anyone who happened to be there at the time arrests were being made—bait anglers, Japanese tourists, and children included.

I suppose none of this has to do with trout fishing, but except to reflect that modern politics can be ruthless in its application of divisiveness. So much so that rural people, squashed to nothing in the crush to go urban, consistently vote against their own interests. Allowing public agencies to be captured by special interests only magnifies the problem. Good luck to you if you're an in-group; too bad if you aren't.

CHAPTER 16

Into the World of TU— Selling Cigars and Catch and Release on Castle Rock Creek

When agencies enact regulations that have no biological significance (usually forced by angling group lobbying), they do not improve trout populations or fishing, but risk losing public credibility and support. Then faced with real resource threats, requiring meaningful restriction regulations, they find little constituent support.

> — SPENCER E. TURNER (retired Missouri fisheries researcher), Wild Trout VI, 1997

I am a great fan of research and pure science but in our increasingly out of control work, I have come to think that our hope [lies in] comradeship between all the players, high and low, who have the wellbeing of our waters at heart.

> — THOMAS McGUANE (author), "The Many Sides of the Wild Trout Issue," Wild Trout VII, 2000

An experimental wild trout regulation allowing the use of natural bait (WBA) was implemented on 14 North Carolina streams following a regulation proposal eliminating the use of natural bait on many streams containing wild trout populations. . . . There were no significant changes in the densities or length-frequency distributions of trout >178 mm. . . . Although natural bait use went from 0% to >50% immediately following the WBA implementation, total catch rates of trout varied little over the 2-year study and were comparable to rates on wild trout streams where natural bait is not allowed. . . .

> — JAMES C. BORAWA and MICKY M. CLEMMONS,
> "Wild Trout Regulations and Natural Bait in
> North Carolina," Wild Trout VII, 2000

"You'd think," said my Trout Unlimited fishing partner, an Italian-American cigar salesman named John, "I could find a fish photo in my own phone." I had decided a month earlier to go undercover with TU and attend their national annual meeting, coincidently to be held in Wisconsin this year. The best part of any TU annual meeting is the field trips before the business begins. John and I were being sported around—along with about forty other anglers—by the generous volunteers of a local chapter.

I couldn't have asked for a better partner. Grizzled looking and tired (he'd just come off a three-day fishing trip to Michigan with friends, and a long night drive), John was scrolling through photos on his phone, looking for the enormous steelhead he'd caught last spring on one of the great coho and steelhead rivers flowing into the New York side of Lake Ontario. Coincidently, we'd grown up a town apart, fishing the same saltwater river. While I was still rigging my rod, John found his phone fish. If I squinted and held the phone away from the light at a certain angle, I could see the head of the great rainbow with an orange fly in the corner of its mouth. Today, smart-phone photos of big fish are the new shrunken heads that tribesmen wore on their belts—either that, or the modern version of penis gourds.

"That's some fish," I said.

"I told the people I was with," said John, "'I'm going to catch that fish with one cast of this fly.'" He held up an orange attractor pattern of some type of fly, used to conquer the spawning steelhead. "They didn't believe me."

I believe that he did catch and release that giant fish, perhaps even with a first or second cast. Sure, these days anyone can Photoshop a trout, but John was credible and he was Italian. Waspish Rhode Islanders like me, unfortunately, tend to stereotype Italian-American Rhode Islanders like John as gangsters—it's shameful, though subconscious. In our blood from years of headlines about Providence mob hits and mob trials during our youth. We see an Italian guy with a two-day beard and track suit and we think Raymond Patriarca and the Marfeo hitman trial. And you don't openly question Mafia about fish (index finger drawn quickly across the jugular), because you don't want to see a dead one wrapped in newspaper on your front step. Rhode Islanders know you gotta be careful.

But I was lucky to be paired with John. To describe him as a well-appointed fly angler is to describe John Wayne as a tough cowboy. Tip to toe, he was armed and ready, down to the leader kit hanging from his Simms vest like a hand grenade and the spare spool protruding from his stomach like a C-rations can. The chest tackle box? It had the girth of a field radio. And he had more flies in it than a user's guide to a bazooka has expanded diagrams. If you're a fly angler like me—who has misplaced much of his gear—then you need people like John. They're walking supply depots. Forgot your magnifying glasses? Can't thread that leader? Can't even see the tippet end? No problem, he will generously lend you a spare pair of magnifiers. Need a snip or a hemostat? He's got several extra. Need a hat, a rod, spare waders, fishing underwear? To top it all off, John has unlimited cigars. This makes him the uber go-to guy.

Castle Rock Creek in Grant County is named for a large outcrop of limestone in its middle reaches. The creek flows through a varied coulee of steep-walled hills and small bottomland farms. It is a favorite among fly fishers. The Harry and Laura Nohr TU chapter holds clinics for children and other fly-fishing educational activities on its banks, and also has been a major force in restoring Castle Rock over the years; they monitor the creek today. Roger Kerr, too, has had a long relationship with Castle Rock. In fact, I'd already been here with Roger and heard his version of the truth, and I'd read a paper he authored on an experimental catch-and-release section here—the first in Wisconsin—back in the 1980s. The best sections of the creek remain catch and release today, much to Roger's dismay.

Does catch-and-release fishing make biological sense on Castle Rock? Or is no-kill fishing here merely a social rule designed to attract a small subset of out-of-town anglers using flies? The answer, according to fish manager Gene Van Dyck, is that catch-and-release fishing can be justified biologically and socially. First, according to Van Dyck, there's little to no reproduction going on in Castle Rock. The silt flows from an upstream tributary take care of that. Second, fishing pressure is heavy. According to Van Dyck, there's as much as four thousand angler hours per year on these sections of Castle Rock (disputed by Roger Kerr). That's a lot of fishing pressure. Third, the creek, with good survival and growth potential, has the capacity to grow and support trophy-sized fish—typically a stated goal in a catch-and-release fishery.

According to the electrofishing data, Van Dyck has grown larger fish here than, say, the higher-density creeks that Jordan Weeks manages farther north. Van Dyck is only carrying five to eight hundred catchable fish per mile. Over a third of these are twelve-plus inches. Stocking 1.75-inch fry gives him replacement fish, and presumably food for the larger fish in the population. Possibly, Castle Rock, with poor trout reproduction, has more fish diversity than a high-density trout stream in Coon Valley, too (I looked at only two years' worth of shocking data, but both years showed higher diversity in Castle Rock than Timber Coulee Creek, from white suckers to fathead minnow, creek chub, bluntnose minnow, johnny darters, central stone rollers, southern redbelly dace, brook stickleback, and mottled sculpin). Socially speaking, poor trout natural reproduction gives Van Dyck an opportunity to cater to catch-and-release (fly) anglers, a group important to creek restoration efforts and the local economy. We should give them what they want, he told me. But has he been overcompensating for this group by giving them special privileges at the exclusion of the local bait fishermen?

Harry Turner thinks so. Turner, seventy years old, retired, a long-time fisherman (worm, spin, fly, you name it, he does it all), is up in arms over the current mix of open water and catch-and-release water on Castle Rock. On the prime sections of Castle Rock, it's three miles of catch-and-release water, flies and lures only, and one mile open to all types of bait. That's out of balance, Harry told me. He's been petitioning the Conservation Congress to get one of those miles of catch and release back to open fishing. It's a practical matter on the one hand and personal on the other. On opening day, he said, that mile that's open to bait is wall-to-wall bait fishermen, while the waters restricted to catch and release are virtually empty. On the personal side, Harry grew up on the banks of Castle Rock, fishing with his father and grandfather. Now he takes his own grandchildren there to fish. His eighteen-year-old granddaughter, he claims, can out–spin fish him.

Harry's campaign is like Kerr's in many ways. He's determined, he counts cars at bridges, and he writes letters to all levels of officialdom, including the governor. Turner's taken his fight through the conventional channels of the Wisconsin Conservation Congress— a strategy Kerr once tried but gave up on after garnering lots of local support, while at the state committee levels he couldn't get them to budge. But bag limits (two fish) and size limits (twelve-inch minimum) don't bother Turner. In fact, Turner thinks the Wisconsin DNR is doing a great job. And he doesn't talk about wanting to bring home more fish. What Turner's arguing for is a quality fishing experience—an objective that used to be solely spoken of in the realm of the fly angler. Bait anglers, lots of whom still come out on opening day, he argues, just don't have enough fishing room. By his own counts there were thirty-four trout fishermen "crammed into one mile of creek," while there were no fishermen in the catch-and-release area next door. "This calculates," he wrote to the Conservation Congress Trout Committee, "to one fisherman fishing every 52 yards of the stream, while no anglers were fishing the remaining three miles of catch and release, artificials-only water. In my opinion, this is not the way to manage the opening weekend fishing pressure and still provide a quality fishing experience with family and friends."

Turner's resolution seemed reasonable, but even with significant local support, it didn't get far. At issue seemed to be the question of fishing pressure in the catch-and-release area, though by Turner's car counts, angling pressure in those three miles throughout the season was modest at best.

Turner said his greatest disappointment was that during the meeting with the Conservation Congress Trout Committee, Gene Van Dyck had waved around the Wisconsin DNR's own trout committee's recommendations for the coming season, saying the department committee had already voted Turner's resolution down. It left Turner feeling like none of his efforts really mattered. That the process was a sham.

Is he giving up then? No, he told me. He's going to a different county with the same resolution next year. And he's written letters to Governor Scott Walker and Wisconsin DNR Secretary Cathy Stepp, inviting them to Castle Rock on opening day. This is a move right out of Kerr's playbook. Go up the ladder; never give up; never give in.

When it comes to catch-and-release fishing in Wisconsin and social conflict, Castle Rock has an interesting history. While Gene Van Dyck was responsible for making nearly four miles of Castle Rock Creek catch and release in 1982, "the first project of its kind in Wisconsin," it was Roger Kerr who pulled together and published the research on its impact to trout populations and people. In his report, the reasons Kerr gives for choosing Castle Rock for no-kill, with only artificial flies and lures allowed, are the same that Gene Van Dyck explained to me: low natural reproduction (trout numbers could be controlled through stocking), excellent water quality, and intense fishing pressure.

What happened to the fish population under this early experiment in catch and release? The numbers and biomass of brown trout increased. Trout over thirteen inches, for example, more than doubled from three to seven per acre, before decreasing in 1980. From the abstract in Roger's report: "Brown trout of hatchery origin increased substantially until 1980 when moderate to severe declines occurred. The maximum number of trout present was 285 per acre in the spring of 1978 and the minimum number present was 99/acre in the fall of 1980. During a nine-month period in 1979 mostly fly anglers (who reported being very satisfied) spent an estimated 3,357 hours fishing Castle Rock and Spring Creek and caught (and released) 5,509 trout. Each trout was caught an average of four times in 1979." According to Roger's report, catch-and-release fishing looks like a winner on the biological side of the register, at least until moderate to severe declines occurred after 1980. That is unless you're a bait fisherman who's been excluded.

Roger's comments on anglers are most interesting, given his current battles. What happened to the angling population at Castle Rock? Whereas before the no-kill designation, fishing pressure was equal on the nearby Big Green, after the designation, fishing pressure doubled on Castle Rock. Fly anglers swarmed to where they expected to find bigger fish. The locals, Roger noted, complained bitterly, but, he wrote, they shouldn't complain because they had about a hundred miles of un-such-regulated water fifteen miles from Fennimore (this is a typical argument made by Roger Kerr's foes today). Why the change since 1980 in Roger's thinking? Because of the angler dropout rates he saw, peaking in the early 1990s . . . and people like Harry Turner.

So I spent an afternoon fishing Castle Rock Creek. Anyone with a valid license can fish it—yet the regulations are designed around a particular kind of method, encouraging a fishing culture that does not represent the full range of fishing styles of the place. That doesn't make a catch-and-release, no-live-bait rule invalid or wrong biologically speaking, but such a rule does invite scrutiny from the social side. That a majority of locals supported Harry Turner's suggested rule change during the annual county-level meeting should count for a lot, perhaps more than one fish manager's skewed view of the anglers he's serving.

Walking back to the truck, I thought of my fishing partner—he'd gone downstream and I'd gone up. We'd lived near each other growing up, but our towns were different worlds. While my town, Barrington, was a park-like suburban town, filled for the most part with business commuters to Providence, John's home, Bristol, was working class and more ethnically diverse. Barrington had a corner drugstore with a soda fountain, but there were no factories or bars. That sort of thing, and all else fascinating, was across the river in Warren—next door to Bristol—with its hulking American Tourister luggage factory just over the bridge and its main street crowded with shoe stores, a record shop, and two movie theaters.

One town up the bay from Warren, Bristol manufactured cables, and yet there were old money estates too; places like the Colt family mansion and Blithewold (turned into a state park and public botanical gardens today). The Colts were descendants of the DeWolf family, slave traders whose fortunes were linked to nearby Newport, plantations in Cuba, and rum manufacturing on nearby Aquidneck Island. While Barrington was new money, upper middle, Bristol had Tweet Balzano's, not far from a Converse sneaker factory; Tweet's was a famously cheap place to eat that served spaghetti by the pound, and where tough, middle-aged, chunky Balzanzo women waited on you when they felt like it. And "shut up your face, you" and don't complain to them, or else. Bristol had a Minuteman Missile silo, while we had tennis courts and a fancy country club that excluded Jewish golfers, Blacks, and Italians, and anyone else with a last name that ended in a vowel, or a string of consonants for that matter. Unfortunately, we belonged to that racist establishment, until my father quit because they wouldn't let an Italian golfing friend of his in.

Why recount the divided culture? It's to show that the gulf between cultures is quickly crossed inside fishing. John and I caught herring out of the same herring run by Barrington High School, on my side of the river. I crossed over by boat to buy bait on his. He fished for striped bass from the Barrington River railroad trestle at night using that herring for bait, while I was casting for bass in the marsh using lures and plugs and then eventually flies. We probably both hit the spring spawning runs of flounder, but from different sides of the river. While cultural differences among trout anglers can look vast, social research shows them to be small and not about the values that matter most, like love of fishing, the sustainability of the catch, and whether the water is cold and clean. Whether we think of trout as sport or food matters little in the overall scheme of conserving fish and their watersheds. Worms or flies don't matter either; what matters is the quality and availability of the world's water to everything that moves, the quality of air and land . . . and good fishing, and fairness.

When I got back to the truck, John, already reclined in a portable lawn chair, was drinking a beer and talking on his cell phone. He's cooler than me, I thought. He's Italian, sipping his beer, all the while making money. Italian fly anglers are cool in a gangsterish way. When he hung up a few minutes later, he said, "I just made a cigar deal that should pay for my next trip down the Snake River this spring." Wow.

Selling cigars, hmmm. "Can I sell cigars too, John? I'm a writer who needs a real job. I can do that," I said. "I can travel, fish, and sell cigars." I'm a cigar traveling fool in the making. John said something about the connections one needs to be an effective salesman of cigars. I pressed a little more until his eyebrows went up in a most mafia-like way. Sometimes a cigar isn't a cigar. I decided to let the cigar matter rest.

Back in the van that took us home to Madison, we had to listen to the success stories of other anglers. That can be boring. Someone caught a double using a dropper on a hopper. *What? If I'd thrown a hopper into Castle Rock Creek, all I'd've gotten was chirp*. Another on the Blue had had a twenty-fish morning. *Fake yawn*. The most entertaining story was the young driver's description of fishing with scuds. He works for the River Alliance of Wisconsin on phosphorus nonpoint-source-pollution issues, a tough mission in an agricultural state where corn prices are through the roof. He described to John his newfound love of pink scuds he ties himself. What is it with pink around here? Friends have taught him how to fish them. He drops them deep and fishes a slow drift across sandy bottoms. Holy crap, he said. Scuds really work. He kills it with scuds. I feigned not listening. But all the way back to Madison, I wondered about that pink scud pattern. I could probably find it online.

CHAPTER 17

Designer
Trout Creeks

O I had never in my life seen anything like that trout stream. It was stacked in piles of various lengths: ten, fifteen, twenty feet, etc. There was one pile of hundred-foot lengths. . . . I went up close and looked. . . . I could see some trout in them. I saw one good fish. I saw some crawdads crawling around the rocks at the bottom.

It looked like a fine stream. I put my hand in the water. It was cold and felt good.

— RICHARD BRAUTIGAN, *Trout Fishing in America*, 1967

It is simply not enough to ask the anglers what they want. The anglers must first know what the options are. It is the job of the fisheries manager to provide that information.

— ROBERT A. BACHMAN, 2002

In Tom Wolfe's *The Electric Kool-Aid Acid Test* (a literary journalistic account of Ken Kesey and the Merry Pranksters, who were a force in the emerging hippy scene in San Francisco in the late 1960s), you were "either on the bus or off the bus," depending on how much LSD-infused Kool-Aid you had drunk and whether you were in on the mind meld. I don't love buses, and I never liked acid trips much, but traveling on a tour bus for eight hours with a group of fanatical TU members—mostly older white males like me, some (like my wise seat mate, TU board member Charles) sporting unusual moustaches, and an assemblage of Wisconsin's finest trout-stream restorers, many of whom worked for the Wisconsin DNR—was a bit like a magical mystery tour. Even though I hadn't drunk the TU Kool-Aid (other than a lot of beer the night before), or even had my complimentary TU breakfast, I knew enough not to underestimate the power of enthusiasm when linked to scientific expertise—two of the three primary forces at work in restoring aquatic ecosystems here, the third being Mother Nature herself.

What is trout creek restoration all about here in Wisconsin? There are many answers to the question, each values-based. If you asked Roger, he would turn your attention to the more important element of wild trout genes, a revolution in fish culture where he can claim some credit. If you asked a TU volunteer from any of the twenty chapters active in the Driftless, you might get an answer conformed in hours of planning, water quality monitoring, fences erected, lunker structures built, scud patterns tied, and brown trout caught. If you asked a DNR biologist, it might be water temperature, cost per foot to restore a creek, trout per acre, or angler surveys. The answer I prefer is from Dave Vetrano, retired fish manager from Vernon, Crawford, and Monroe Counties (Jordan Weeks's territory today). He said he doesn't even use the word restoration anymore. Because it's not necessarily obvious what we're restoring. He sounds like he's talking out of Aldo Leopold's playbook. Leopold often complained that he was never sure what the overharvested, eroded, highly impacted forests of the Southwest needed restoring to. Vetrano says his focus today is grazing systems; new ways to use the land that creeks flow through. He speaks about the vital link between community health and restored trout creeks. Soil and high school students are among the natural resources he's interested in cultivating today.

The Blue River, in the northeast corner of Grant County in southwestern Wisconsin's Driftless Area, flows north into the Wisconsin River, a distance of only twenty miles from source to mouth. About a hundred of us had climbed out of tour buses and now stood—with landowners, Nohr chapter TU volunteers, and a smattering of fisheries experts—on the banks of the Blue. I felt vaguely ill, perhaps from too much coffee. Hip deep in the water below us, an electrofishing crew made up of techs Lloyd Meng and John Bunker waited for the word from managers Gene Van Dyck and Bradd Sims to start their generator and work the boat one hundred yards downstream, electrified wand waving through the water, nets at the ready.

The Blue is one of the region's larger streams by measure of base flow. It doesn't have as many springs as some creeks nearby, but it has a large upper watershed. This is Class 2, special-regulations water. It has low trout-reproduction values, downstream of where we were standing anyway, so it's stocked with upwards of ten thousand wild fingerlings annually. When I say wild, I mean that these are from eggs that came from populations of brown trout reproducing successfully in the wild. Their biological clocks are well tuned to seasonal patterns of light and cold, and they know how to survive. Wisconsin jumped full-throttle into hatchery technologies that favored wild genes over domestic in 1995—right on cue, as the nation's top trout scientists were recognizing this approach as the most effective and efficient way to provide high quality fishing to American anglers. These fingerling trout spend a minimum time inside a concrete fish tank at the hatchery before they're put back where they belong.

Where we stood, at the head of a small valley, we could see the Blue meandering through meadows, under pine- and oak-covered slopes and large limestone outcrops. This is a scenic stretch and according to TU volunteers and officials, there are public-access easements all along it, making it friendly to anglers, many of whom travel long distances to get here. Many a Chicagoan has fished here, and you can see the appeal. It's catch-and-release, special-regulations water, making it especially friendly to fly anglers, but a blank on the map if you fish with worms.

If the Blue had been heavily reengineered, it didn't appear so. Robert Hunt's sixth principle in his book *Trout Stream Therapy* is to "disguise artificiality. . . . Restore aesthetic conditions as quickly as possible." That principle was adhered to here. The Blue looked wild and untouched. Aldo Leopold would have liked this view. To him, a laudable result of land restoration was the creation of beauty and function both. Looking downstream, there were no scarred banks, very little sign of riprap or channelizing structures, just a thin creek weaving through grass and sedge. As evidence that restored beauty and utility can transform people, the hundred of us stood on the bank, watching the fish techs shocking and netting fish. From perhaps a hundred-yard section, they netted sixty or so fish for the well in the boat. Mostly brown trout, a few in the fourteen-inch range. Fishing over the water of this narrow, winding creek must be a dire challenge, but for the willing, the wild fish are there.

To have good fishing, you need good water. Two miles upstream from where we stood are the headwaters of the Blue, near Route 60 in Iowa County. Route 60 runs north-south along a so-called ridge— really more of a rounded mesa top. It's these areas that support intensive row-crop agriculture. With corn prices high, there is endless corn on the tops, gobbling up acres that conservation reserve programs once took out of production. Intensive row cropping is the enemy of wild trout and much else that likes a cold creek for home. Farmers looking to optimize profits increasingly draw groundwater from deep wells to irrigate corn, to grow it faster. Pulling out so much ground-water can reduce spring discharges. Farmers looking for the highest yields employ heavy inputs of nitrate and phosphate fertilizer, which ends up as runoff pollution. Then, to rapidly remove water from land surfaces seasonally, they may add drainage tiles, which contribute silt, salts, warmed surface waters, chemical pollution, and increased flood intensity.

Still, the Blue's water seemed to be holding up pretty well, and it was growing large trout. The restored Blue also was growing other fish too. Gene Van Dyck reported that sculpin populations had increased over 500% in recent years, and so had white suckers and some native fish like creek chub and shiner populations. I had posed the question to him on Castle Rock: Had the lack of successful brown trout reproduction benefitted other species? Stated another way, was brown trout reproductive success on other creeks creating monocultures of brown trout, and were the very high densities of brown trout found in some Class 2 streams showing downward-trending growth? The average age of Jordan Weeks's brown trout in Timber Coulee was 4.5 years, for example, and their average size was just above ten inches. Van Dyck's fish in Castle Rock average closer to eleven inches at roughly the same age. Were the relationships significant, or the variances just too small to draw any conclusions?

Back on the bus, headed to Big Spring, a tributary of the Blue, we heard from the experts. David Rowe, area fisheries supervisor, talked about the political challenges of resource management—among them, dropping funding levels in the department for land acquisition. On the other hand, he said, there were surprising new sources of funding for easement acquisition coming from the Legislature; six million earmarked for the current fiscal year. Rowe described a master planning process that was now a guideline for trout management. Trout streams are vital local recreational resources, he said, like hard coin that can provide urbanizing communities with recreation and open-space opportunities, ecosystem services, including flood control, and jobs and businesses with customers. There's no downside, assuming the whole community is brought into the process. Rowe went on to describe the threats to trout creeks in the Driftless, including climate change. These spring creeks seem immune to warming, but recent devastating floods in Boscobel and other towns along the Wisconsin and Mississippi were a reminder that two-hundred- and five-hundred-year flood events appear to be more frequent now. Though restored creeks are more resilient, base flows are higher than they have been in years, and that contributes to flooding and potential erosion.

Rowe also said that they are learning not to armor banks, and instead, to let them move. This is an idea I recognized from the writings of George Perkins Marsh in the 1860s. I'd heard earlier from Weeks that a trend in restoration is to fix fundamental issues, like removing pollution sources and restoring basic environmental functions, and then let the river work itself clean. Other challenges in the watersheds closest to Madison (Dane County) include sprawl (and the growth of impervious surface areas as towns expand), growing frack sand mining, and the aforementioned boom in corn ethanol. There are no regulations currently limiting field runoff, and the bulk of nutrient pollution—all the way to the Gulf of Mexico—is from tiling corn and bean fields in places like this. This is all biology, it seems, but the importance of social buy-in and support was lost on no one.

As far as trout growth, it was Matthew Mitro who said on the bus that, with feral brown trout, they were getting to the point where biologists were seeing slower growth in some high-density populations. "We could afford," he said, "to have higher harvests of trout." Jordan Weeks had said the same. The question in Wisconsin's Driftless Area, with low bag limits and voluntary catch and release, was how those higher harvests might be achieved, and by whom. The Wisconsin TU members I talked to didn't seem interested in liberalizing regulations or extending the season year round, or at least into March or April. Not at all. The fish resource is prime. Their feelings may change if they see a drop in trout numbers and size that can be linked to density. Or if they see brown trout populations outcompeting native brook trout in their favorite reserve. Trout populations fluctuate; it isn't always clear why.

Big Spring, as suggested by its name, has a large spring at its source. Water tumbles out of the side of a wooded bluff a hundred feet above the valley floor. Many of us walked the short distance up a mowed trail to the spring, and a few walked down the creek looking for brook trout. I walked partway back with a biologist, talking about water flow and temperature. He was explaining that the lowest flows of the summer now are higher than the historic average flows across the last hundred years, according to Unified Soil Classification System (USCS) flow monitors. There is a huge amount of recharge capacity in the fractured limestone bedrock, and the groundwater discharges slowly, evenly, and cold. He's seen water temperature drop by a whole degree, thanks in part to better overhead cover. Water comes out at 48°F. That's too cold for brown trout. However, brown trout thrive when the water begins to warm downstream between the bridges. There, the browns—at well over a thousand fish per mile (this in a creek that is only twenty feet wide)—outcompete brook trout, so brook trout have been pushed out of most of the creek below this bridge. This is concerning to the department (the Wisconsin DNR recently has instituted a brook trout refuge plan).

Todd, the project point person from TU's Harry and Laura Nohr chapter (the lead chapter at the 2013 TU annual meeting), talked about project partners. Restoring creeks takes partners. The Big Spring project, unfolding over years, had grown into an ecosystem-wide approach. Partners brought interest and expertise in birds, amphibians, insects, and native grasslands. A typical project today accomplishes multiple goals. The practical side of an ecosystem-wide approach at Big Spring was that it attracted interest and funding from a more diverse stakeholder base. Volunteers have added shallow wetland scrapes for frogs, turtles, and waterfowl. There might be wood duck boxes erected, and piles of stones in upland areas for snake hibernacula. While beaver ponds were being drained and dams removed to protect water quality in the Driftless (I don't see how draining wetlands improves anything from a total biodiversity standpoint), bat boxes were going up and plans were in the offing to increase the use of native plants (the barriers being that natives sometimes grow more slowly and floods bring in regular loads of non-native seeds).

The audiences for creek restoration in the Driftless were in an expansive mode, from mushroom-gathering groups to grassland bird enthusiasts. As trout culture has shifted to what sociologist Stephen Kellert described as "naturalistic"—with a growing interest in biodiversity and what is native—the goals of trout creek restorers have shifted strategically as well, to become socially inclusive. Do we need more brown trout in Big Spring? Questionable. Though a sustainable Class 1 fishery with no more stocking would be economical. But do we need a broader coalition, more aware and involved citizenry? More people like these volunteers? You betcha.

TU chapters and Spurgeon Vineyards & Winery had partnered to provide us conservation tourists with a lunch of bratwurst on buns, boiled onions, baked beans, and coleslaw. It was a great lunch that I overate with relish, literally. Including a second bratwurst and a second heap of greasy onions, which in hindsight I shouldn't have. Mary Kerr works part time at Spurgeon. We are very good friends . . . I think. Mary turned me into a Green Bay Packers fan, a big deal since I have been a long-term Patriots fan, so I owe her a large debt of gratitude.

I had visited the winery with Mary during one of her shifts there and she weighed me down with bottles of sweet elderberry wine. In fact, before lunch I went searching, hoping to find her in the tasting room, which was open for TU business, and busy. The father of the owner of Spurgeon, Mary told me, lost his hands in a farm accident. He'd been behind the effort to open the winery. What does one do when one loses one's hands? You don't whine about it, she told me, or sit on them. Mary as much as told me, you go to work making good wine. That's one of the reasons I like Spurgeon wine—an admirable founder. Wisconsin's farmers in general seem to be a worthy class of no-nonsense hard workers. Elderberry wine is not California pinot. It's fruity, summery. If you want to bring some of Wisconsin's summer back home so you can sip it all the cold winter long by a woodstove in Vermont, you go to Spurgeon, and you buy as many bottles of elderberry wine as you can afford (*paid for by the Wisconsin Elderberry Wine Council*) to fit in a Toyota Prius (54 miles per gallon).

I didn't find Mary in the tasting room; I was relieved. Truth be told, I felt a little bit like a traitor on this tour, and I was afraid I might run into Mary and have to explain why I was consorting with Kerr's devil TU-ers. Would she understand that this was undercover work? Would she blow my cover? Mary Kerr is a loyal soldier to husband Roger and every bit as good a fisher. I wanted to maintain my good relations with Mary, who I suspect is the only person in the world who can contain Roger Kerr's ornery excesses.

Over lunch, I had another chance to talk with biologists. To paraphrase, sure we can stand to harvest more trout, Scott Stewart told me. Then, to paraphrase, Gene Van Dyck added: Look, more than 70% of the people who fish in this region now are fly anglers, and yet only 15% of creek mileage is oriented to fly anglers here. If anything, we should do more for this group, not less. They're the ones working with us to restore these creeks. They're paying their way.

True fact about TU volunteers. But I don't agree with his logic. Taxpayers from all over Wisconsin, and the country for that matter, are paying for creek restoration in Wisconsin. Federal NRCS funds count for the largest share by far. TU members deserve lots of credit. But their volunteer work shouldn't buy them privilege. The farmers of the 1930s pulled their weight years ago, but a rural people from a farm economy in decline—one moving away from farming, or hanging on—may have little incentive, little time to devote to trout and their creeks. Read David Rhodes's novel *Driftless* to get a picture of this fading rural population, and ask yourself if it should be excluded from more creeks because it isn't in the club to restore them. These communities paid their dues, and they represent a powerful potential voice for conservation. Volunteer firemen in Vermont may not give a hoot about planting trees on the Ottauquechee, but they should be able to go down there and fish with worms, and catch those twelve brook trout in mountain streams if they want.

TU members love what they do. Love and the satisfaction of good work for the public good is its own reward. Having said that, rural people in a changing economy need jobs. Trout fishing guide or shop owner or innkeeper are good jobs that pay bills. A trout can provide a meal, but a job is needed to pay the rent and pay for most meals.

As we drove off in the buses, Roger's angry words were ringing in my head. I was seeing in my mind's eye the chart showing the drop in Wisconsin's trout anglers since the trout stamp program was enacted in the late 1970s. It showed dropping angler interest that corresponded to increasing minimum-size limits and lowered bag limits—a dropout that accelerated dramatically when the present stream class system was enacted in 1990. There are undoubtedly many factors involved in angler dropout nationwide, reflecting changes in society, values, and demographic shifts. But I was seeing numbers from a Colorado study and from Robert Hunt's work on Lawrence Creek in the 1960s and angler drop-off in Yellowstone, showing the elasticity of the response among certain anglers to stricter regulation, not only when a virtual catch-and-release area was created, but when minimum lengths were raised by only two inches and reduced bags of several fish were enacted. Anglers walked. It's not that stricter regulations aren't needed in a crowded world. It's about whom they exclude. Who volunteers their time for improving trout habitat is beside the point. Whether a special regulation is needed to improve a trout population is the question, and it's a biological one. In heavily fished waters, catch and release has proved a valuable biological tool in some cases. Had special regulations achieved their desired effect here? Was it regulations that produced the abundance in these creeks? No. Studies like one at Elk

Creek (Mitro and Kanehl 2011) suggest not. Had regulations caused thousands of anglers to walk, through the 1970s and 1980s? Yes, in the context of the rise of destination fisheries and the emerging urban fishing clientele. Local anglers began looking elsewhere as they were shown the door, sometimes not so subtly. Rules, however finely crafted with all users in mind, work in mysterious ways that have more to do with psychology and less to do with rules' actual effect on the catch. We migrate to where we're welcomed.

Fifteen minutes into our drive to Bear Creek, my stomach began to lurch in an unusually powerful way. As far as my stomach was concerned, UPS was on the way. Very soon. I have the guts of a vulture that eats from ten-day-old roadkill. Nothing upsets my system. Nothing. I've eaten up and down the street vendors of southern Mexico and the open markets of Central America, and I've been desperately ill from it only once or twice—so naturally, my thoughts turned to poison, and to Mary. Bloody Mary Kerr.

Could Mary Kerr have poisoned the bratwurst? She could have done so easily, slipping into the kitchen after hours. She had the keys. She could have laced the TU-ers' bratwurst with *Salmonella* or some other such biological weapon. I looked around for other signs of extreme discomfort and saw none. I seemed to be the only person who had been poisoned by Mary, and I was in agony. We were miles from our destination and there was no emergency toilet on the bus. In times like these, you put on your heroic dark glasses and try to enter a higher state, a hallucinogenic state, where, out of your body, you can ride like a Merry Prankster on the bus of pain. Literally, sweat it out. The alternatives are not pretty. You pray for a reprieve, but you know what's coming.

While we rode on, Steve Born—a legendary visionary of some note, author of books (*Exploring Wisconsin Trout Streams*, among others), an angling academic and trout activist, highly regarded—lectured in a spirited fashion on the massive plate tectonic forces at work deep in the earth, shaping the bedrock that gave rise to the parent materials of this native black soil. He described the iron-rich waters of a covering sea, beginning two billion years ago. Five hundred million years ago, the seas retreated, leaving Cambrian sandstone hills and petrified cross-bedded dunes where the shore once lay. Slowly, in concert with the workings of my screaming intestines, he brought us up through the ages. Four hundred million years ago, he said, more seas invaded, more sandstones were formed. Life and its carbon and limestone, including the great dolomites dipping toward the Mississippi, painted the world brown. He ended with a dramatic description of the last seventy thousand years of glacial activity. As if with a massive clap of thunder, the glaciers came and went—mile-high ice sheets, faces shearing off and many tons of ice crashing to the ground. Then he described, in lay physics, the miracle of this glacier-free zone—the Driftless, with its absence of glacial drift, its abundant loess, wind-blown soils from the west. His lecture, I will never forget. I felt it in a very personal way, all the way through my guts, trying to explode.

By the time the bus rolled to a stop, I was near to passing out, crippled with abdominal tectonic shift. I'd made my exit plan and hurried discreetly to the woods, hoping not to drop trow there by the swinging bus door, as the rest of the crowd streamed out.

My notes of Bear Creek and our visit to Black Earth Creek close to Madison soon after are sketchy at best. There are whole pages of scrawl I can't even read. I was ill, sweating, only half there.

What I discerned is that Bear Creek was developed by the Aldo Leopold chapter. The Bear Creek tab, about $650,000, came mostly from the farm bill and NRCS, as so much of the funding for these projects does. Diesel, 25% of project cost. Fifteen times more soil hauled away than rock put in place. Zen garden, where only special people go. That's what it seemed. That they were creating a creek-like park, where quiet religious anglers could work out difficult spiritual problems streamside, while coaxing up the brown trout in a mutually beneficial communion. Let me prick you Mr. Humble but Oh So Smart Brown Trout with Spots—I promise to not eat you so that my unknown friends, my fly-fishing brethren, can prick you again and again, while the internal order of my mind/body is restored.

The mechanics of earthmoving are important. I learned that. In my altered state, I wrote that, thanks to Henry Koltz's Milwaukee chapter, chapters and projects once on life support down here in the Driftless have been revitalized. Urban chapters moving into rural areas. An urban guerilla action. That real work—trying something hard—gives life.

I wrote that we are all colonists, still, on this land. I know I am. We can't own it; if we're lucky, we might help it along.

At the end of the day, was I on the bus or off the bus? Did I care? At Black Earth Creek, I wrote that Fred Wolf, whose family had sold at a bargain price a strategic easement, looked like Paul Newman with a broken leg; that old men from Madison come hunting deer on Fred's land and cut his fences and their britches to get through. Bait-fishing bastards from Montana. So he has posted his land. "Because these men are too fat," I wrote, and then, in a scrawl that I can barely read: "To know history is to make history." Who said that?

"There is love fest going on. It's all around me," I wrote. The trout creek restoration movement has its trench-working heroes, its villainous Roger Kerrs, its distant funders, its hangers-on.

Government, a local representative said, doesn't have to be dysfunctional. <u>So true</u>, I wrote.

Bent over in pain, I recalled something I already knew about Black Earth Creek, and as I walked along, tripping on the good feelings around me and the bad feelings in me, my mind flipped back through the index cards trying to recall what I knew . . . Months ago, Roger had sent me shocker survey results for a section of Black Earth Creek. The data were from the 1970s. They showed two hundred plus pounds of wild brown trout per acre, over two thousand fish per mile, even with heavy exploitation and a bag limit of ten fish per day back then, a very healthy and sustainable fishery. Black Earth was his proof of the fallacy of modern bag limits. These are data he must have sent to a hundred different people.

Meanwhile, the creek restorers were having their well-deserved day. Scott Stewart was recognized, and Steve Born, for their years of staying power; such a project requires that. Dave Vetrano was hailed as truly one of the world's greatest trout stream restoration experts, though Dave wasn't using the words "creek restoration" anymore. I wrote it in my notebook, that it's Dave who's using wild trout to drive social and environmental change.

Where was that bad fairy, Roger Kerr? His invitation never arrived in the mail. And I missed his sustained protest. His role as gadfly brings all the self-congratulation into sharper focus. The old world is bad:

farmers eating trout; poachers and incest. The new world and new farmers like Paul Newman are good. There is a giant massive trout under there waiting to emerge, waiting, waiting to catch us all, and release us and catch us, over and over again. But if Roger thinks nothing has changed, he's wrong. Change is the rule. The ultimate rule, what we can count on. Will a robust rural existence return? Did it ever really exist?

Thinking back, I remember the deluge of testimonials. There was a cacophony of celebrating going on, and I felt strangely hollowed out. It was an unwelcomed feeling. Taking stock and celebrating success is vital. I remembered my own pride of conservation work, when it was farms we were conserving, and public access to a river, and putting public trails on privately conserved lands. Thousands of acres along another river. I did that. For a while, I was chair of a non-profit organization that protected rivers (Vermont River Conservancy). I have traveled and lectured across Central Europe after the Wall came down, to teach a people how to create a culture of private land conservation when all they knew was government mandate. I was proud of the land conservation I achieved. Why the hell did I decide to change course and write words for a living? Doubt creeps in. It always does. I felt disembodied at Black Earth. Split in two by Roger Kerr and his battles. Lost. Why was the last great worm fisherman in Wisconsin making me feel so much like shit? Why the cognitive dissonance, and now the diarrhea?

There is a great necessity to give thanks and credit where credit is due. People work hard for long years to restore lands that have been badly mangled. Restoration and renewal: That is our primary task. The earth is covered in broken bodies and half measures. Like Richard Brautigan's used trout stream for sale in a warehouse in San Francisco, all is fragmented. The last words I can discern in this particular shit-stained notebook of mine are "working together."

Acid trip or no acid trip, magical mystery tour or no, *Salmonella* poisoning at the hand of sweet Green Bay Packers fan Grandma Kerr or not, when I got back on the bus and took my place next to the man with his amazing moustache, his generous view, his history as an enlightened teacher, and the pistol he bought for his wife, I felt I had finally lost all sense of myself. I was dropping into piscine narcosis, a stupor from the drug of ecstatic trout creek restoration.

CHAPTER 18

TU Annual Meeting
September 25, 2013
Middleton, Wisconsin
Marriott Hotel

Now I truly believe that we in this generation must come to terms with nature, and I think we're challenged as mankind has never been challenged before to prove our maturity and our mastery, not of nature, but of ourselves.
> — RACHEL CARSON, "The Silent Spring of
> Rachel Carson," *C.B.S. Reports*, 1963

So long as our focus remains on fish and fisheries management, we are talking to ourselves. . . . Our challenge is to build a framework . . . that allows us to turn recovery of trout and salmon from a defensive, reactive, and reactionary game to the forward-looking, positive, and solution-oriented outlook that local communities can rally behind and that can recover wild trout and salmon. In short, it entails reconnecting people to the lands and waters that sustain them.
> — CHRIS WOOD (CEO of Trout Unlimited), "The Future
> of Wild Trout: Protecting, Reconnecting, Restoring, and
> Sustaining our Wild Trout Legacy," Wild Trout IX, 2007

No matter how highly we anglers think of ourselves as conscientious con-
servationists and enlightened citizens, the rest of the world is no longer im-
pressed. . . . Do I know what we should become instead of what we are? Not
really. But I do have some ideas of how the world of wild trout might look
if we succeed. . . . [It] is a world in which a typical calendar or coffee-table
book about the so-called great American wildlife species would include . . .
the desert pupfish or the mottled sculpin . . . in which good sportsmanship
would again be—especially in the minds of the urban non-angling public—
synonymous with good citizenship. . . . In this new world a wild trout confer-
ence . . . would [have] more of the traditional adversaries with whom we are
now learning to collaborate. There would also be social scientists, non-angling
environmental activists, general-interest journalists, educators, congressional
staffers, and even those passionate and politically savvy folks from the animal
welfare movement. And a much higher percentage of all these people from
all these groups would be female. . . . If there is ever to be such a brave new
world of wild trout, some of us veterans of the older world are going to have
the hardest time living in it. But that's a price worth paying if it means we get
to keep the trout.

— PAUL SCHULLERY, Closing Summary, Wild Trout IX, 2007

A s I stood bleary eyed in the Marriott foyer on the first day of Trout Unlimited's annual conference, my thoughts flashed to Hunter S. Thompson's *Fear and Loathing in Las Vegas.* Thompson showed up drug addled to cover a convention of cops trying to figure out how to fight the drug war, and then wrote a paranoid book about it. While all around me were schools of well-dressed, white, male, hardworking, fly-fishing board members and other believers of the truest sporting faith on Earth, I was carrying a rock in my heart. I didn't look the part of an activist angler either. Having stayed up long past midnight in a Madison pub to watch the Red Sox beat the Tigers in playoff baseball, and then having slept on the ground, I wouldn't have passed a sniff test. But mainly, I wasn't feeling a part. Not yet. Hanging out with an anti-TU trout-regulations protester had had its psychic costs. I had cast far to adopt Roger Kerr's TU-opposing views. Now I was feeling the dislocation of coming home to an unfamiliar place. I had my doubts about the entire writing enterprise too. Who was I kidding? I'd spent a lot of time with Roger stripping out line to make that long cast, only to find a tangle deep in my own reel. I have my own resentments around the issues of fairness, power, and privilege in America. I came of age in the early 1970s when you blamed Authority, any authority . . . for any ill. I discovered the fly when trout fishing was less fishing and more Quixotic quest. Is that all I had? That I oppose cultural divides, and yet here I was teasing them out? Was I inventing? What's there to oppose?

Why had I come to the TU annual meeting in the first place? Resentment and blame have no place in a revival tent full of local chapters and higher ups trying to figure out what to do.

Two common penetrating themes came out of my two days of wandering the halls of TU. First, these old white knights of the fly-fishing guilds are tireless and won't be calling it quits anytime soon; second, there's a lot of frustration at the Round Table. Too few bodies; too much work. The world, as Paul Schullery noted in 2007, isn't paying attention to the angle of the back cast much these days. While more rivers and fish need saving and the dragon of climate change scorches the earth, popular culture is wading off in a new direction, guided by cell phone app. That's a hard reality to bear when you consider that TU's work is legacy building. The irony is that TU has never been more effective, gotten more done, raised more money, or had more to crow about at year's end.

And there's the second irony: In spite of a culture in flux, I think TU's going to figure it all out, for a few reasons.

First, because of the women in the room. One of the distinguishing characters of a TU annual conference is that it's attended mostly by old white guys . . . but also by this much smaller group of remarkable women, like queen fish that control the direction of the school. Women were in all the key locations. They ran the conference with a high degree of Midwestern efficiency. They were biologists staffing rivers and social researchers. They were as comfortable with wild fish in the field as they were in a public meeting. They ran chapters; they raised a lot of money. Then there were the women political leaders and activists. Wisconsin's DNR Secretary Cathy Stepp welcoming TU conference goers over breakfast; EPA Administrator Gina McCarthy giving a lunchtime address (in a heavy Boston accent that sounded funny in flat-affectation Wisconsin); and Nanci Morris—fishing guide, mother, and landscape activist dubbed "Queen of the Naknek"— giving the keynote. She's one of those remarkable kitchen-table activists you know is going to win against a proposed conglomerate gold mine high up the Naknek. TU women may be far fewer in numbers, but still the takeover is imminent. None too soon.

Women entering into leadership roles in natural-resource fields is yet another trend that emerged in the 1970s. When I transferred into a wildlife ecology program at UVM in 1975, Mollie Beattie was already there doing her master's degree in forestry. She went on to become the first woman to direct the US Fish and Wildlife Service. The last time I heard her speak publicly, she was serving as director and it was at my own annual meeting—a land trust—years ago, where she invoked Aldo Leopold's "Thinking Like a Mountain" essay. I have always had trouble with thinking like a mountain. Mountains don't think. Mountains just are. And yet, when Mollie described thinking like a mountain, it all made sense. Thinking like a mountain . . . cut a doorway into that mountain. When Mollie died too young, I reflected on what I knew about her motivations: She never picked up a fly rod, as far as I knew, but probably did more for coldwater fisheries than any previous director. What attracted her to the field? What's most attractive now? As Bob Heine—a conference-goer from Missouri—told me, the lobby work, the restoration focus, the education focus, these are attractive and compelling. The relationship between human health, community resiliency, and the health of the waters is compelling. Community building is compelling, and so is a big-tent approach.

Second: The food revolution underway in the countryside gives hope. Millennials are flocking back to land in places like Wisconsin and Vermont to start local farm businesses, restaurants, and all manner of artful living on the land. There's the local-food movement, farm-to-school programs, and Slow Food. No rural place worth its salt lacks a farmers market. Food is a fundamental leverage point when it comes to conserving land and water. New farmers are pushing a reset button. How food is grown, what food is grown, who grows it, who can afford it, and how it's distributed are emerging as central community-organizing questions across the countryside. Trout savers have an important stake in the matter of water, and they have a knowledge base of community organizing and land restoration to share as communities try to knit themselves resilient food systems. And since fish are a food with a history of sustaining people, good health, and good taste, the fisheries experts are needed at the dining table.

Third: Information and knowledge. The complexity of the world is being answered for the first time by the complexity of the computer models that imagine it. In TU, we have a crowd, a new type of crowd that can source and share the data. Most of that crowd may only exist online in the future. But that's efficient. On the other hand, hang out in the small workshop sessions if you want to get a glimpse of what crowdsourcing can achieve. That's where the hope and frustration are. At the program level, volunteers dope out who's going to do what. Work—somehow, painfully, without a set process for deciding—gets done. Plans are made and actions are taken regardless of the odds of success. A small citizen science regiment will head out after the conference to monitor water temperatures, for example. They'll establish protocols, site temperature-monitoring stations, and eventually cover the entire Mountain West with a network of citizen scientists. It's love, a form of love anyway; they do it for love, and that drives everything.

Fourth: Love. Love gives hope for the prospects of trout, trout fishing, and the culture of small fishing places. While we want to be loved for what *we* loved in this life, after a certain age we sense that civilization has long since left our shores. Never mind. We left too. We press on with an elegant false cast. And we lay out plans that extend far beyond us. Love—we don't even remember when it first entered. All we know is that it did, that it was good, and that it looks somewhat like a fish we plucked out across a very uncompromising current one night.

President Chris Wood's state-of-TU-union address early on the first day quoted William Faulkner on love and action, the fundamental quotient. "What's worth writing about is only the pulls of heart and love, honor, pity, pride, and sacrifice." You could read that as *what's worth protecting*. The answer isn't only fish and streams. Wood saw in trout-saving a reflection of the whole community. "We are making the world a better place, and building community in otherwise fractured places," he added.

That's what I came to hear from TU. That TU sees its role as repairing fractured communities, fractured people. There are too many hurting, neglected places, urban and rural. What better role for a fishing organization than creating a culture of restoration? But the fix can't be rules only. When it comes to rules, more of Steve Dewald's anthropological view is needed, and more of the likes of Robert Ditton, who tried to pull back the curtain a little on the nature of rural people and the impacts to a people's sense of place that seemingly small changes can have.

I came to the TU annual conference in Wisconsin to see the TU of today, to learn something about the culture of one of our preeminent conservation organizations, highly respected and deserving the praise. A group that has shaped the culture of trout fishing over the past sixty years more than any other. I came thinking it was TU's vision I was after—something to provide relief to the view of the organization I got from Roger Kerr. Now I know it was my own vision I needed, and that without it, I'd never be able to wade my way back through my own notes.

My vision for the future of trout fishing isn't exactly Roger's, though it came from him. Roger's years of resentment over what he saw as TU dominating policy-setting when it came to trout rules and his old employer Wisconsin DNR had grown into a kind of haunting. Wisconsin's Driftless Area in places suffers from a mutant wild abundance, and bag limits and seasons aren't changing to reflect that abundance— Roger wants that to change and he wants the local anglers back and able to fish a longer season that makes sense according to the seasons of rural life. That flight of local anglers and traditions, he can't let that go. Roger is right about a lot of things: The rules do not explain the abundance of brown trout; the link between abundance and the poor condition of the fish in some creeks has its roots in the density of trout and the absence of significant harvesting; the relationship between a new generation of social rules and angler decline; the effect of wild brown trout genes and the positive impact of restoration on natural reproduction and survival; the social impacts of a destination fishery on rural anglers; the need for social science—all these came from Roger, to me, through a regular supply of personal letters, trout counts, publications, and fishing.

If I were King Tut and was the keeper of the trout fishing vision for the Driftless, I'd decree, no more exclusive trophy fisheries that ban live bait. Driftless, with its miles of lightly fished creeks and abundant trout, can sustain more harvests, especially in this age of catch and release. Keep the slot limit and amp up the bag limit. Too often, trophyism leads to limited public access by tackle restriction, prohibitive costs, or the lack of long river accesses to walk and fish, a blue-collar alternative to drift boats and guides. If destination trophy fisheries are important to economic development, then let the developers and business people have their go. Just don't let them close off waters from the people of all economic abilities living nearby, and don't exaggerate the economic benefit claims or hooking mortality losses. Make public access the goal, and work with private landholding interests that would close off land. Make private economic gains subservient to science and the public good. We need fewer trophy fisheries for the few, and more clean and accessible rivers for the many.

Instead of Trout Unlimited, why not a Fisheries Limited? Isn't that the more pressing work? The same set of science and organization skills apply. Trout are a limited resource, limited to places with cold water. That leaves a lot of fish without a champion. There are too many silos in fisheries research. Trout still get the lion's share of resources, but the public is moving on.

Renew the TU philosophy and really live by it. I've always liked TU's philosophy statement. I think TU founder Art Neumann penned it. While Neumann, who recently passed away, hated and blamed local bait anglers for the poor fishing on rivers in northern Michigan, his take on the TU philosophy was and still is profound: "Take care of the fish, then the fishing will take care of itself." Neumann was declaring that TU will focus on the qualities of land and water use and human understanding that are fundamental to good, abundant fish and healthy aquatic systems. The problem is that the "fishing will take care of itself" part of Neumann's philosophy has been a difficult hands-off approach for TU, with so much trout fishing passion in the room. The fishing enterprise today is ably handled by trained state- and federal-level biologists and social scientists. While TU anglers have every right—and an obligation—to stay involved in public processes having to do with fishing management issues, TU's primary value as a partner to state and federal agencies is in building constituencies and enlarging public support for and involvement in their steward- ship work. Spending resources fighting for rule changes that have little impact on the health of aquatic communities or fishing quality is a lost opportunity. Special regulations projects that don't meet very narrow biological and social science justification thresholds should be opposed by TU nationally.

Respect local traditions and cater to the visions of rural commu- nities. Become the organization known for standing firm for equity and scientific honesty. In the not-too-distant past, rural people were as victimized by industry as their local rivers were. For example, in a telling statement about the formation of the Great Smoky Mountains National Park, where 1,400 families with small in-holdings were removed, a park anthropologist makes the point that the mountain people of the region, prior to industrial logging and coal mining, lived in a manner economically akin to the people of the eastern valleys and Piedmont. Poor in monies, but rich in just about everything they needed. During and after industrial logging (80% of the old growth was logged off by timber barons before the park was created), the inhabitants became impoverished, ill, and reliant on jobs in mining and logging that routinely killed them. Ironically, they got blamed for decimating trout populations when it was the same acid mine spoils, rail lines, and log drives that killed trout and were killing them. Don't let this happen again in the name of conserving nature. Be the conservation organization that reaches into communities, that helps make connec- tions, not widen differences. Support communities in imagining their own conservation work from within even if it means harvesting and eating a fair number of trout.

We need the truth seekers, the artists, the marginalized, the political activists, immigrant populations, the Black Lives Mat- ter-ers, the boldest and brave who are able to say *this is who I am, and this is my community and we belong.* Restoring nature restores the meaning and value of individual lives. Boldness and ri sktaking is what got TU to where it is today. Create a conservation movement that people can dance to, that puts at the center the immigrant angler with a ten-dollar rod and a family recipe for trout curry. We need to open up to a diverse community.

Pay attention to the importance of fishing culture to rural life today. Too often, the wild trout vision has been framed in terms of the urban angler with money and mobility. Special regulations are framed as an inevitable marketing necessity to this group. Highly mobile urban fly anglers are valuable but shouldn't be privileged when it comes to rule making. Demographics suggest that the future story of trout fishing has rural anglers alive and well. The 21% dropout of trout anglers between 1991 and 2011 (a 38% drop after adding in population growth) is skewed to the urban; the relative decline of trout anglers in rural America is less than in urban America (Maillett 2011). Small-town anglers belong as solidly in the middle of any future vision for trout fishing in America as urban populations, and the growth potential may be there. According to Maillett's report, based on the last US Fish and Wildlife national survey, rural people value all freshwater fishing, including trout fishing, more than urban anglers do. Women and families are an increasing demographic in some types of non-trout freshwater fishing. There is potential in these figures to increase the number and diversity of people who care enough to get involved in stewardship work.

Embrace the eco-friendly hatchery. Rather than another battle over hatcheries and stocking—one of TU's most sacred cows—TU could ask itself how it might go about growing the culture of restoration in America by growing positive relations to hatcheries. Hatcheries could play an increasingly important role in restoring native fish. The state-of-the-art hatchery today is a classroom, living museum, and open scientific laboratory combined. Hatcheries play a key role in inspiring and educating future anglers. Hatcheries are here to stay. A generation from now, TU may still be fighting hatchery projects, but the culture will judge that irrelevant.

The real work is almost always the long game. The long game is social change driven by the transformation of human beings and communities. TU is clearly in it for the long game. The long game is never a waste of time. That means doubling down on the next generation. There are so many cool spinoff projects that link to fish and water, schools, camps, and water bodies of all types, and so many underserved communities, urban, rural and in between. Surely, TU could double the energy and money it puts towards education and find urban and rural partners that can take its money and grow it, and grow the impact.

My own experience of TU's annual meeting was inspiring, and inspiration wasn't limited to the president's pep talk. I met a wide range of ordinary folks who have devoted a significant chunk of their lives in service to a greater good. Who will do this work in the future?

Just before the wrap-up of President Wood's address to a plenary session, before the lights came back up, I looked over my right shoulder and noticed for the first time a large block of people, mostly younger, sitting toward the back. It was the TU staff. The group that literally has our backs. The next generation is ready to replace us as we drop like spent mayflies onto the stream. It's the likes of them and their generation that will take the controls, reset the course—given all the data and wisdom from the old pilots here in the room—and head us to a heretofore unknown and different place. What holistic model of a new society do they carry? What will their new kind of person look like? What will the people of the future value most? How will they live their values? How will they make their way back into rural lands, back into the wild? What type of fish and fishing experience is waiting for them? What stranger will they meet and befriend out there? There is Nature, her needs and requirements. Then there is Culture, our values, our ways, and our diverse beliefs. The future rests in the unity of both. I hope the new people's working agenda might include, in the same breath of our most worthy environmental work, the bringing about of peace among warring tribes. It's entirely doable, but there are major preoccupations too, from the realities lost to the virtual, to growing class warfare.

As for those who have found a place comfortably within this restoration establishment, with their love of fly angling—yes, there is a practical and a spiritual value to knowing that a certain bug at a certain time hatches out of its old self and floats for a moment on the film before taking flight. And there is magical value, too, where, by the powers of mind and a fishing rod, time can be stilled and the mind transcended. We may know by the waiting stillness between casts what we have to do. That all said, a worm on a hook makes a tempting bait, and a trout poached in white wine a tasty dish.

Over the next day and a half, I met members of the local chapter that I should probably join; drank too much whiskey at the fish fry at the DDD (Death's Door Spirits). I spent too much money I didn't have on raffle items I didn't win (trying to shoot the moon by shooting most of my budget on a fishing kayak). I met a guy over dinner who has the impossible life goal of catching and releasing every species of native fish in the world. All thirty thousand of them. He's now my people, and I have adopted that impossible goal myself, though only at the Vermont scale (sorry fish—we torture you because we love you). I sat with the mostly unsung heroes of the coldwater fisheries conservation movement, and it became, over time, a comfortable place.

There is something I can do. Take water temperature measurements, for instance. And there's a small, ancient dam on a feeder brook that needs removal . . . Everyone can do something to help along the natural world, fish and all. Even Roger Kerr's barrage of letters to the editors, many under pseudonyms, should be considered a contribution. Roger is a constant reminder that we have to do a better job of listening, of being drawn into rural communities, their knowledge sets and their customs. No future fishery needs to be built without the broad backing of virtually every interest. Why not hold to a standard of consensus? So what if some never come in from the cold. Make it a point to angle for the hardest fish.

As for Roger Kerr, he finally got his wished-for arrest citation for breaking the rules, his act of civil disobedience, something he had tried to bring about for twenty years. Crawford County Warden Cody Adams responded to seventy-five-year-old Kerr's admission of harvesting eight brown trout: four from Saunders Creek and four from his home river, the Big Green. The possession limit for brown trout is five. That put him three over. In one respect, his act got him what he wanted. Front-page news in the *La Crosse Tribune* (Sunday, July 27, 2014). On the other hand, it wasn't the publicity he'd hoped for. There was no wave of public support, and the experts piled on against him. A few weeks later, having been intent on a jury trial, he settled out of court and paid his fine. He wrote to me: "I was never a defendant in a courtroom in my life. I thought I would have an ulcer or have a heart attack (or both) so my body was 'unhappy' with me. . . . I sent two blank checks to my lawyer to pay my fines." Shortly after that letter of discouragement, he wrote to say he was done protesting and would retire from his effort to stamp out bad rules. I sent him a letter of congratulations and a collection of Robert Behnke's writings. Behnke is a favorite of Roger's. But then a month later Roger was back to protesting. Lately he's been sending his mailings to Iowa and to state-level politicians in Wisconsin. Some of them are writing back, and Roger continues to build his argument for healthy local trout-fishing communities based on longer seasons, fewer bait restrictions, bigger bag limits, and simpler rules. Part of me is glad Roger's back. I admire him. There's an old crusader's adage that applies to Roger. It goes something like, "I may not have changed anyone or anything, but at least they haven't changed me." I constantly remind Roger that the rules are changing in Wisconsin—only a small percentage of Wisconsin's trout stream miles are now managed as trophy waters, and Justine Hasz has vowed publicly to simplify the regulations. Roger is winning. Even John "Duke" Welter, head of TU's Driftless program, has professed to eating trout, sharing his favorite recipe in a recent issue of the Wisconsin TU's newsletter.

After the TU banquet wound down, the awards made, the raffle winners selected, and the new board members welcomed, it was time for me to move on. In the rain and the dark of Saturday night, I headed west. I intended to fish the Bighorn and then the Yellowstone with friends living in Pray, Montana, before entering Yellowstone National Park for Wild Trout XI. But with a federal government divided, gridlock in Congress, and a threatened government shutdown, would the Wild Trout Symposium, celebrating the first forty years, happen at all? As an alternative, I could drop down into Colorado to fish the upper wilderness reaches of the White. Or maybe I'd visit the Rio Grande. There's always Cochetopa Creek in the San Juans, with its browns and its brook trout invaders, and that isolated tribe of cutthroat trout protected by a waterfall. All that wild space full of fish for a good next lost ramble. What's not to like?

SOURCES AND NOTES

Introduction: Everglades City, Florida

The *National Survey of Fishing, Hunting, and Wildlife-Associated Recreation* (posted online), a collaborative effort between federal and state agencies conducted every five years since 1955, is the most important source of state-by-state statistics on the demographics and economics of sport fishing. The 2011 survey finds Florida as the top US destination when it comes to recreational sport fishing, both in terms of numbers of out-of-state visitors who travel to fish in Florida, and overall expenditures. See also *The Economic Impact of Saltwater Fishing in Florida*, a report by the Florida Fish and Wildlife Conservation Commission. Many states conduct their own recreational angler surveys; statistics can differ slightly between state and federal surveys; state surveys often contain more detailed information on angler demographics.

Author Peter Matthiessen's three historical "mystery"—novels including the first and best known, *Killing Mister Watson*—about early twentieth-century culture in Florida's Ten Thousand Islands mangrove forests and the Everglades ecosystem, have been edited, shortened, and collected under one title: *Shadow Country*.

The Randell Research Center in Pineland, Florida, is dedicated to the long-term research of ancient indigenous Calusa culture centered in the mangrove system of the Gulf Coast of southern Florida.

According to recent reports, 85% of all commercial marine fisheries are now being exploited up to or beyond their biological limits. See "Unsustainable Seafood: A New Crackdown on Illegal Fishing" by Richard Conniff. (*Yale Environment 360*, April 22, 2014, http://e360.yale.edu/feature/unsustainable_seafood_a_new_crackdown_on_illegal_fishing/2758/).See also the Pew Charitable Trusts' US Ocean Conservation Program, particularly the Federal Ocean Policy recommendations. A network of marine sanctuaries has been established by NOAA (National Oceanic and Atmospheric Administration) under their Office of National Marine Sanctuaries, in partnership with the US National Park Service and other federal and state natural resource agencies.

For every effort at the state and federal level to manage commercial and recreational fisheries sustainably, there is pushback (often legal challenges) from organized groups. These may be based in the commercial, recreational fishing industries or organized as unaffiliated lobby and educational organizations (some set up as 501(c)(3) non-profit organizations). See, for example, www.theFRA.org (the Fishing Rights Alliance).

Aldo Leopold calls for "a new kind of people": see Julianne Lutz Newton's *Aldo Leopold's Odyssey: Rediscovering the Author of A Sand County Almanac*

(Washington DC: Island Press, 2006), page 266. The idea that natural-resource conservation action and other social behavior change begins with personal transformation: people changing inside—Leopold frames it as "a new kind of people"—is at least as old as Plato, the Irish prelate, Philosopher Bishop Berkeley and his immaterialism, and many ancient idealists too numerous to mention. Rachel Carson and George Perkins Marsh, to name two modern environmentalists, also picked up on this theme. Community-based social marketing is another related development in the field of social change.

Chapter One: Wild Brook Trout and the Social Rule

Bachman, Robert A. "Integrating the Ecological and Human Dimensions of Trout Management." Proceedings of Trout and the Trout Angler II workshop, La Crosse, WI, July 2000.

Conniff, Richard. "Unsustainable Seafood: A New Crackdown on Illegal Fishing." *Yale Environment 360*, April 22, 2014.

Detar, Jason E., and Robert Carline. "The Contemporary Role of Special Regulations in Wild Trout Management: Evaluation of Biologist Views in the Eastern and Midwestern United States." Proceedings of Wild Trout Symposium XI, West Yellowstone, MT, September 2014.

Ditton, Robert B., Stephen M. Holland, and David K. Anderson. 2002. "Recreational Fishing as Tourism." *Fisheries* 27 (3): 17-24.

Jackson, Robert M. "Why, Why, Why?: The Human Dimensions of Trout Angling Motivations and Satisfactions." Proceedings of Wild Trout Symposium IV, Yellowstone National Park, MT, September 1989.

Lee Wulff—conservationist, artist, writer, fishing innovator, promoter of no-kill "on our best trout waters," teacher, sage, and guru—left a lot of content in his wake. One of the best compendiums of his writings is John Merwin's *The Compleat Lee Wulff: A Treasury of Lee Wulff's Greatest Angling Adventures* (New York: Dutton, 1989). Merwin's book includes an early magazine piece in *Collier's* extolling the lowly worm as a trout bait of choice, despite the "whispering campaign against it." *Trout on a Fly* (Guilford: Lyons Press, 1986) is an excellent, short read on Wulff. In it, he trashes the hatchery trout in no uncertain terms.

Two of Wisconsin's best-known trout fishing columnists and book authors, Len Harris, author of *The Stream of Time* and *Brigadoon Creek*, and Jay Ford Thurston, columnist and author of *Spring Creek Treasure*, write prosaically of trout fishing adventure throughout the Driftless region. These two know the region and its creeks, proving yet again the unwritten rule that if you want to connect with fish, seek out local fishing titles and expertise.

Lucy Crawford's *The History of the White Mountains* (Portland: B. Thurston, 1886) is Ethan Allen Crawford's story as told by his wife Lucy Crawford in the year of his death, 1846. She draws on Ethan's journals, including his forays on the Saco and Ammonoosuc and up to Ethan Pond to fish, trap, and guide. Jack Noon's *Fishing in New Hampshire: A History* (South Sutton: Moose Country Press, 2003), with an introduction by John McPhee, describes fishing from colonial days forward, including information gleaned from the first years of biennial reports of the NH Fish and Game

Commission (beginning in 1894). His treatment of early trout fishing in the White Mountains includes accounts of overharvesting, shrinking sizes of fish, disappearing spawning runs of lamprey and Atlantic salmon, and old-growth fish in old-growth forests. M.F. Sweetser's early guide to exploring the White Mountains includes references to the difficulties of walking through the old forest, and trout growing unmolested in isolated ponds and streams.

The Complete Fly Fisherman: The notes and letters of Theodore Gordon (New York: Charles Scribner's Sons, 1947), edited with an introduction by John McDonald, gives a great picture of not only Gordon but also trout fishing and fishing literary styles of the day. *The Fishing in Print: A Guided Tour Through Five Centuries of Angling Literature* (New York: Winchester Press, 1975), edited by Arnold Gingrich and John Groth, contains much good information on Gordon's life; also, *American Trout Fishing by Theodore Gordon and a Company of Anglers*, edited by Arnold Gingrich (New York: Alfred A. Knopf, 1966).

For trout research and restoration in New Hampshire, see New Hampshire Fish and Game and the various papers and working references of John Magee, including: MacCartney, James M., John A. Magee, and John J. Field. "Restoring Trout Habitat in Difficult to Access Areas Using Mobile Wood Additions." Proceedings of Wild Trout Symposium XI, West Yellowstone, MT, September 2014.

Dianne Timmins, coldwater fisheries biologist for New Hampshire Fish and Game, has done work on brooktrout migratory patterns in northern New Hampshire (see her poster presentation, "Migration Patterns of Wild Adult Brook Trout in Northern New Hampshire" at Wild Trout XI, 2014).

Compensatory mortality is the idea that mortality in wild populations, especially in the first year of life, is density dependent. Or, as Robert Behnke stated at a symposium on wild trout management in San Jose, California, in 1977, "the more trout killed by anglers, the fewer trout lost to natural mortality and vice versa." James McFadden references compensatory mortality in relation to brook trout populations in Michigan streams in "A Population Study of the Brook Trout, *Salvelinus Fontinalis*" (Wildlife Society, 1961). Other references in the 1960s and 1970s include David S. Shetter in 1967 and Russell F. Thurow. R-selection in population ecology refers particularly to reproductive strategy for species in unstable environments (numerous web references).

Chapter Two: Trout Fishing and the Diminishing Rural Class

George Perkins Marsh's *Man and Nature: Or, Physical Geography as Modified by Human Action* was published in 1864 (New York: Charles Scribner's Sons). His "Report, Made Under Authority of the Legislature of Vermont, on the Artificial Propagation of Fish" (Burlington: Free Press Print, 1857) was also ahead of its time. Stephen C. Trombulak's *So Great a Vision: The Conservation Writings of George Perkins Marsh* (Hanover: University Press of New England, 2001) contains many of Marsh's best-known addresses, including his fisheries report. David Lowenthal's *George Perkins Marsh: Prophet of Conservation* (Seattle: University of Washington Press, 2000) is the definitive biography. Marsh's address "Human Knowledge: a Discourse Delivered before the Massachusetts Alpha of the Phi Beta Kappa Society, at Cambridge, August 26" (New York: Charles C. Little and James Brown, 1847) is less well known and shows some of the influence of his cousin James Marsh's ideas on his writings.

Vermonter James Marsh, an older cousin of George Perkins Marsh, is an acknowledged original source of the American transcendentalism movement—the movement many assume started with Ralph Waldo Emerson, Henry David Thoreau, and other religious leaders, poets, and essayists in and around Concord and Boston, Massachusetts. James Marsh grew up on a farm in Hartford, Vermont, attended Dartmouth College, and at the age of thirty-two became president of the University of Vermont. Peter Carafiol's biography *Transcendent Reason: James Marsh and the Forms of Romantic Thought* (Gainesville: University Press of Florida, 1982) is a good place to begin. Diane Yoder's M.A. thesis, *Satisfying the Head as Well as the Heart: James Marsh, Samuel Taylor Coleridge and the American Transcendentalist Movement* (Antioch University McGregor, 2009), is a clearly written description of Marsh's radical thinking on unity at the heart of the transcendentalist movement, and the role of reason and thinking in spiritual understanding.

Vermont conducted an angler survey in 2009, published in 2010, showing a 33% decline in anglers between 1999 and 2009. The angler survey was prepared by Nancy A. Connelly and Barbara A. Knuth, respectively of the Human Dimensions Research Unit and the Department of Natural Resources at Cornell University. It's titled "The Potential Use of Specialized Fishing Regulations for Improving Wild Trout Stream Fisheries in Vermont" (Vermont Department of Fish and Wildlife, Study No. VIII, 1999).

Chapter Three: Worms and Trout and Hooking Mortality, Oh My!

Wulff, Lee. "The Lost Art of Fishing with a Worm." *Collier's.* April 16, 1954.

Carline, R. F., T. Beard, Jr., and B. A. Hollender. 1991. "Response of Wild Brown Trout to Elimination of Stocking and to No-Harvest Regulations." *North American Journal of Fisheries Management* 11: 253-266.

Detar, Jason E., and Robert Carline. "The Contemporary Role of Special Regulations in Wild Trout Management: Evaluation of Biologist Views in the Eastern and Midwestern United States." Proceedings of Wild Trout Symposium XI, West Yellowstone, MT, September 2014.

The history and current management of the Spring Creek fishery in Pennsylvania is covered well in:

Carline, Robert F., Rebecca L. Dunlap, Jason E. Detar, and Bruce A. Hollender. "The Fishery of Spring Creek: A Watershed Under Siege." 2011. The Pennsylvania Fish and Boat Commission: Technical Report Number 1.

Hooking mortality studies are too numerous to read or cite. I found a 2005 report from the Ontario Ministry of Natural Resources that was particularly helpful because of its broad scope:

Casselman, S.J. "Catch-and-Release Angling: a Review with Guidelines for Proper Fish Handling Practices." Ontario Ministry of Natural Resources, Fish and Wildlife Branch, Fisheries Section. Using a meta-study of 118 catch-and-release studies and estimating a 16% average mortality rate, the Ontario report lays out the state of the art of catch-and-release practice as it was in 2005. The report notes that all but 5% of anglers in Ontario partake in catch and release today.

Several hooking mortality studies on trout are worth mentioning because they represent a then-and-now contrast:

Mason, J.W. and R.L. Hunt. 1967. "Mortality Rates of Deeply Hooked Rainbow Trout," *Progressive Fish-Culturist* 29 (2): 87-91. This was an early hooking mortality study conducted in a hatchery setting that looked at the mortality of deeply hooked fish (up to 70%). Trout hooking mortality studies evolved over the years to consider fish in moving water, where much lower rates of deep hooking and hooking mortality were discovered.

High, Brett, Kevin A. Meyer, and Christopher L. Sullivan. "Performance of Circle Hooks When Bait Fishing for Stream-Dwelling Trout." Proceedings of Wild Trout Symposium XI, West Yellowstone, MT, September 2014. This study shows that use of circle hooks results in a lower incidence of deep hooking than conventional J hooks, especially when fished actively rather than passively (11% rate of deep hooking with active fishing versus 17% with passive fishing).

Schill, Daniel J. 1996. "Hooking Mortality of Bait-Caught Rainbow Trout in an Idaho Trout Stream and a Hatchery: Implications for Special Regulation Management." *North American Journal of Fisheries Management* 16: 348-356.

Schill, Daniel J., J.S. Griffith, and Robert E. Gresswell. 1986. "Hooking Mortality of Cutthroat Trout in a Catch-and-Release Segment of the Yellowstone River, Yellowstone National Park." *North American Journal of Fisheries Management* 6: 226-232.

Chapter Four: Pere Marquette River: Hooked on Dollars

Borgelt, Bryon G. "Flies Only: Early Sport Fishing Conservation on Michigan's Au Sable River," PhD diss., University of Toledo, 2009. This is an excellent overview of an early clash of fishing cultures over regulations, access, fishing styles, and economics in northern Michigan.

Bryan, H. "A Social Science Perspective for Managing Recreational Conflict." Proceedings of the Seventh Annual Marine Recreational Fisheries Symposium, Fort Lauderdale, FL. Published by Sport Fishing Institute, Washington, D.C., 1982: 15-22.

Gigliotti, L. M. and R. B. Peyton. 1993. "Values and Behaviors of Trout Anglers, and their Attitudes Toward Fishery Management, Relative to Membership in Fishing Organizations: a Michigan Case Study." *North American Journal of Fisheries Management* 13: 492-501.

Hicks, Charles E., Lawrence C. Belusz, Daniel J. Witter, and Pamela S. Haverland. 1983. "Application of Angler Attitudes and Motives to Management Strategies at Missouri's Trout Parks." *Fisheries* 8 (5): 2-7.

Jackson, Robert M. "Why, Why, Why?: The Human Dimensions of Trout Angling Motivations and Satisfactions." Proceedings of Wild Trout Symposium IV, Yellowstone National Park, MT, September 1989. This was one of the first papers presented at the symposium by a bona fide psychologist. Jackson was a professor of psychology at the University of Wisconsin—La Crosse at the time. Abraham Maslow published his hierarchy of human needs in 1943. His theory postulated eight stages of human need, beginning with the most basic—physiological—and ending with self-actual-

ization and transcendence beyond the self. Individuals would need to satisfy earlier needs before progressing to the next level. Jackson's work used a parallel thought process
to describe a hierarchy of motivations distinguishing types of trout anglers in Wisconsin. Other writers, particularly Lee Wulff, have described trout angling in terms of a hierarchy of values.

Kellert, Stephen R. "Perceptions of Animals in American Society." Transactions of the 41st North American Wildlife and Natural Resource Conference, Washington, D.C., March 1976: 533-546.

Peyton, R. B. and L. M. Gigliotti. "Anglers, Attitudes, and the Au Sable: For Whom Does the River Flow?" Proceedings of Trout and the Trout Angler in the Upper Midwest Workshop, La Crosse, Wisconsin, 1988.

The Public trust doctrine holds that certain natural resources—fish and game, for example—cannot be owned and managed for private benefit, but held for the benefit of all.

The Federation of Fly Fishers's documentary film describing the founding years, *Never Name the River,* is highly entertaining, and as a record of the massive shift in culture going on in trout fishing, contains early thoughts on the link between fly fishing and conservation, including cautions about linking the two.

Talleur, Richard W. "The Economic Effect of No-Kill Regulations on Communities." Proceedings of Wild Trout Symposium IV, Yellowstone National Park, MT, September 1989.

Chapter Five: The Last Great Worm Fisherman

David Rhodes's book *Driftless* (Minneapolis: Milkweed Editions, 2009) is a humorous and highly compelling account of small-town life in the present day Driftless. A must-read for anyone traveling to the Driftless Area.

The Physical Geography of Wisconsin by Lawrence Martin (Madison: Wisconsin Geological and Natural History Survey [Issue 36], 1916) is essentially a bibliography of early research, including over a hundred references to the early cultures and geographic and geological explorations of the Driftless region.

Exploring Wisconsin's Trout Streams: The Angler's Guide by Steve Born, Jeff Mayers, Andy Morton, and Bill Sozogni (Madison: University of Wisconsin Press, 1997) contains an excellent description of the geography of the Driftless Area and provides the local and traveling angler with an essential guide to trout fishing in Wisconsin.

The Land Remembers: The Story of a Farm and its People by Ben Logan (Chanhassen: NorthWord Press, 1999) is a sweet recollection of life in the Driftless, growing up on a Crawford County farm. Roger Kerr told me that if I wanted to know what Mary Kerr's life was like growing up, I should read Ben's book.

Faast, T.S., and S.K. Sahnow. "Regaining Public Trust . . . and Keeping It!" Proceedings of Wild Trout Symposium VIII, Yellowstone Nation Park, MT, September 2004.

Mitro, Mathew G. "Stocking Trout of Wild Parentage to Restore Wild Populations: An Evaluation of Wisconsin's Wild Trout Stocking Program." Proceedings of Wild Trout Symposium VIII, Yellowstone National Park, MT, September 2004.

Much else of what I initially received in the way of information on the history of Wisconsin's wild trout stocking program and regulations came through personal interviews with Roger Kerr or inside nearly two hundred personal letters I received from him. They contained recollections, interviews, copies of technical reports, minutes from public meetings of the Wisconsin Conservation Congress, Wisconsin DNR hearings and planning sessions, and newspaper articles and commentaries by Roger Kerr and others. These will be donated to the Boscobel Public Library. The rest of the information came, by and large, from my own research, interviews, and travels in Wisconsin.

Chapter Six: The Best Way to Fix Wild Trout

Fryin' Magic is available online, but not on grocery store shelves in Vermont or New Hampshire, as far as I can tell. Get some today.

Fruit wines do seem to be a specialty of the Driftless Area (see Chapter Ten). My plantation of elderberry is now well established.

Wilma Smith's Vegetable Salad recipe (compliments of Mary Kerr): Add 1 can (14 oz, well drained) each of corn, tiny beans, and cut green beans to a glass or Tupperware bowl (Wilma says, do not use a metal bowl). Then add ½ cup chopped green pepper, ½ cup chopped red pepper, ½ cup chopped celery, and ½ cup chopped (mild) onion. Dressing: In a separate bowl combine ¼ cup canola (or other salad oil, but do not use olive oil), 1 tsp salt, ½ tsp pepper, ½ cup cider vinegar (do not use regular vinegar), ¾ cup sugar. Stir well, then add vegetables and stir well again. Let stand overnight in refrigerator and stir occasionally.

Chapter Seven: The Trout Explosion in Southwestern Wisconsin

I'm convinced that restoring trout creeks and then managing them for sustainable, healthy trout populations and highly opinionated anglers is a matter of art, science, and insanity. Several papers are worth reading in relation to the restoration of Coon Valley and the creeks that run through it. Unfortunately, much of the Aldo Leopold correspondence is lost. There are a few items in the Leopold archives at the University of Wisconsin in Madison. Very few.

Mitro, Matthew G., Jordan Weeks, and David Vetrano. "Trout Angling on Timber Coulee Creek Then (1984) and Now (2008)." Wisconsin DNR Fisheries Research and Wisconsin DNR Fisheries Management, La Crosse, WI, 2008. This Timber Coulee study comparing angler surveys from 1984 and 2008 has been available online at the Wisconsin Department of Natural Resources site, but is no longer (Wisconsin TU published an abridged version). For a picture of how effective habitat restoration on Wisconsin spring creeks can be, read researcher Matthew Mitro's study of Elk Creek trout production before and after restoration: Mitro, Matthew, and Paul Kanehl. 2011. "Trout Population Response to Instream Habitat Restoration in Elk Creek." Wisconsin Department of Natural Resources, Fisheries

Research Division.

Thurow, Russell F., and Daniel J. Schill. "Conflicts in Allocation of Wild Trout Resources: an Idaho Case History." Proceedings of Wild Trout Symposium V, Yellowstone National Park, MT, September, 1994.

Chapter Eight: The Best and Worst of a Destination Fishery

In many ways, the social impact of destination trout fisheries is the main topic of this book. In the Driftless Area, a destination fishery exists in some shape or form, and the question is: Have the rules, policies, promotional materials, statistics, and vast efforts at creek restoration used to shape this social fishery had a dampening impact on local trout fishing participation? The answer I got from one side, including Trout Unlimited members and officials in the department, is that there is no proven negative correlation. The official line tends to be that no one really knows how to explain the dropout of local anglers. Roger Kerr and a handful of others say the proof is writ large.

This is what is known: 1.) A majority of fisheries biologists feel special regulations are justified merely on social grounds and that such regulations can discourage some anglers from participation. See: Detar, Jason E., and Robert Carline. "The Contemporary Role of Special Regulations in Wild Trout Management: Evaluation of Biologist Views in the Eastern and Midwestern United States." Proceedings of Wild Trout Symposium XI, Yellowstone National Park, MT, September 2014. 2.) It's not clear what role Wisconsin's special rules have played in trout increases. See: "UW-Stevens Point study points to improved trout population statewide," Wisconsin Department of Natural Resources, Weekly News, February 22, 2011, http://dnr. wi.gov/news/weekly/?id=263#art1. This article summarizes a study done by Nancy Nate, Andy Fayram, and Joanna Griffin of the UW-Stevens Point Fisheries Analysis Center, analyzing sixty years of survey records. 3.) And finally, trout anglers often vote with their feet when new special regulations are applied (either flocking to that fishery or leaving that fishery). See: Hunt, Robert L. 1970. "A Compendium of Research on Angling Regulations for Brook Trout Conducted at Lawrence Creek, Wisconsin." Wisconsin Department of Natural Resources, Madison, Wisconsin, Research Report 54.

Mitro, Matthew G., Jordan Weeks, and David Vetrano. 2008. "Trout Angling on Timber Coulee Creek Then (1984) and Now (2008)." Wisconsin DNR Fisheries Research and Wisconsin DNR Fisheries Management, La Crosse, WI.

Welter, John (Duke). "Wild Trout and the Driftless Area: An Expanding Draw for Angling Tourism." Proceedings of Wild Trout Symposium XI, West Yellowstone, MT, September 2014.

Robert Ditton's work stands out as a rare attempt to determine the social cost of destination fisheries to local angler communities. From the Academy of Leisure Sciences: "Dr. Ditton was the first to specialize in outdoor recreation research in coastal and marine settings. He now focuses on the human dimensions of fisheries. He was a Sea Grant researcher for 20 years, and developed a graduate program in marine recreation resources management in the Department of Recreation, Parks and Tourism Sciences at Texas A&M. Along with numerous research articles and reports, he co-authored the book, *Coastal Resources Management*. He served five years as Editor of *Leisure Sciences* and, also, as Associate Editor of *Leisure Sciences*, the *Journal of Leisure Research*, and *Coastal Zone Management*."

Fedler, A. H. and Robert B. Ditton. 1986. "A Framework for Understanding the Consumption Orientation of Recreational Fishermen." *Environmental Management* 10 (2): 221-227.

Ditton, Robert B., Stephen M. Holland, and David K. Anderson. 2002. "Recreational Fishing as Tourism." *Fisheries* 27 (3): 17-24. In this paper, Ditton asks a set of questions pertaining to the impact of destination fisheries—the influx of non-resident anglers—on local fishing communities. As of 2002, there were no clear answers.

Chapter Nine: Lawrence Creek and the Lost Anglers

Hunt, Robert L. 1970. "A Compendium of Research on Angling Regulations for Brook Trout Conducted at Lawrence Creek, Wisconsin." Wisconsin Department of Natural Resources, Madison, Wisconsin, Research Report 54.

Today the effects on trout populations of bag limits, size limits, slot limits, catch-and-release rules, hook and barb, lure, bait and fly-only are generally well understood by the fish managing community, but that was not the case in the late 1960s and early 1970s. That's why Robert Hunt's paper on lessons from Lawrence Creek—at a time when the impacts of rule changes, including non-consumptive regulations like no-kill, low-kill and terminal-tackle restrictions including fly-fishing only, were still poorly understood—was important. Less understood and rarely discussed (and this is still the case today) was the impact of non-consumptive regulations on fishing participation across the wide spectrum of angler groups. Hunt touches on the problem in 1974 at Wild Trout I, and a few other managers allude to it (Art Whitney: "Creel, Size, Seasons and Angling Methods"; Ralph Abele: "The Political Area"; and John D. Varley: "The Yellowstone Fishery").

At Wild Trout II in 1979, moderator Starker Leopold's summary of the symposium is fascinating for its lack of mention of angler society, though it contains an early personal recollection of overharvests of cutthroat trout on the Yellowstone prior to superintendent Jack Anderson's move to establish no-kill on the Yellowstone River and a fishing ban at Fishing Bridge—a move Leopold strongly endorses (he goes on to make a persuasive argument for watershed-wide planning). Angler dropout comes up only in John D. Varley's paper, "Catch and Release Fishing in Yellowstone Park." Robert Behnke's opening remarks, as discussion leader of a research panel, hits on topics that will remain at the top of wild trout research agendas for years to come (genetics of wild trout, impacts of special regulations—he cries out for more research—and environmental improvements to streams); special rules' impact on fishing participation is not one of them. He does state here that "Under most circumstances, unless we are dealing with particularly a long-lived trout population with low natural mortality rates, special regulations will not work a dramatic change to produce more older larger trout if the annual angling kill is much less than 50% of the catchable size trout." Much of Wild Trout II, however, with fly anglers like Lee

Wulff, Marty Seldon, Greg Lilly, Nat Reed, and Pete Van Gytenbeek, is a full-court press for no-kill regulations.

At Wild Trout III in 1984, the impact of catch-and-release regulations on angler participation comes up only in several cases, but more often than not in its relationship to increased crowding on streams that have such regulations (Gardner Grant, Gerald Barnhart, and Robert Engstrom-Heg's paper: "A Synopsis of Some New York Experiences with Catch and Release Management of Wild Salmonids"). Jerry Wells's paper "Restrictive Regulations: the Montana Experience" outlines the generally positive impacts of catch-and-release rules on selected fisheries in Montana without looking at angler impacts. Though touching on the social impacts of non-consumptive rules (anglers in Colorado widely supported the new rules and managers generally believed in allowing some harvest), R. Barry Nehring and Richard Anderson's paper "Catch and Release Management in Colorado: What Works? How, When, Where, Why?" notes that catch-and-release rules, applied in a big way in 1979, were generally successful, leading to more large fish and higher catch rates. In some fisheries, such as the South Platte, with upwards of five thousand hours per acre year of fishing pressure at the time, there were no good alternatives to catch and release. Ronald D. Jones reports in "Ten Years of Catch and Release in Yellowstone Park" that angler participation initially dropped and then rose to record levels (in catch-and-release sections of the Yellowstone, native cutthroat trout were caught back then at an average rate of 9.7 times per season—they stayed in the system up to three years and had an approximate recreational value of $45 per fish!).

Wild Trout IV in 1989 has lots of papers focused on the successes and failures of no-kill experiments. D. W. Chapman's paper "Visiting Hours Only, or: Catch and Release Revisited" starts with this: "We rarely acknowledge that catch and release fisheries limit entry in sport fishing." His paper takes a look at the biological and social impacts of formally limiting entry, say, by permit systems, etc. It's a fascinating study in which he references angler responses to Idaho's attempt to restrict a section of the Big Wood River to catch and release and artificial lures only.

Wild Trout V in 1994 contains an important contribution to understanding angler conflict in trout fishing. Russell F. Thurow and Daniel J. Schill's paper "Conflicts in Allocation of Wild Trout Resources: an Idaho Case History" looks at angler conflict in the Big Wood River system, including Silver Creek. There are many gems in this paper, and I was tempted to reprint large sections verbatim in this book. Some points worth repeating here: "Lewynsky (1986) suggests continual elimination of bait anglers from special regulations fisheries may be the result of poor goal definition by regulating agencies. . . . 87% of Idaho trout anglers used bait in 1994. . . . Depending on management goals and other factors . . . hooking mortality from bait may be acceptable. . . . To achieve the broadest base of support for special regulations, unnecessary restrictions should be avoided."

Lewynsky, V.A. 1986. "Evaluation of Special Angling Regulations in the Coeur d'Alene River Trout Fishery." Master's thesis, University of Idaho, Moscow.

Chapter Ten: A Bluegill Insight

Much beloved humble little bluegills get a surprising amount of attention in fisheries management circles in Wisconsin. New proposed regulations in Wisconsin, radically reducing bag limits, are opposed by Roger Kerr.

Ditton, Robert B., David K. Loomis, and Seungdam Choi. 1992. "Recreation Specialization: Re-conceptualization from a Social Worlds Perspective." *Journal of Leisure Research* 24 (1): 33-51.

"NRB Approves Fish, Wildlife Rule Change Options for Spring Hearings," *Wisconsin Outdoor News,* February 20, 2015.

Chapter Eleven: Melancthon Creek, Fishing Rules, and the Psychology of Social Change

Much of the material in this chapter comes either from an interview with John Slaney during the summer of 2013 and John's files—now in my possession—or from the files of Roger Kerr. It was Slaney's stand against emergency trout rules on the Melanchthon that spurred the creation of Roger Kerr's Pine Melanchthon Group of trout regulations protesters. With significant help from Roger Kerr, John Slaney was able to repeal the new restrictive rules on the Melanchthon.

Lee Fahrney's op-ed piece can be found in the May 10, 2007 edition of *The Monroe Times.* Warden Mike Nice's letter is in John Slaney's file in my possession; so are copies of the minutes of various meetings of the Richland Conservation Commission, Roger Kerr's petition, and original letters and correspondence with the Wisconsin DNR.

The March 21, 2008 edition of *Wisconsin Outdoor News* contains an article on the Prairie River conflict over the repeal of trophy regulations, with quotes from Richard Ament, Duke Welter, Ed Harvey (chair at the time of the Wisconsin Conservation Congress), and Joe Hennessy, regulations specialist for the Wisconsin DNR.

Steve Dewald's remarks to Wisconsin TU in 2002 are found also in the proceedings of the 2000 Trout and the Trout Angler II conference, held in La Crosse, Wisconsin. His remarks and opinions are also available in the May 2007 edition of *Wisconsin Outdoor Journal*, in an article titled "Complicated Regulations Stem from Trophy Trend." The 2002 conference paper provides greater detail. Also presenting papers: Robert Behnke, Robert Hunt, Robert Ditton, and Robert Bachman. Also, Stephen M. Born ("The Role of Trout Anglers in the 21st Century") and many other distinguished researchers.

Petchenik, Jordan. "Results of the 2011 Survey of Lapsed Wisconsin Inland Trout Anglers," Wisconsin Department of Natural Resources, Bureau of Fisheries Management, May 2012.

Chapter Twelve: The Perfect Crossover Angler

Interviews and field trips. Anecdotal matters.

Chapter Thirteen: The Sand County

The Leopold Outlook 13 (1).

Leopold, Aldo. *The River of the Mother of God and Other Essays by Aldo Leopold.* Edited by Susan L. Flader and J. Baird Callicott. Madison: The University of Wisconsin Press, 1991. (See particularly two essays: "The Pig in the Parlor," 1925, and "Coon Valley: An Adventure in Cooperative Conservation," 1935.)

Chapter Fourteen: Lost in the Driftless

Leopold, Aldo. *The River of the Mother of God and Other Essays by Aldo Leopold.* Edited by Susan L. Flader and J. Baird Callicott. Madison: The University of Wisconsin Press, 1991.

Chapter Fifteen: The Ones that Got Away

This chapter is based partly on an interview with Jordan B. Petchenik in the late summer of 2013 and Petchenik's survey of lapsed trout anglers in Wisconsin, published in 2012.

Petchenik, Jordan. "Results of the 2011 Survey of Lapsed Wisconsin Inland Trout Anglers," Wisconsin Department of Natural Resources, Bureau of Fisheries Management, May 2012.

For an additional summary and discussion of the findings, see:

Petchenik, Jordan, R. Scot Stewart, Matthew G. Mitro, and Marty P. Engel. "A Plausible Explanation for Lapsed Trout Fishing Participation in Wisconsin." Proceedings of Wild Trout Symposium XI, West Yellowstone, MT, September 2014. Notably, this is the first paper presented at the Wild Trout Symposia across its forty-year history that's devoted to trout angler decline.

American Fishing Tackle Manufacturers Association. 1990. Fishing motivation study. Barrington, Illinois.

Fedler, Anthony J., and Robert B. Ditton. 2011. "Dropping Out and Dropping In: A Study of Factors for Changing Recreational Fishing Participation." *North American Journal of Fisheries Management* 21 (2): 283-292.

Fedler, Anthony J., Robert B. Ditton, and M.D. Duda. 1998. "Factors Influencing Recreational Fishing and Boating Participation: Strategic Plan for the National Outreach and Communication Program." Sport Fishing and Boating Partnership Council, Washington, D.C.

Maillett, Edward. "Trout fishing in 2011: a Demographic Description and Economic Analysis." Addendum to the 2011 National Survey of Fishing, Hunting, and Wildlife-Associated Recreation; US Fish and Wildlife Service, 2011.

Responsive Management and Southwick Associates. 2012. "Understanding Activities that Compete with Recreational Fishing." Prepared for the American Sportfishing Association, Arlington, Virginia.

Ritter, Christine, Robert B. Ditton, and R. J. Riechers. 1992. "Constraints to Sport

Fishing: Implications for Fisheries Management." *Fisheries* 17 (4): 16-19

Schor, Juliet. 1991. *The Overworked American: the Unexpected Decline of Leisure.* New York: Basic Books, 1992.

Sutton, Stephen G. 2007. "Constraints on Recreational Fishing Participation in Queensland, Australia." *Fisheries* 32 (2): 73-83.

Wainberg, J., Thomas Kida, and James F. Smith. 2010. "Stories vs. Statistics: The Impact of Anecdotal Data on Professional Decision Making." *Social Science Research Network*, http://ssrn.com/abstract=1571358.

Chapter Sixteen: Into the World of TU—Selling Cigars and Catch and Release on Castle Rock Creek

Conversations and interviews on the stream.

Phone interviews with Gene Van Dyck, fisheries manager, Wisconsin DNR.

Behnke, Robert. 1989. *Trout* Magazine, Vol. 2.

Kerr, Roger. 1982. "A Five-Year Study of Brown Trout Populations and Angling Success in the Castle Rock Creek Fish-for-Fun Area, Grant County, Wisconsin." Fish Management Report 111, Wisconsin Department of Natural Resources, Bureau of Fish Management.

Chapter Seventeen: Designer Trout Creeks

Hunt, Robert L. *Trout Stream Therapy.* Madison: University of Wisconsin Press, 1993.

Mitro, Matthew, and Paul Kanehl. 2011. "Trout Population Response to Instream Habitat Restoration in Elk Creek." Wisconsin Department of Natural Resources, Fisheries Research Division.

Chapter Eighteen: TU Annual Meeting – September 25, 2013 – Middleton, Wisconsin – Marriott Hotel

Dempson, J.B., D. G. Reddin, and M. F. O'Connell. 1998. "To What Extent Does Catch and Release Contribute to Mortality in Atlantic Salmon?" Canadian Stock Assessment Secretariat Research Document 98/99, Department of Fisheries and Oceans.

Dewald, Steve. "Enforcing and Communicating Fishery Regulations in Wisconsin: A Conservation Warden's Perspective." Proceedings of Trout and the Trout Angler II workshop, La Crosse, WI, July 2000.

Gallagher, Nancy L. *Breeding Better Vermonters: The Eugenics Project in the Green Mountain State.* Hanover: University Press of New England, 1999.

Maillett, Edward. "Trout Fishing in 2011: A Demographic Description and Economic Analysis." Addendum to the 2011 National Survey of Fishing, Hunting, and Wildlife-Associated Recreation; US Fish and Wildlife Service, 2011.

Faast, T.S., and S.K. Sahnow. "Regaining Public Trust...and Keeping It!"

Proceedings of Wild Trout Symposium VIII, Yellowstone National Park, MT, September 2004.

www.ingramcontent.com/pod-product-compliance
Lightning Source LLC
LaVergne TN
LVHW091917270525
812231LV00009B/514